We all need to b  even our most
cherished teache ritten a highly
charitable and g Til's approach
to apologetics f challenges Van
Tilians to think ca.... s have perceived
problems in Van Til's work and presents an oppo..... .ty for an equally
charitable reply where the deflection of 'misunderstanding' could be
set aside in favor of real discussion about how to gain more common
ground. Mathison should be commended for his humility and diligence
to move the discussion forward in the best of ways.

HARRISON PERKINS
Pastor, Oakland Hills Community Church (OPC),
Farmington Hills, Michigan.
Author, *Righteous by Design: Covenantal Merit and Adam's Original Integrity.*

Debates about apologetic methodology in the Reformed world often
generate more heat than light and sometimes devolve into verbal knife
fights on social media. Keith Mathison instead refreshingly shines
exegetical and theological light upon this debated topic. Through a
careful and patient exposition of Cornelius Van Til's presuppositional
apologetics method, he presents a charitable and fair-minded critique.
But far from an ivory tower debate, Dr Mathison shows how clarity on
apologetic methodology does not merely vindicate a particular school
of thought but rather better equips Christians to defend the faith once
delivered to the saints and returns Reformed Christians to their classical
confessional heritage.

J. V. FESKO
Harriett Barbour Professor of Systematic and Historical Theology,
Reformed Theological Seminary, Jackson, Mississippi.
Author, *Reforming Apologetics: Retrieving the Classic
Reformed Approach to Defending the Faith.*

Van Til's presuppositional apologetics dominates much of the Reformed
world and even beyond. Critiques of Van Til are usually met with charges
of being anti-Reformed. This book by Keith Mathison might just upend
all that. Using Van Til's own extensive writings, Dr Mathison shows that
Van Til's apologetic not only lacks exegetical support, it runs counter to
whole swaths of biblical teaching. He also shows how it runs counter to
the Reformed confessions and systematic theologies. This book exposes
real concerns and substantive errors of Van Til's apologetic method. But
don't miss an underlying current in the book. Many in the Reformed
world tend to debate about apologetics rather than actually practice it.

This book is ultimately a clarion call to the actual and so urgent defense of the faith. We all owe Dr Mathison a huge debt for this gift.

STEPHEN J. NICHOLS
President, Reformation Bible College, Sanford, Florida.
Author, *Track: A Student's Guide to Apologetics.*

My introduction to Van Tillian apologetics was via a secondary source. I took a course at RTS in apologetics taught by Dr Greg Bahnsen in the mid-1970s. Bahnsen was formidable in class. His debates with Gordon Stein on the existence of God have become legendary. Since then, I have attempted to read Van Til, grasp his method, and failed to be convinced. Not least, has been the issue that there are several different 'takes' on Van Til's apologetical method. Whether one agrees with Dr Mathison's conclusions or not (I, for one, find him utterly convincing), this book must be read and studied. You will be the better for reading this book, not least it will help you provide a better account of 'the faith once delivered to the saints.'

DEREK W. H. THOMAS
Teaching Fellow, Ligonier Ministries,
Retired Senior Minister, First Presbyterian Church (ARP),
Columbia, South Carolina.

Keith Mathison is the ideal author to write this kind of critique of Cornelius Van Til: namely, someone with no personal ax to grind and who does not appear overly eager to pick a fight. Indeed, were the reader to put *Toward a Reformed Apologetics* down halfway through, he might be forgiven were he to assume that Mathison is himself a Van Tilian, so charitable and clear is his presentation of Van Til's thought on Van Til's own terms. Mathison deftly shows the *prima facie* plausibility of Van Til's argument, with its dazzling symmetry and apparent explanatory power. All this makes the second half of *Toward a Reformed Apologetics* – wherein Mathison demonstrates that Van Til's apologetic system, despite its aesthetic appeal, is unbiblical, non-confessional, theologically novel, historically dubious, philosophically incoherent, and practically disastrous – all the more potent. My only mark against Mathison is that he did not write this book fifteen years ago.

SAMUEL G. PARKISON
Assistant Professor of Theology,
Gulf Theological Seminary, United Arab Emirates.
Author, *To Gaze Upon God: The Beatific Vision in
Doctrine, Tradition, and Practice.*

R.E.D.S.
REFORMED,
EXEGETICAL
AND
DOCTRINAL
STUDIES

# TOWARD A REFORMED
# APOLOGETICS

## A CRITIQUE OF THE THOUGHT
## OF CORNELIUS VAN TIL

# KEITH A. MATHISON

SERIES EDITORS J.V. FESKO & MATTHEW BARRETT

MENTOR
*Encouraging Christians to Think*

Copyright © Keith A. Mathison 2024

Paperback ISBN 978-1-5271-1229-2
Ebook ISBN 978-1-5271-1233-9

10 9 8 7 6 5 4 3 2 1

Published in 2024
in the
Mentor Imprint
by
Christian Focus Publications Ltd,
Geanies House, Fearn, Ross-shire,
IV20 1TW, Great Britain.

www.christianfocus.com

Cover design
by Pete Barnsley

Printed by
Bell & Bain, Glasgow

# CONTENTS

*To all of my students, past and present, at Reformation Bible College.*

# Series Preface

Reformed, Exegetical and Doctrinal Studies (R.E.D.S.) presents new studies informed by rigorous exegetical attention to the biblical text, and engagement with the history of doctrine, with a goal of refined dogmatic formulation.

R.E.D.S. covers a spectrum of doctrinal topics, addresses contemporary challenges in theological studies, and is driven by the Word of God, seeking to draw theological conclusions based upon the authority and teaching of Scripture itself.

Each volume also explores pastoral implications so that they contribute to the Church's theological and practical understanding of God's Word. One of the virtues that sets R.E.D.S. apart is its ability to apply dogmatics to the Christian life. In doing so, these volumes are characterized by the rare combination of theological weightiness and warm, pastoral application, much in the tradition of John Calvin's *Institutes of the Christian Religion*.

These volumes do not merely repeat material accessible in other books but retrieve and remind the Church of forgotten truths to enrich contemporary discussion.

MATTHEW BARRETT
J. V. FESKO

# Preface

When asked whether I would have any interest in writing a book on the thought of Cornelius Van Til, I have to admit that I was initially reluctant. The debate in North American Presbyterian and Reformed churches over Van Til's teachings began in the 1940s, and it continues to the present day. There is little indication, however, that Reformed Christians are any closer to consensus now than they were so many decades ago. Not only is it a long-standing and entrenched debate, it has also often been an acrimonious one. Serious charges and countercharges have been made by both proponents and opponents of Van Til's doctrines. The question I had to ask myself was whether there was anything constructive I could offer.

I was first introduced to the debate over Van Til's teachings in 1992 when I transferred from Dallas Theological Seminary to Reformed Theological Seminary in Orlando. At DTS, most of the discussion and debate among students and faculty had to do with eschatological questions (My first semester at DTS coincided with the Gulf War in Iraq, and this prompted a *lot* of eschatological speculation there). I do not recall ever hearing or being involved in a discussion on apologetics while at Dallas. All of that changed dramatically when I arrived at RTS in Orlando. The faculty of RTS in 1992 included Richard Pratt (b. 1953), R. C. Sproul (1939–2017), and Ronald Nash (1936–2006). Each of these men had a distinctive view of apologetics, and each had very strong opinions about the teachings of Van Til.

Richard Pratt was a proponent of Van Til's presuppositionalist apologetics and taught it from a perspective shaped to some degree by John Frame. R. C. Sproul, on the other hand, was an opponent of Van Til's presuppositionalism. He argued for 'classical apologetics.' Ronald Nash argued for a view he called 'inductive presuppositionalism.' He was also very critical of Van Til. I had only recently become convinced that Reformed theology was the system of theology found in Scripture, so navigating my way through this new debate as I went from class to class was very disorienting and sometimes discouraging.

During my years at RTS, I was still in the process of coming to grips with the system of Reformed theology. As a former dispensationalist, it was all very new to me. I was trying to wrap my head around things like covenant theology, infant baptism, and amillennial eschatology. But the apologetics debate was always there, in almost every classroom and, it seemed, in almost every student discussion. Remaining neutral as a student at that school during those years was not a live option. Initially, I was inclined toward Van Til's view, but ultimately I was swayed in a different direction. Some of this was a result of reading the great Reformed scholastic theologian Francis Turretin (1623–1687). The first volume of the English translation of his *Institutes of Elenctic Theology* was published during my time in seminary.

In 1996, after graduating from RTS, I began working for Ligonier Ministries, the teaching ministry of R. C. Sproul. After several years, I became an associate editor of *Tabletalk* magazine. By that time, I had a settled view with regard to the debate over Van Til, but I never considered writing anything substantial on the subject. I had other areas of interest. Then, in 2011, I began teaching at the newly founded Reformation Bible College, and students sometimes wanted to talk about Van Til. In some ways it was like being back at RTS. For years, if a student asked my opinion on the subject, I would share it privately. I still saw no reason to write anything.

All of this changed because one of the courses I began teaching at Reformation Bible College after several years was the Doctrine of God class. As I did more and more reading on this subject in preparation for my lectures, I discovered that some very unusual things were being taught about God by some prominent evangelical and Reformed theologians. One of the things that immediately struck me was the fact that among those who were teaching these unusual things were two of the most prominent Van Tillian scholars alive today, namely John M. Frame and K. Scott Oliphint. I began to wonder whether this was a coincidence or not. I wondered whether there was something in Van Til's own thought that had caused two of his most prominent and influential students to publish works that appeared to depart dramatically from the doctrine of God taught in the Westminster Confession of Faith.

In 2017, John Frame wrote a critique of James Dolezal's book *All That is in God: Evangelical Theology and the Challenge of Classical Christian Theism.* Toward the end of that year, I wrote a response to Frame's critique. That online article, titled 'Unlatched Theism,' was my first public response to any Van Tillian on any subject. I then spent much of 2018 and the first half of 2019 reading a stack of Van Til's books and articles in an attempt to discover whether there was anything in Van Til's works that might have led Frame in the direction he was taking on the doctrine of God. As I read Van Til, however, I also took notes on other issues and questions as they arose.

Ultimately, although I did not find anything obvious in Van Til that would conclusively explain why certain Van Tillian scholars were teaching what they were teaching about God, I decided to write a friendly critique of Van Til regarding issues in his works that I found to be confusing, frustrating, or otherwise problematic. This somewhat lengthy piece was published at *Tabletalk* online in August 2019 with the title 'Christianity and Van Tillianism.' The title ruffled quite a few feathers, and I received more feedback concerning it than I did concerning the content.

Given that feedback, a few words concerning my choice of that title are perhaps in order before proceeding. I used that title for a few different reasons. It was obviously a deliberate allusion not only to J. Gresham Machen's *Christianity and Liberalism*, but also to Van Til's *Christianity and Barthianism* and his *Christianity and Idealism*. Machen and Van Til both used versions of the 'Christianity and ...' title to critique a certain position, so my use of the 'Christianity and ...' title was in part a tongue-in-cheek allusion to all three since I was attempting a critique of certain elements of Van Tillianism. There was also a deliberately provocative reason for using it. Although I certainly don't think Van Tillianism is in the same category as liberalism or Barthianism, I do have concerns about the direction certain proponents of Van Tillianism are going with the doctrine of God.

The few responses to the content of my article that I saw suggested that it was simply another rehashing of the same tired arguments that had been repeatedly answered by Van Til and others over the decades. Some suggested that I completely misunderstood Van Til's thought. One prominent Van Tillian said that the article revealed my need to read more of Van Til. Initially, I thought I had read enough of Van Til to grasp what he was saying, but the person who made this comment has spent his career studying Van Til's works. I had spent about a year and a half reading him, so I took that suggestion to heart.

That brings us back to the invitation I received to write this book. As I said, I was hesitant to accept it. I had no interest in writing anything else on this subject if I was, in fact, failing to understand Van Til and if what I wrote was not going to be helpful in some way. I had no interest in writing on this topic again unless I thought I could offer something constructive to the debate. Repetition of the same old arguments and the repeated claims and counterclaims of misunderstanding are tiresome and of no interest to anyone on either side of this debate.

In the end, after much prayer and counsel from friends, I decided to accept the invitation to write, but I determined that I would not publish it unless I was as certain as I could be that I had properly understood and accurately represented Van Til's system of thought. To that end, I determined to do three things. First, I decided that I would read everything Van Til wrote, and that meant carefully re-reading even those works I had already completed. Thankfully, there is an electronic edition of the complete works of Cornelius Van Til available through Logos, and Logos was gracious enough to provide a complimentary copy of this collection. Second, I determined to read every book, dissertation, article, and chapter on Van Til that I could locate. Third, I decided that I would ask recognized Van Tillian scholars for their feedback on questions that arose during my research.

My prayer is that this work will honor the labors of our brother in Christ, Cornelius Van Til, who is now present with our Lord. He, along with J. Gresham Machen and many other faithful men, stood firm against the tide of modernism in the early twentieth century. He also recognized the dangers of Barthianism when many others were being carried away. Van Til's goal was to construct a consistently Reformed apologetic method. Many are convinced he achieved that goal or that, at the very least, he made great strides toward achieving that goal. Others still have concerns. Because of his widespread influence, whether he achieved that goal or not remains a topic worthy of careful consideration.

There are several people to whom thanks are due. First, thank you to J. V. Fesko and Matthew Barrett for inviting me to write this book for their outstanding R.E.D.S. series. I greatly appreciate their confidence that I could write something constructive on this topic. I hope that I have done so. Second, I want to thank my lovely wife Tricia for her continual encouragement. Thank you also to my colleagues on the faculty of Reformation Bible College: Levi Berntson, Matthew Dudreck, Ben Shaw, and John Tweeddale. These gentlemen patiently listened to me talk about one subject for months on end. I also want to thank James N. Anderson, John M. Frame, John Muether, K. Scott Oliphint, and Lane G. Tipton, all of whom are Van Tillian scholars, and all of whom answered my questions at various points during the research for this book. Special thanks are due to James N. Anderson and Lane G. Tipton for extended discussions. While these men and I differ in our opinions of Van Til's thought, they were very generous with their time.

Several people read all or part of the manuscript at various stages and provided invaluable feedback along the way. Thank you to Levi Berntson, Christopher Cleveland, Matthew Dudreck, Juan Estevez, Aaron Garriott, Harrison Perkins, Ben Shaw, and Scott Swain. Their feedback saved me from several embarrassing mistakes. It should go without saying that any remaining errors are entirely my responsibility, but I'll say it anyway. Any remaining errors are entirely my responsibility.

Thank you to Daniel Peeler and Michael Farrell, the librarians at Reformation Bible College and Reformed Theological Seminary Orlando respectively, for their help in obtaining certain difficult to access books and articles. Thank you to Logos for providing the electronic edition of the collected works of Cornelius Van Til. Thank you to Ludwig van Beethoven for providing great background music for writing. Finally, thank you to all of the students at Reformation Bible College who have sat in my classes since 2011. Your love for the Lord Jesus Christ and for his church has been a constant source of encouragement to me for well over a decade. I dedicate this book to each one of you.

# Introduction

*Three things are certain in life: death, taxes, and debates over Cornelius Van Til.*

JAMES N. ANDERSON

Cornelius Van Til was born in the Netherlands in the village of Grootegast on May 3, 1895 to Ite and Klazina Van Til.[1] His family emigrated to the United States in 1905 and moved to Highland, Indiana where his father worked as a farmer. Van Til's parents were faithful members in the Christian Reformed Church (CRC) and raised him and his siblings in that communion.[2] In 1914, he took the first steps toward formal ministerial training by enrolling at Calvin Preparatory School in Grand Rapids, Michigan. Then in 1921, he enrolled at the Theological Seminary of the CRC (later re-named Calvin Theological Seminary). In 1922, he moved to the east coast to enroll at Princeton Theological Seminary in New Jersey where he would earn both his ThB and ThM. He also earned his MA and PhD from Princeton University.

After serving for a year as a CRC pastor in Michigan, Van Til accepted an offer to join the faculty of Princeton Seminary in 1928 as

---

1. For a detailed biography of Cornelius Van Til, see John R. Muether, *Cornelius Van Til: Reformed Apologist and Churchman* (Phillipsburg: P&R Publishing, 2008). This section is indebted to Muether's outstanding work. An older biography of Van Til is William White, Jr.'s *Van Til: Defender of the Faith* (Nashville: Thomas Nelson Publishers, 1979). Readers should be aware, however, that White's biography, while informative, occasionally veers toward uncritical hagiography.

2. For a helpful introduction to some of the cultural and ecclesiastical context within which the Van Til family and other Dutch immigrants lived, see James D. Bratt, *Dutch Calvinism in Modern America: A History of a Conservative Subculture* (Grand Rapids: Wm. B. Eerdmans Publishing Company, 1984).

an instructor in apologetics. When the seminary was reorganized several weeks after his appointment, and he, J. Gresham Machen (1881–1937), and others recognized that it was now inevitably moving in a more liberal direction, Van Til resigned and returned to the pastorate in Michigan. His stay did not last long, however, because in 1929 he accepted an offer to join the faculty of Westminster Theological Seminary along with Machen and other former Princeton Seminary faculty.[3]

In 1936, Van Til transferred his ministerial credentials and joined the newly formed Presbyterian Church of America, which would soon change its name to the Orthodox Presbyterian Church (OPC). He was an active churchman in the OPC for the remainder of his life. Van Til would faithfully serve as a professor at Westminster Theological Seminary until his retirement in 1972, and he would faithfully serve as a minister in the OPC until his death on April 17, 1987.

During his lifetime, Cornelius Van Til wrote numerous books, pamphlets, articles, reviews, essays, and sermons.[4] He also wrote unpublished class syllabi that he often distributed to interested enquirers around the country and around the world. His hundreds of seminary students would go on to fill pulpits in the OPC and other denominations. As new Reformed seminaries and Christian colleges were established, faculty positions were often filled by his former students. Through his writings and through the impact of his many students, Van Til became one of the most influential Dutch-American Reformed theologians of the twentieth century.

## Van Til's Goal

Van Til's goal, from the time he was in seminary, is probably best expressed in the title of one of his privately published pamphlets: 'Toward a Reformed Apologetics.'[5] In this work he explains, 'It is

---

3. Muether, *Cornelius Van Til*, 60-62. During his tenure at Westminster Seminary, Van Til taught thirty-eight different courses. For more details on this part of his life, see Timothy I. McConnel, 'The Historical Origins of the Presuppositional Apologetics of Cornelius Van Til,' (PhD diss, Marquette University, 1999), 17-18.

4. See Greg L. Bahnsen, *Van Til's Apologetic: Readings and Analysis* (Phillipsburg: P&R Publishing, 1998), xvii. Bahnsen points out that Van Til wrote around thirty books and published syllabi and wrote around 220 articles and reviews.

5. Cornelius Van Til, 'Toward a Reformed Apologetics' (Philadelphia, 1972) in Cornelius Van Til and Eric H. Sigward, *The Pamphlets, Tracts, and Offprints of Cornelius Van Til*, Electronic ed. (Labels Army Company: New York, 1997).

because the Reformed Faith alone has an essentially sound, because biblical, theology, that it alone has anything like a sound, that is, biblical method of challenging the world of unbelief to repentance and faith.'[6] John Muether has helpfully summed up Van Til's basic point: 'Reformed theology demanded a Reformed apologetic.'[7] In other words, in all of his works Van Til begins with the assumption of the truth of Reformed theology as expressed in the Reformed confessions. He was raised in the Christian Reformed Church, using the Three Forms of Unity (the Belgic Confession, the Heidelberg Catechism, and the Canons of Dordt). When he joined the OPC, he subscribed to the Westminster Standards. These confessions provided him with his theological foundation.

Van Til believed that these Reformed confessions expressed the system of theology found in Holy Scripture. As we shall see, he also believed that Reformed theologians had come to adopt apologetic methodologies that effectively undermined their own confessions. He believed that traditional apologetic methods compromised many Reformed doctrines. He sought, therefore, to develop a theory and method of apologetics that would be completely consistent with confessional Reformed theology.[8] An understanding of this point will help us as we seek to grasp Van Til's foundational commitments. His arguments, even though often couched in philosophical terminology, are primarily theological. His ultimate starting point is not some abstract metaphysical or epistemological position. His starting point is the doctrine of God found in the Reformed confessions.

## Van Til's Audience

As an ordained minister of the Gospel, Van Til's audience was, in one sense, the constituency of the entire Reformed church, and he sometimes wrote works for such a general audience.[9] There is another sense, however, in which

---

6. Ibid.

7. Muether, *Cornelius Van Til*, 114.

8. Muether, *Cornelius Van Til*, 18. See also Jim S. Halsey, *For a Time Such as This: An Introduction to the Reformed Apologetics of Cornelius Van Til* (Phillipsburg: Presbyterian and Reformed Publishing Company, 1976), 13; K. Scott Oliphint, introduction to Cornelius Van Til, *A Christian Theory of Knowledge*, ed. K. Scott Oliphint (Glenside: Westminster Seminary Press, 2023), xi.

9. See, for example, the many articles he wrote for *The Banner*, *The Presbyterian Guardian*, *Torch and Trumpet*, and *Christianity Today* (not the same as the *Christianity Today* in publication today).

we can speak of more specific audiences. I believe that we can discern at least two such audiences. First, the fact that many of Van Til's most important works were originally published as class syllabi indicates that the initial immediate audience of these works was the student body at Westminster Theological Seminary. In other words, one of his most important audiences consisted of aspiring pastors situated in a rigorous academic context.

Van Til also wanted to address the educated elite of his day, particularly those who had some training in philosophy.[10] Van Til explains, 'Reformed theologians the world over are concerned with the question how they may speak significantly to the leaders of thought today.'[11] Van Til wanted to respond to and 'challenge the best thought of our age.'[12] This explains why many pages of his works are filled with the names of the most prominent scientists and philosophers of his time. It is also one reason why Van Til's work can be difficult to follow at times since many of those who were the intellectual elite of his day are virtually unknown in our day.

## Van Til's Major Influences

Like all theologians, Van Til was influenced by the men under whom he studied and by the men whose works he read. Van Til himself claimed that his understanding of philosophy was strongly influenced by Herman Dooyeweerd (1894–1977), D. H. Th. Vollenhoven (1892–1978), and H. G. Stoker (1899–1993). Van Til writes,

> In trying to develop a Christian totality view, the writer has had much help from the *Philosophy of the Cosmonomic Idea* as set forth by professors D. H. Th. Vollenhoven and Herman Dooyeweerd of Amsterdam, and by Professor H. G. Stoker of Potchefstroom. It was, in particular, Dr Dooyeweerd's detailed analysis of the history of philosophy that was of much help.[13]

---

10. Cornelius Van Til, *The Defense of the Faith*, 4th ed. (Phillipsburg: P&R Publishing, 2008), 45.

11. Cornelius Van Til, *The Theology of James Daane* (The Presbyterian and Reformed Publishing Company: Philadelphia, 1959), 7.

12. Cornelius Van Til, introduction to B. B. Warfield, *The Inspiration and Authority of the Bible*, ed. Samuel G. Craig (Phillipsburg: The Presbyterian and Reformed Publishing Company, 1948), 4.

13. Cornelius Van Til, *An Introduction to Systematic Theology,* 2nd ed. (Phillipsburg: P&R Publishing, 2007), 13. See also Cornelius Van Til, 'Herman Dooyeweerd: A Personal Tribute,' *Westminster Theological Journal* 39/2 (Spring 1977): 319-27.

Van Til found Dooyeweerd especially helpful in opposing 'the synthesis philosophy of the middle ages.'[14]

With regard to theology, Van Til says that his most important influences outside of Scripture and the Reformed confessions were John Calvin (1509–1564), Abraham Kuyper (1837–1920), Herman Bavinck (1854–1921), and Benjamin B. Warfield (1851–1921).[15] Van Til often refers to the first chapters of John Calvin's *Institutes* when he discusses key elements in his theory of knowledge.[16] Abraham Kuyper influenced Van Til's concept of the antithesis, but Van Til followed B. B. Warfield rather than Kuyper in insisting that Christianity is objectively defensible.[17]

Arguably, however, Herman Bavinck is Van Til's most significant theological influence.[18] Nathaniel Gray Sutanto, for example, observes that Van Til likely presupposes 'Bavinck's dogmatics as the system of theology that he would defend.'[19] More work needs to be done, but the theological connection between Bavinck and Van Til appears strong. In addition to the names mentioned above, John Frame also lists Louis Berkhof (1873–1957), J. Gresham Machen (1881–1937), and Geerhardus Vos (1862–1949) as important theological influences.[20]

---

14. Cornelius Van Til, *Christianity in Conflict*, Philadelphia: Westminster Theological Seminary, 1962–64 in Cornelius Van Til and Eric H. Sigward, *The Pamphlets, Tracts, and Offprints of Cornelius Van Til*, Electronic ed. (Labels Army Company: New York, 1997). For an overview of Dooyeweerd's thought, see Andree Troost, *What is Reformational Philosophy? An Introduction to the Cosmonomic Philosophy of Herman Dooyeweerd*, trans. Anthony Runia, ed. Harry Van Dyke (Paideia Press, 2012).

15. Van Til, *The Defense of the Faith*, 2.

16. For example, see Cornelius Van Til, 'Common Grace: Second Article,' *Westminster Theological Journal* 8, no. 2 (May 1946): 192.

17. Van Til, *The Defense of the Faith*, 351-52.

18. Muether, *Cornelius Van Til*, 56. See also Laurence R. O'Donnell, III, '*Kees Van Til als Nederlandse-Amerikaanse, Neo-Calvinistisch-Presbyteriaan apologeticus*: An Analysis of Cornelius Van Til's Presupposition of Reformed Dogmatics with special reference to Herman Bavinck's *Gereformeerde Dogmatiek*,' (ThM thesis, Calvin Theological Seminary, 2011), ix.

19. Nathaniel Gray Sutanto, 'From Antithesis to Synthesis: A Neo-Calvinistic Theological Strategy in Herman Bavinck and Cornelius Van Til,' *Journal of Reformed Theology* 9, no. 4 (2015): 348.

20. John M. Frame, *Cornelius Van Til: An Analysis of His Thought* (Phillipsburg: P&R Publishing Company, 1995), 20-23.

## Van Til's Major Interpreters

Although this book is primarily focused on the thought of Cornelius Van Til himself, an examination of his teaching cannot ignore his many interpreters and the sometimes different ways in which they have developed his views. Muether explains, 'Debates over Van Til's teaching have divided his followers, who have created competing versions of the Reformed apologist.'[21] As a result of these divisions, there are now several different versions of Van Tillianism.[22] It should be noted that with a few exceptions, most of these versions are a result of differences in emphasis rather than differences in substance. It is helpful to be aware of these different versions of Van Tillianism, however, because an author's particular emphasis can affect the way in which that author understands the whole of Van Til's system of thought.[23]

### Reconstructionist Van Tillians

One of the first published explanations and defenses of Van Tillianism was written by Rousas J. Rushdoony (1916–2001), the father of twentieth-century reconstructionism.[24] Rushdoony's son-in-law, Gary North

---

21. Muether, *Cornelius Van Til*, 15.

22. In the secondary literature, one will find the spelling 'Van Tillian' and 'Van Tillianism' as well as 'Van Tilian' and 'Van Tilianism.' I have chosen to use the spelling 'Van Tillian' and 'Van Tillianism' throughout for no other reason than the necessity of choosing one.

23. Most of the labels I have chosen to use in this section are not used by Van Tillians themselves. I have coined most of them solely for the purpose of helping readers note the different emphases found among different Van Tillian theologians. My use of these labels is certainly not intended to imply that any Van Tillians I have grouped under one label *necessarily* reject the emphases of Van Tillians I have grouped under a different label. For example, my use of the label 'Redemptive Historical Van Tillians' is not intended to imply that other Van Tillians reject the idea of redemptive history as an important element of Van Til's thought.

24. Rousas John Rushdoony, *By What Standard? An Analysis of the Philosophy of Cornelius Van Til* (Vallecito, CA: Ross House Books, 1958). Christian Reconstructionism is the term for a view that combines Reformed theology, theonomic ethics, Van Tillian presuppositionalism, postmillennial eschatology, and a generally transformationalist understanding of the church's relation to culture. In addition to Rushdoony, other important early reconstructionist authors include Gary North, Greg L. Bahnsen, Kenneth L. Gentry and Gary DeMar. Although he has apparently rejected the label, Douglas Wilson teaches, in a modified form, many of the main doctrines of the original reconstructionist movement. For an in-depth study of Rushdoony and the origins of Reconstructionism, see Michael McVicar, *Christian Reconstruction: R. J. Rushdoony and*

(1942–2022), a prolific writer and publisher of reconstructionist books, edited a *Festschrift* for Van Til entitled *Foundations of Christian Scholarship*.[25] He also wrote and edited books accusing Westminster Theological Seminary of abandoning Van Til's legacy.[26] The reconstructionist Van Tillian who was most influential in the spread of Van Til's specific apologetic ideas, however, was Greg L. Bahnsen (1948–1995). Not only did Bahnsen write one of the most thorough examinations of Van Til's thought in print, he also taught Van Tillian apologetics in a way that made it relatively easy for Christians without a PhD in philosophy to understand.[27] Reconstructionist Van Tillians have tended to emphasize Van Til's doctrine of the antithesis and the corresponding rejection of neutrality in any field of human activity or thought. They are best known for the application of this principle to the field of political theory.[28]

## *Triperspectival Van Tillians*

Few, if any, of Van Til's students have written as extensively on his apologetic system of thought as John M. Frame (b. 1939). In 1995, Frame published *Cornelius Van Til: An Analysis of his Thought*, which to

---

*American Religious Conservatism* (Chapel Hill: The University of North Carolina Press, 2015). On Wilson and the contemporary manifestation of reconstructionism in the United States, see Crawford Gribben, *Survival and Resistance in Evangelical America: Christian Reconstruction in the Pacific Northwest* (Oxford: Oxford University Press, 2021).

25. Gary North, ed., *Foundations of Christian Scholarship: Essays in the Van Til Perspective* (Vallecito, CA: Ross House Books, 1979).

26. See Gary North, ed., *Theonomy: An Informed Response* (Tyler, TX: Institute for Christian Economics, 1991) and Gary North, *Westminster's Confession: The Abandonment of Van Til's Legacy* (Tyler, TX: Institute for Christian Economics, 1991). Both of these books were published in response to William S. Barker and W. Robert Godfrey, eds., *Theonomy: A Reformed Critique* (Grand Rapids: Academie Books, 1990). The latter book contained chapters written by the faculty of Westminster Theological Seminary.

27. For his in-depth examination of Van Til's thought, see Bahnsen, *Van Til's Apologetic: Readings and Analysis* (Phillipsburg: P&R Publishing, 1998). For his more popular level presentations of Van Tillian apologetics, see his *Always Ready: Directions for Defending the Faith*, ed. Robert R. Booth (Atlanta: American Vision, 1996) and his *Presuppositional Apologetics: Stated and Defended*, ed. Joel McDurmon (Powder Springs: American Vision Press, 2008).

28. For reconstructionist writings on this subject, see, for example, Rousas J. Rushdoony, *Christianity and the State* (Vallecito, CA: Chalcedon/Ross House Books, 1986); Gary North, *Political Polytheism: The Myth of Pluralism* (Tyler, TX: Institute for Christian Economics, 1989); and Greg L. Bahnsen, *Theonomy in Christian Ethics*, 3rd ed. (Nacodoches, TX: Covenant Media Press, 2002), 311-458.

this day remains the most comprehensive study of Van Til's teaching in print.[29] Like Bahnsen, Frame has also written more popular level presentations of Van Tillian apologetic principles and method as well as numerous articles and essays.[30] Two features, in particular, distinguish Frame's interpretation of Van Til from that of most other Van Tillians. First, Frame has been quicker than other Van Tillians to reject or revise significant aspects of Van Til's thought. This revisionism is evidenced throughout his *Analysis*, and it has been criticized by other Van Tillians.[31] Second, Frame has developed a somewhat obscure element of Van Til's thought (the 'fields of revelation') into what he calls 'triperspectivalism.'[32] Triperspectivalism is a distinctive and unique approach to theological method based on Frame's epistemological views.[33] The triperspectival method shapes many of Frame's major written works.

## *Redemptive-Historical Van Tillians*

The particular emphasis of what I am calling 'Redemptive-Historical' Van Tillianism is the reading of Van Til through the lens of the eschatology

---

29. Frame, *Cornelius Van Til: An Analysis of His Thought*.

30. See, for example, his *Apologetics to the Glory of God* (Phillipsburg: P&R Publishing Company, 1994), which has been republished in a revised and expanded form as *Apologetics: A Justification of Christian Belief* (Phillipsburg: P&R Publishing Company, 2015). Most of his articles on topics related to apologetics have been collected in his *Selected Shorter Writings*, 3 vols. (Phillipsburg: P&R Publishing Company, 2014–2016) and his *On Theology: Explorations and Controversies* (Bellingham, WA: Lexham Press, 2023).

31. For an example of Frame's criticism of Van Til, see his discussion of the antithesis in *Cornelius Van Til: An Analysis of His Thought*, 187-210. For Van Tillian criticisms of Frame, see Greg L. Bahnsen, *An Answer to Frame's Critique of Van Til: Profound Differences Between the Traditional and Presuppositional Methods* (Glenside: Westminster Seminary Bookstore, n.d.); Mark W. Karlberg, 'John Frame and the Recasting of Van Tilian Apologetics: A Review Article,' *Mid-America Journal of Theology* 9, no. 2 (Fall 1993): 279-96; and William D. Dennison, *In Defense of the Eschaton: Essays in Reformed Apologetics*, ed James Douglas Baird (Eugene, OR: Wipf & Stock, 2015), 21-22.

32. On 'fields of revelation,' see Van Til, *An Introduction to Systematic Theology*, 121-22. Frame points to Van Til's discussion of the different 'fields of revelation' as a source of inspiration for his perspectival approach in his *Cornelius Van Til: An Analysis of His Thought*, 119.

33. On triperspectivalism, see John M. Frame, *Theology in Three Dimensions: A Guide to Triperspectivalism and its Significance* (Phillipsburg: P&R Publishing Company, 2017). See also John M. Frame, *The Doctrine of the Knowledge of God* (Phillipsburg: P&R Publishing Company, 1987) and Vern S. Poythress, *Symphonic Theology: The Validity of Multiple Perspectives in Theology* (Phillipsburg: P&R Publishing Company, 1987).

of Geerhardus Vos (1862–1949). The most prominent example of this distinctive approach to Van Til is found in the writings of William D. Dennison (b. 1949). In his book *In Defense of the Eschaton*, for example, Dennison approaches the Van Tillian antithesis through the lens of the Vosian eschatological overlap of the two ages.[34] He argues that although the believer lives in two worlds because of the overlap of the ages, he is a member only of the age to come.[35] The believer stands 'in heaven – in the *age to come* – pointing the unbeliever to heaven.'[36] A distinctively redemptive-historical/eschatological approach to Van Til is also found in the apologetic writings of Richard B. Gaffin, Jr.[37]

## Covenantal Van Tillians

I am calling this version of Van Tillianism 'Covenantal' in part because of the desire of its proponents to do away with the term 'presuppositionalism' as a descriptive label for Van Til's apologetic views. They argue instead for the label 'Covenantal Apologetics.' The main proponent of 'Covenantal Van Tillianism' is K. Scott Oliphint (b. 1955).[38] Oliphint's distinctive emphasis is his approach to the Van Tillian antithesis primarily through the lens of Adam and Christ as the covenant heads of two distinct peoples: covenant breakers and covenant keepers respectively.[39]

## Systematic Trinitarian Van Tillians

The most prominent scholar representing this type of Van Tillianism is Lane G. Tipton (b. 1967). Although Tipton observes redemptive-historical and covenantal elements in Van Til's thought, his emphasis

---

34. Dennison, *In Defense of the Eschaton*, 106-111. See also Dennison, *Paul's Two-Age Construction and Apologetics* (Eugene, OR: Wipf & Stock, 2000).

35. Dennison, *In Defense of the Eschaton*, 106.

36. Ibid., 107.

37. See, for example, Richard B. Gaffin, Jr., 'Some Epistemological Reflections on 1 Cor. 2:6-16,' *Westminster Theological Journal* 57, no. 1 (Spring 1995): 109.

38. See K. Scott Oliphint, *Covenantal Apologetics: Principles & Practice in Defense of Our Faith* (Wheaton: Crossway, 2013).

39. Although it would be possible to place William Edgar (b. 1944) in a category of Van Tillians strongly influenced by Francis Schaeffer, I would also include him in this category because he has publicly stated his agreement with the idea of replacing the label 'presuppositionalism' with 'covenantal apologetics.' See Peter A. Lillback, 'Interview with Dr William Edgar.' *Unio cum Christo* 3, no. 1 (Apr 2017): 253.

is on Van Til's doctrine of the Triune God as foundational to all that he teaches. According to Tipton, 'The ontological Trinity provides the architectonic principle in Van Til's theology and apologetic.'[40] Tipton has fully explained his views in his doctoral dissertation as well as in his book *The Trinitarian Theology of Cornelius Van Til*.[41] Tipton also emphasizes Van Til's teaching on the aseity of God and his corresponding insistence on rejecting the application of any form of 'correlativism' to God.[42]

## Analytic Van Tillians

James N. Anderson (b. 1973) has argued for an interpretation of Van Til that recognizes more compatibility between Van Til and contemporary analytic philosophy than might be expected given Van Til's educational context and certain of his philosophical emphases.[43] While recognizing clear points of tension, Anderson notes several affinities between Van Til and analytic philosophy including their shared criticism of British idealism and their shared interest in transcendental arguments. He argues furthermore that Van Tillians could benefit by engaging with the recent work of analytic philosophers and borrowing from their 'toolkit.' Time will tell whether this approach to Van Til gains a foothold among a larger number of Van Tillians.[44]

---

40. Lane G. Tipton, 'The Function of Perichoresis and the Divine Incomprehensibility,' *Westminster Theological Journal* 64, no. 2 (Fall 2002): 289.

41. See Tipton, 'The Triune Personal God: Trinitarian Theology in the Thought of Cornelius Van Til,' PhD diss, Westminster Theological Seminary, 2004 and *The Trinitarian Theology of Cornelius Van Til* (Libertyville, IL: Reformed Forum, 2022).

42. Correlativism is a term Van Til used to describe 'a mutually interdependent relationship.' See Cornelius Van Til, 'Presuppositionalism, Part 1,' *The Bible Today* 42, no. 7 (Apr 1949), in Cornelius Van Til and Eric H. Sigward, *The Articles of Cornelius Van Til*, Electronic ed. (Labels Army Company: New York, 1997). As we will see, Van Til taught that God is not in a mutually interdependent relationship with His creation and that any such correlativism is antithetical to Christian theism.

43. James N. Anderson, 'Van Til and Analytic Philosophy' in *Thinking God's Thoughts After Him: Essays in the Van Til Tradition*, 2 vols. ed. Bradley Green (Eugene, OR: Wipf & Stock, forthcoming).

44. Although it is not a separate version of Van Tillianism, John Frame has helpfully described what he calls 'Movement' Van Tillianism in his *Cornelius Van Til: An Analysis of His Thought*, 8-18. A 'Movement' Van Tillian would be a person who falls into one of the categories of Van Tillianism discussed above but who treats Van Til as if he is effectively above all criticism.

## Reconsidering the Van Til Debate

In 1971, E. R. Geehan published a *Festschrift* in honor of Cornelius Van Til titled *Jerusalem and Athens*. The book contained numerous chapters written by men who were supportive of Van Til's thought, but it also contained several chapters that were highly critical of his views. Van Til himself wrote extensive responses to many of these chapters. At the beginning of the book, he expressed his reason for doing so, saying, 'I hope that by doing this we may be of help to one another as together we present the name of Jesus as the only name given under heaven by which men must be saved.'[45] This comment is significant and worth considering.

Van Til indicates here that he saw his interaction with these critics as a means by which brothers in Christ might 'be of help to one another.' In other words, he saw these critics, not as enemies, but instead as fellow ministers of the gospel of Jesus Christ. This is an important point for those on both sides of this debate to remember. Van Tillians and non-Van Tillians who are confessionally Reformed should recognize that we agree on the vast majority of theological issues. We are not enemies. However, because Van Til spent the bulk of his career writing and speaking about the smaller number of issues on which we disagree, we can easily fall into the trap of thinking the two sides of this debate are in complete disagreement on every doctrinal issue. This is not the case, and if all of those on both sides could acknowledge this, perhaps the debate could be turned in a more constructive direction.

The debate over the teachings of Van Til began in the 1940s and over the decades became increasingly mired in acrimony and confusion.[46] I believe each side shares some of the responsibility for this. As we will see, because of his desire to create a completely consistent Reformed apologetic, Van Til often stated and implied that all the Reformed theologians of earlier centuries (with the possible exception of John Calvin) had unwittingly compromised the teaching of Scripture. The

---

45. Cornelius Van Til, 'My Credo,' in *Jerusalem and Athens: Critical Discussions on the Philosophy and Apologetics of Cornelius Van Til*, ed. E. R. Geehan (Phillipsburg: P&R Publishing Company, 1971), 3.

46. I am considering the 1948 and 1949 articles by J. Oliver Buswell and Cornelius Van Til in *The Bible Today* as the first real public volley in the debate over Van Til's apologetic thought. The next phase would begin in the early 1950s in the pages of *The Calvin Forum*.

same was stated and implied about those of his Reformed contemporaries who did not share his views on apologetics. Of course, this did not sit well with his critics.[47] On the other hand, many of these early critics suggested that Van Til's philosophy was little more than baptized idealism in spite of his many criticisms of idealist philosophy. Some went so far as to accuse him of an implicit pantheism.[48] Of course, this did not sit well with Van Til.

For many decades, there has been a lack of understanding on both sides. For various reasons, critics of Van Til have misunderstood elements of his teaching. Some of this is perhaps due to Van Til's use of obscure philosophical terminology intended, as mentioned above, to speak the language of the educated elite of his day. Some of this is perhaps due to Van Til's style of writing. John Muether describes his prose as 'dense and tedious.'[49] Mark Garcia speaks of 'his often impenetrable and painful prose, and his sometimes maddening revisionist use of vocabulary.'[50] Frame observes that it is 'very difficult to pin down precisely what Van Til believes on a given specific topic.'[51] A lack of clarity on the part of Van Til, then, is likely part of the reason for the continual misunderstanding of his teaching, but some of the misunderstanding has also likely been due at times to a lack of careful reading and charity on the part of his critics.

---

47. The problem was exacerbated when other Van Tillians suggested that those who disagreed with Van Til were deceptive and had all manner of sinful motives. Rushdoony, for example, refers to Van Til's Reformed critics as 'ostensibly Calvinist.' He adds, 'The difficulty most people experience is not with Van Til's writing but with his God; it is essentially He whom they find inacceptable and offensive.' See Rushdoony, *By What Standard*, 6, 98. Bahnsen titles a chapter on non-Van Tillian approaches to apologetics, 'Not Lying to Defend the Truth,' implying that non-Van Tillians are liars. In that chapter he specifically uses the words 'immoral' and 'duplicity' to describe non-Van Tillian approaches. See Bahnsen, *Always Ready*, 99, 100.

48. See, for example, Cecil De Boer, 'The New Apologetic,' *The Calvin Forum* 19, no. 1-2 (Aug–Sept 1953): 3-7; Jesse DeBoer, 'Professor Van Til's Apologetics, Part I: A Linguistic Bramble Patch,' *The Calvin Forum* 19, no. 1-2 (Aug–Sept 1953): 7-12; Clifton J. Orlebeke, 'On Brute Facts.,' *The Calvin Forum* 19, no. 1-2 (Aug–Sept 1953): 13-17; and Jesse DeBoer, 'Professor Van Til's Apologetics, Part II: God and Human Knowledge,' *The Calvin Forum* 19, no. 3 (Oct 1953): 27-34.

49. Muether, *Cornelius Van Til*, 125.

50. Mark Garcia, preface to *In Defense of the Eschaton: Essays in Reformed Apologetics*, ed. James Douglas Baird (Eugene, OR: Wipf & Stock, 2015), xv.

51. Frame, *Cornelius Van Til: An Analysis of His Thought*, 34.

David Filson rightly notes that critics of Van Til should 'listen carefully to what Van Tillians are actually saying and avoid superficial reaction and simplistic definitions and rejections of terms and phrases that must be taken as part of an apologetic system.'[52] This is a reasonable request, but the same courtesy should be extended by Van Tillians to non-Van Tillians. Van Til's supporters also need to listen more carefully to what his critics are saying and 'avoid superficial reaction and simplistic definitions.' It seems to me that both sides of this debate have plenty of room for improvement when it comes to careful and charitable listening and speaking. When we disagree, it is important that we first make every attempt to clearly understand both what is being said and the precise nature of the disagreement in order that we might, as Van Til said, 'be of help to one another' and in order that we might seek the peace and purity of the church.

But why continue the debate at all? I am convinced that most on both sides have grown weary of the same old criticisms and countercriticisms.[53] Furthermore, if it is true that confessionally Reformed theologians involved in this debate agree on most elements of their theology anyway, why not drop it and move on? In my opinion, we cannot simply drop the issue because it remains a very significant issue. Important biblical doctrines are involved, and truth matters. Furthermore, it does not do justice to the labors of Van Til himself to pretend that the concerns he raised were of no consequence. He was concerned that Reformed theologians had for centuries adopted an approach to apologetics that undermined their own theology. That is a serious concern and one that, if true, must be addressed.

It is also important to observe that Van Til has had an enormous influence in the twentieth century, and that influence has extended into the twenty-first century. Through his writings and through the work of his many students, Van Til's teaching has had a profound influence on Reformed churches and educational institutions around

---

52. David Owen Filson, 'The Apologetics and Theology of Cornelius Van Til,' *Foundations* 79 (Nov 2020): 57.

53. K. Scott Oliphint, for example, writes: 'But in my experience, many students of apologetics are growing weary of an almost interminable discussion of principles only. This is understandable. An apologetic that can do little more than continually talk about itself is not worth the effort exerted or ink spilled over it.' See Oliphint, *Covenantal Apologetics*, 25.

the world. If there are errors in his thought, then the effects of those errors will be magnified due to his influence. If any significant errors exist in his thought, they can be found only if we subject his ideas to careful critical consideration.

As James Anderson, himself a Van Tillian, has observed, 'Van Til's ideas invite criticism – indeed, they deserve criticism.'[54] As Anderson also notes, we cannot claim 'that Van Til is beyond criticism, or that his work does not need refinement, correction, and even rejection at points.'[55] Another Van Tillian scholar, Lane Tipton, has similarly observed:

> By 'critical' I mean that we should be willing, where necessary, to subject Van Til to refinement and perhaps correction. We ought to pursue greater biblical fidelity and dogmatic precision in all of our work. Investigating the work of Van Til is no exception. Thus we should not have an *a priori* commitment blindly to defend Van Til simply because he taught something. Nor should we have an *a priori* commitment blindly to oppose him at every point simply because he taught something. We should engage neither in wholesale rejection of Van Til nor in idealized hagiography of the man and his theology. We ought to aspire to sincere engagement, careful analysis, and scholarly assessment of his work.[56]

I agree. Sincere engagement is needed. Van Til's work is important, and it is because his work is important that it deserves such careful critical evaluation. Only if Van Til's work was insignificant could we drop the issue.

## What This Book Is and Is Not

A few words are necessary to explain what this book is and what it is not. In the first place, this book is a modest attempt to clear the air of as much misunderstanding as possible after decades of sometimes tedious and often acrimonious debate. Second, it is an attempt to present in a relatively concise and understandable way the structure of Van Til's thought, showing the manner in which each part builds upon another. Third, it is an attempt to explain what I believe to be legitimate concerns with some aspects of the Van Tillian system of thought. My working

---

54. James N. Anderson, 'Presuppositionalism in the Dock: A Review Article,' *Reformed Faith & Practice* 7, no. 1 (May 2022): 85.

55. Ibid.

56. Tipton, *The Trinitarian Theology of Cornelius Van Til*, 59.

assumption (my presupposition) is that all Reformed Christians involved in this debate, whether Van Tillian or non-Van Tillian, sincerely desire to follow Scripture faithfully. My hope is to move the discussion among such Van Tillians and non-Van Tillians in a more constructive direction.

On the other hand, this book is *not* an attempt at exhaustive analysis of every version of presuppositionalism. I will not be analyzing the views of men such as James Orr or Abraham Kuyper, whose works influenced Van Til's apologetic system of thought.[57] Nor will I be analyzing the views of men such as Gordon Clark or Francis Schaeffer who offered alternative forms of 'presuppositionalism.'[58] It is not that the teaching of any of these men is unimportant or unworthy of careful consideration, but for the sake of my primary objectives, I have limited the scope of this book to a consideration of Cornelius Van Til's thought.

This book, however, is also *not* an attempt at exhaustive treatment of every aspect of Van Til's thought.[59] It is limited to an examination of the basic ideas that lay the groundwork for his controversial apologetic claims and to an examination of those claims themselves. Finally, this book is not intended to provide a full defense or exposition of 'traditional apologetics.' My goal in this book is to clear the air of as much misunderstanding of Van Til as possible. I am convinced that it will be possible to carry on a constructive discussion of Reformed apologetic principles and methodology only when these distractions are removed. In short, I am not attempting to do everything in this book.

---

57. For a good introduction to James Orr, see Ronnie P. Campbell, Jr., 'James Orr: Defender of the Christian Worldview,' in *The History of Apologetics: A Biographical and Methodological Introduction*, eds. Benjamin K. Forrest, Joshua D. Chatraw, and Alister E. McGrath (Grand Rapids: Zondervan Academic, 2020), 429-44. On Abraham Kuyper, see James D. Bratt, *Abraham Kuyper: Modern Calvinist, Christian Democrat* (Grand Rapids: Wm. B. Eerdmans Publishing Co., 2013) and Peter S. Heslam, *Creating a Christian Worldview: Abraham Kuyper's Lectures on Calvinism* (Grand Rapids: Wm. B. Eerdmans Publishing Co., 1998).

58. The most helpful introduction to Gordon Clark is Douglas S. Douma, *The Presbyterian Philosopher: The Authorized Biography of Gordon H. Clark* (Eugene, OR: Wipf & Stock, 2016). For a good introduction to Francis Schaeffer, see William Edgar, 'Francis Schaeffer: Cultural Apologist,' in *The History of Apologetics: A Biographical and Methodological Introduction*, eds. Benjamin K. Forrest, Joshua D. Chatraw, and Alister E. McGrath (Grand Rapids: Zondervan Academic, 2020), 509-519.

59. Readers interested in a more comprehensive study of Van Til's thought should begin with Frame's *Cornelius Van Til: An Analysis of His Thought* and Bahnsen's *Van Til's Apologetic: Readings and Analysis*.

I am attempting to make one small step in a constructive direction. If successful, more steps can then be taken by those interested in doing so.

The approach I will take in my summary of Van Til's teaching requires some explanation. A number of authors who have sought to provide a summary or overview of Van Til's thought have structured their outlines in terms of philosophical categories. John Frame, for example, outlines Van Til's thought under four major headings: the metaphysics of knowledge, the ethics of knowledge, the argument for Christianity, and the criticism of unbelief.[60] Because Van Til's theory of knowledge (i.e., his epistemology) is the thread that runs through every step in his apologetic system of thought, this is a very helpful approach that provides much insight. I believe it can, however, prove difficult for those Christian readers who lack any philosophical training. It can hinder such readers from grasping the most important connections in Van Til's thought.

For these reasons, I have decided to structure my summary of Van Til's thought in a different way. I believe it is far less difficult for most Christian readers to understand the connections in Van Til's thought if it is approached through explicitly biblical/theological categories, starting with the doctrine of the Triune God and then moving to the doctrines of creation, the fall, and redemption. If we begin with the doctrine of the Triune God and are able to understand first what Van Til says concerning God's infinite knowledge of himself and the facts he eternally decreed, we will then be in a position to understand everything else he teaches. This starting point will also help us see clearly how and why the doctrine of God is foundational to everything Van Til says about knowledge throughout his system of thought.[61]

When we turn next to what Van Til says about creation, our understanding of what he has said about God's omniscience will enable us to grasp the way in which the Creator-creature distinction provides the foundation for his doctrine of the 'analogical' relation of human

---

60. See the Table of Contents in Frame, *Cornelius Van Til: An Analysis of His Thought.*

61. It is important to note that Frame clearly recognizes the foundational nature of Van Til's doctrine of God for everything else he taught (See, for example, Frame, *Cornelius Van Til: An Analysis of His Thought*, 53). I am not suggesting otherwise. My point here has to do with the overall *structure* of the summary, the *arrangement* of the parts. In other words, my table of contents does not look like Frame's table of contents.

knowledge to God's knowledge. Once this element of Van Til's thought is understood, we can then grasp what he says about the effects of the fall on human knowledge as well as the qualifications he makes that are grounded in God's common grace. We will then be able to understand Van Til's teaching about the division among human beings that results from God's work of redemption – the 'antithesis' between believers and unbelievers and the corresponding antithesis between their respective interpretive principles and systems of knowledge. Once we grasp Van Til's doctrine of the antithesis, we will be able to understand the apologetic implications of that antithesis. We will be able to understand why Van Til's apologetic, dependent as it is on his theory of knowledge, requires a presuppositional method. In short, if we are to understand Van Til's apologetic methodology, we must first understand the doctrinal context of his epistemology.

I will, therefore, proceed in Part One to present a basic summary of Van Til's thought. I will move step by step from his doctrine of God to his doctrine of creation and revelation, from his doctrine of the fall and common grace to his doctrine of redemption and the antithesis. I will trace the key idea of knowledge through each of these chapters. Only after these doctrines are explained will I move finally to the apologetic implications of these ideas and explore Van Til's apologetic methodology. The goal of the chapters in Part One is simply to clear away misconceptions about Van Til's teaching and present it in a concise, accurate, and understandable manner.

In Part Two, I will then attempt to explain as clearly as possible my remaining concerns with Van Til's thought. I will look first at some biblical concerns, asking whether Van Til's system is consistent with Scripture. I will then turn to certain philosophical concerns with a focus on trying to bring some clarity to the long-standing debate concerning idealist 'influence' on Van Til's thought. In the remaining chapters, I will discuss some of my theological, historical, and practical concerns. The goal of the chapters in Part Two is to clear away misconceptions by helping readers better understand why some confessionally Reformed believers have not embraced Van Tillianism.

It may be that some of my concerns and some of the concerns of other non-Van Tillians are unwarranted. But it may also be that some of those concerns have not been carefully considered and are worthy of further study. My hope is that these chapters will be read in the spirit in which they are intended and that Van Tillians will respond in the way that Van Til responded to his critics in the introduction to *Jerusalem and Athens*. My hope is that these pages will be used to further the discussion among Van Tillians and non-Van Tillians so that as brothers in Christ we might 'be of help to one another.'[62]

---

62. A note regarding citations of Van Til's works: A large number of Van Til's works, particularly his unpublished works and articles in more obscure publications, are available to those without easy access to his archives only in *The Works of Cornelius Van Til* edited by Eric Sigward (New York: Labels Army Company, 1997). I have made extensive use of this resource, but readers should be aware that those publications available only on Logos sometimes do not include page numbers.

# PART ONE:

# Considering The Thought of Cornelius Van Til

# CHAPTER ONE

# The Triune God

If we are to understand the apologetic thought of Cornelius Van Til, we must first recognize the importance of acknowledging that he was a Christian minister in the Reformed theological tradition. He was raised in the Christian Reformed Church and later became a minister in the CRC before transferring his credentials to the Orthodox Presbyterian Church. In the early twentieth century, when Van Til served as a minister, these were both confessionally Reformed bodies, and Van Til adopted their confessions as his own. Without hesitation he expresses his 'allegiance to the Reformed Faith as set forth in its historic creeds.'[1] This means that the theology of the Reformed confessions provides the overarching doctrinal context for Van Til's apologetic system of thought.

Van Til devoted his entire adult life to propagating and defending the theology of the Reformed confessions.[2] He was not interested in the defense of any sort of 'common denominator' or 'core' form of Christianity.[3] He agreed with the Old Princeton theologian B. B. Warfield that 'Calvinism is just religion in its purity,' and it was Calvinism or Reformed theology that he intended to defend.[4] His goal throughout his life was to develop an apologetic methodology that would be consistent

---

1. Van Til, *The Defense of the Faith*, 1. The fact that this statement is made on the first page of one of his most important apologetic works is not without significance.

2. Ibid., 23.

3. Ibid., 43.

4. Ibid. Cf. B. B. Warfield, *Selected Shorter Writings*, 2 vols. (Phillipsburg, N.J.: P&R Publishing Company, 2001), 1:389.

with the theology of the Reformed confessions.[5] He firmly believed that all other apologetic methodologies lacked such consistency.[6] Given Van Til's goal, the necessity of understanding his Reformed theological context is evident.

Reformed theology developed during the Protestant Reformation, a reformation of the theology and worship of the late medieval western church.[7] The Reformation began in the early sixteenth century with Martin Luther (1483–1546) and quickly spread.[8] Unlike Lutheran theology, which had its origins in one individual, namely Luther himself, Reformed theology developed as several tributaries merged over time to form one confessional tradition. Men such as Huldrych Zwingli (1484–1531), William Farel (1489–1565), Martin Bucer (1491–1551), Peter Martyr Vermigli (1499–1562), Heinrich Bullinger (1504–1575), and John Calvin (1509–1564) all contributed to this tradition and laid the foundation stones of Reformed theology and worship. In the 1550s and 1560s some of the most important early Reformed confessions and catechisms were written. Among these were the French Confession (1559), the Scots Confession (1560), the Belgic Confession (1561), and the Heidelberg Catechism (1563).

As various cities, regions, and nations gradually broke away from Rome and adopted the teaching of the Reformers, a need arose for the theological training of pastors for the new Reformed churches. As educational institutions of various kinds were created to accomplish this goal, theological texts suited for these schools were also written. The era of Reformed scholasticism saw the production of numerous theological works that built upon the work of the first generation of Reformers and worked out the details of the theology of the Reformed confessions.[9]

---

5. Van Til, *Christian Apologetics*, 2nd ed. (Phillipsburg: P&R Publishing, 2003), 86, 124; cf. also, Van Til, *The Defense of the Faith*, 28-29, 43.

6. Van Til, *Introduction to Systematic Theology*, 92, 94, 100.

7. See Matthew Barrett, *The Reformation as Renewal: Retrieving the One, Holy, Catholic, and Apostolic Church* (Grand Rapids: Zondervan Academic, 2023).

8. For a helpful introduction to the history of the Reformation, see Nick Needham, *2000 Years of Christ's Power*, vol. 3, *Renaissance and Reformation*, rev. ed. (Fearn: Christian Focus, 2016).

9. On Reformed Scholasticism, see Willem J. van Asselt, *Introduction to Reformed Scholasticism*, eds. Joel R. Beeke and Jay T. Collier, trans. Albert Gootjes, Reformed Historical–Theological Studies (Grand Rapids: Reformation Heritage Books, 2011); Carl

Among the most important Reformed theologians of this era were men such as Girolamo Zanchius (1516–1590), Zacharius Ursinus (1534–1583), Amandus Polanus (1561–1610), William Ames (1576–1633), Johannes Wollebius (1589–1629), Francis Turretin (1623–1687), Petrus van Mastricht (1630–1706), and Herman Witsius (1636–1708). The high point of mature confessional Reformed theology was reached in the Westminster Confession of Faith (1646).

As Enlightenment philosophy expanded its reach and influence, many theologians in the churches began to embrace rationalism. This led to a transitional period in the development of Reformed theology in the latter half of the seventeenth century, and as the seventeenth century gave way to the eighteenth century, the classic era of Reformed orthodoxy gradually ended.[10] This did not mean the complete end of helpful Reformed theological texts, however. In the eighteenth century, the works of Bernardinus de Moor (1709–1780), and John Brown of Haddington (1722–1787) stand out. In the nineteenth century, important Reformed theological works were written by men such as John Dick (1764–1833), Charles Hodge (1797–1878), William G. T. Shedd (1820–1894), Abraham Kuyper (1837–1920), and Herman Bavinck (1854–1921). In the early twentieth century, Kuyper and Bavinck continued their work, and theologians such as B. B. Warfield (1851–1921) and Louis Berkhof (1873–1957) also contributed to the Reformed theological heritage.

Cornelius Van Til stood firmly in this early twentieth-century, confessionally Reformed theological tradition. As a young man, he was taught the theology of the Three Forms of Unity. As a minister in the Orthodox Presbyterian Church, he was required to subscribe to and teach the doctrines of the Westminster Confession of Faith and the Larger and Shorter Catechisms. These Reformed confessions summarize the system of theology found in Scripture, the theology that provides the doctrinal context for Van Til's apologetic system of thought. His commitment to this confessional Reformed theology is evident throughout his works, but it is particularly important for our purposes as we turn to his doctrine of God.

R. Trueman, and R. Scott Clark, eds., *Protestant Scholasticism: Essays in Reassessment*, eds. Alan P. F. Sell, et al, Studies in Christian History and Thought (Eugene, OR: Wipf & Stock, 2005).

10. Richard A. Muller, *Post-Reformation Reformed Dogmatics*, vol. 1, *Prolegomena to Theology*., 2nd ed. (Grand Rapids: Baker Academic, 2003), 84.

## The Doctrine of God

The doctrine of the Triune God is the cornerstone of Cornelius Van Til's apologetic thought.[11] Everything else that he teaches concerning knowledge and its apologetic implications builds directly upon what he says about God and ultimately depends for its coherence on what he says about God. Chapter two of the Westminster Confession of Faith provides Van Til with the basic theological framework within which he develops his doctrine of God. This confession explains that God 'is infinite in being and perfection, a most pure spirit, invisible, without body, parts, or passions; immutable, immense, eternal, incomprehensible, almighty, most wise, most holy, most free, most absolute; working all things according to the counsel of his own immutable and most righteous will, for his own glory; most loving, gracious, merciful, long-suffering, abundant in goodness and truth, forgiving iniquity, transgression, and sin; the rewarder of them that diligently seek him; and withal, most just, and terrible in his judgments, hating all sin, and who will by no means clear the guilty' (WCF, 1.1). Article 1 of the Belgic Confession, although much briefer, states the same basic doctrine: 'We all believe in our hearts and confess with our mouths that there is a single and simple spiritual being, whom we call God – eternal, incomprehensible, invisible, unchangeable, infinite, almighty; completely wise, just, and good, and the overflowing source of all good.'[12]

This God is also Triune. There is plurality as well as unity in God. The Westminster Confession explains: 'In the unity of the Godhead there be three persons, of one substance, power, and eternity: God the Father, God the Son, and God the Holy Ghost: the Father is of none, neither begotten, nor proceeding; the Son is eternally begotten of the Father; the Holy Ghost eternally proceeding from the Father and the Son' (WCF, 2.3). Article 8 of the Belgic Confession provides further explanation:

> … we believe in one God, who is one single essence, in whom there are three persons, really, truly, and eternally distinct according to their

---

11. Van Til, *An Introduction to Systematic Theology*, 15; cf. also Van Til, *Christian Apologetics*, 23.

12. Jaroslav Pelikan and Valerie Hotchkiss, eds., *Creeds and Confessions of Faith in the Christian Tradition*, vol. 2, *Creeds and Confessions of the Reformation Era* (New Haven: Yale University Press, 2003), 407.

incommunicable properties – namely, Father, Son, and Holy Spirit. The Father is the cause, origin, and source of all things, visible as well as invisible. The Son is the Word, the Wisdom, and the Image of the Father. The Holy Spirit is the eternal power and might, proceeding from the Father and the Son. Nevertheless, this distinction does not divide God into three, since Scripture teaches us that the Father, the Son, and the Holy Spirit each has his own subsistence distinguished by characteristics – yet in such a way that these three persons are only one God. It is evident then that the Father is not the Son and that the Son is not the Father, and that likewise the Holy Spirit is neither the Father nor the Son. Nevertheless, these persons, thus distinct, are neither divided nor fused or mixed together. For the Father did not take on flesh, nor did the Spirit, but only the Son. The Father was never without his Son, nor without his Holy Spirit, since all these are equal from eternity in one and the same essence. There is neither a first nor a last, for all three are one in truth and power, in goodness and mercy.[13]

## The Attributes of God

God's infinite and perfect knowledge is the attribute most directly relevant to an understanding of Van Til's apologetic system of thought, but God's knowledge must be understood in relation to his other attributes. In several places in his writings, Van Til offers a summary discussion of the attributes of God. Following Herman Bavinck, he typically begins with the attribute of independence, which he defines in terms of God's self-existence (or aseity).[14] He writes: 'First and foremost among the attributes, we therefore mention the independence or self-existence of God (*autarkia, omnisufficientia*).'[15] Herman Bavinck summarizes the main features of this divine attribute:

Now when God ascribes this aseity to himself in Scripture, he makes himself known as absolute being, as the one who *is* in an absolute sense. By this perfection he is at once essentially and absolutely distinct from

---

13. Ibid., 409.

14. The order in which Van Til discusses the incommunicable attributes of God also follows the order in which Bavinck discusses them in his *Reformed Dogmatics*. Bavinck begins with independence before moving to immutability, infinity, unity, and simplicity. See Herman Bavinck, *Reformed Dogmatics*, vol. 2, *God and Creation*, ed. John Bolt, trans. John Vriend (Grand Rapids: Baker Academic, 2004), 152.

15. Van Til, *An Introduction to Systematic Theology*, 327.

all creatures. Creatures, after all, do not derive their existence from themselves but from others and so have nothing from themselves; both in their origin and hence in their further development and life, they are absolutely dependent. But as is evident from the word 'aseity,' God is exclusively from himself, not in the sense of being self-caused but being from eternity to eternity who he is, being not becoming. God is absolute being, the fullness of being, and therefore also eternally and absolutely independent in his existence, in his perfections, in all his works, the first and the last, the sole cause and final goal of all things.[16]

Note that God's independence describes God's other perfections or attributes (including his knowledge). Van Til makes an additional point about God's independence saying, 'that God is in no sense correlative to or dependent upon anything beside his own being.'[17] Correlativism is a term Van Til uses to speak of a 'mutually interdependent relationship.'[18] God cannot be both independent and mutually interdependent. Therefore, since God *is* independent of all creatures, God is *not* correlative to any creature.

The truth of God's independence leads Van Til to an affirmation of divine immutability. As Van Til observes, 'The immutability of God is involved in his aseity.'[19] He then quotes Herman Bavinck with approval, saying that God is 'unchangeable in his existence and essence; as he is in his thought and will, in all his purposes and decrees.'[20] Note that immutability describes God's *thought* in his *decrees*. Immutability is, thus, tied to God's knowledge. Regarding immutability, Van Til explains that, 'God does not and cannot change since there is nothing besides his own eternal being on which he depends.'[21] In other words, God cannot change precisely *because* God is independent. To deny immutability, therefore, is to deny independence, and to deny independence is to affirm correlativism.

---

16. Bavinck, *Reformed Dogmatics*, vol. 2, *God and Creation*, 152.

17. Van Til, *Christian Apologetics*, 24.

18. Cornelius Van Til, 'Presuppositionalism, Part 1,' in Cornelius Van Til and Eric H. Sigward, *The Articles of Cornelius Van Til*, Electronic ed. (Labels Army Company: New York, 1997).

19. Van Til, *An Introduction to Systematic Theology*, 333.

20. Ibid.

21. Van Til, *Christian Apologetics*, 24.

Van Til recognizes that Scripture uses anthropomorphic language such as 'repentance' (e.g., Gen. 6:6-7) to speak of God, but he argues that this language does not undermine the doctrine of divine immutability. It does not mean that God's being changes. As Van Til puts it, 'The Scriptures speak anthropomorphically of God, and could not do otherwise, but for all that, God, in himself, is immutable.'[22] Not only does anthropomorphic language not undermine divine immutability, neither creation nor the incarnation undermine it either. Van Til explains, 'The movements of history are not determinative of the self-sufficient activity of God; when God created the world by the determination of his will there was no change in himself. When the second person of the Trinity became incarnate there was no change in God.'[23]

It is important to grasp the points that Van Til is making in these remarks. In the first place, the anthropomorphic language used in Scripture to describe God's relation to his creatures does not contradict what Scripture teaches about divine immutability. Van Til clearly objects to any use of anthropomorphic language to downplay or deny the attribute of immutability.[24] Second, Van Til insists that God's act of creation did not change God in himself. God remained immutable even as he created the heavens and the earth. Third, the incarnation of the Son did not change the divine nature.[25] One of the properties of the

---

22. Van Til, *An Introduction to Systematic Theology*, 334.

23. Ibid., 337. See also Bavinck, *Reformed Dogmatics*, vol. 2, *God and Creation*, 153. For a traditional Reformed defense of this same point, see Francis Turretin, *Institutes of Elenctic Theology*, ed. James T. Dennison, Jr., trans. George Musgrave Giger (Phillipsburg: P&R Publishing Company, 1992–1997), 1:205.

24. Some Van Tillians, such as John Frame, are concerned with the opposite problem. They are concerned that the doctrine of immutability is being used to deny the anthropomorphic language of Scripture. See, for example, Frame, *On Theology: Explorations and Controversies* (Bellingham, WA: Lexham Press, 2023), 106-107. Those Van Tillians who have either rejected or redefined the doctrine of immutability, have fallen into what Van Til called 'correlativism' in the process. Ironically, the 'correlativist' views of such Van Tillians would have been rejected by Van Til himself in the strongest terms.

25. In its statement of the hypostatic union of the divine nature and human nature in the Person of the Son, the Definition of Chalcedon affirms, 'the property of both natures is preserved.' See Jaroslav Pelikan and Valerie Hotchkiss, eds., *Creeds and Confessions of Faith in the Christian Tradition*, vol. 1, *Early, Eastern, and Medieval* (New Haven: Yale University Press, 2003), 181.

divine nature is immutability, and this property was preserved in the incarnation of the Son. In short, it is important to understand that Van Til does not pit the biblical doctrines of creation, incarnation, covenant, or anything else against the biblical doctrine of divine immutability.

God's independence or self-existence also leads Van Til to an affirmation of the attribute of infinity. Van Til writes, 'The infinity of God is also involved in his aseity. By the infinity of God is meant the boundless fulness of his being. God is limitless in his existence, and therefore in his attributes.'[26] Unlike the being of finite creatures, the fulness of God's being is not limited by either time or space. Thus, God is eternal as well as omnipresent. Furthermore, the attribute of infinity informs our understanding of God's other attributes. God's goodness is without limits. His power is without limits. Most significant for our purposes, his knowledge is without limits.

Van Til moves next to the divine attribute of unity. He explains, 'By the unity of God we mean that God is one God, and that he is not composed of parts. We therefore speak of unity of singularity and of unity of simplicity.'[27] As Bavinck explains, the unity of singularity means 'that there is but one divine being and, consequently, that all other beings exist only from him, through him, and to him.'[28] The attribute of simplicity refers to the fact that God is non-composite. He is not composed of parts of any kind. If God were composed of parts of any kind, he would not be independent. A composite being is dependent upon its constituent parts and upon a composer.

In addition to these incommunicable attributes, it is important for our purposes at this point to discuss more fully one of God's communicable attributes, namely, his knowledge. It is important to discuss God's attribute of knowledge because knowledge is the key theme that runs through each major building block in Van Til's system of thought. God's infinite and perfect knowledge, his omniscience, is foundational to his

---

26. Van Til, *An Introduction to Systematic Theology*, 335.

27. Ibid., 341. Van Til here is using the language of Bavinck. See Bavinck, *Reformed Dogmatics*, vol. 2, *God and Creation*, 170. For a fuller contemporary discussion of the doctrine of divine simplicity, see James E. Dolezal, *God Without Parts: Divine Simplicity and the Metaphysics of God's Absoluteness* (Eugene, OR: Pickwick, 2011); cf. also Steven J. Duby, *Divine Simplicity: A Dogmatic Account* (London: T&T Clark, 2016).

28. Bavinck, *Reformed Dogmatics*, vol. 2, *God and Creation*, 170.

system. If we miss what Van Til teaches concerning God's knowledge, we will miss his starting point and misread everything that follows.

Van Til affirms the attribute of divine omniscience. This means he affirms that God is eternally and perfectly all-knowing. God, as Van Til explains, 'knows his own being to its very depths in one eternal act of knowledge. There are no hidden depths in the being of God that he has not explored.'[29] Because God is independent and infinite, God's knowledge 'is absolutely comprehensive and self-contained.'[30] Furthermore, Van Til emphasizes the point that God knows the meaning of every proposition 'in all the fullness of its significance because he knows it in relationship to all other propositions …'[31] We will return to the significance of this doctrine below, but at this point we merely note that according to Van Til, it is in God's omniscience that we discover the solution to the problem of human knowledge.[32] We must await a discussion of God's divine decree, however, before the full significance of this attribute for his system of thought becomes completely clear.

## The Trinity

Van Til's discussion of the attributes of God uses the traditional language of classical theism as found in the Reformed confessions and mediated through Reformed theologians such as Herman Bavinck. When he turns to the doctrine of the Trinity, however, Van Til elaborates on the way in which the term 'person' applies to God using language that departs from traditional terminology and is, thus, much more controversial. Van Til, for example, writes:

> We turn from our consideration of the incommunicable attributes of God to that of his triunity. The fact that God exists as concrete self-sufficient being appears clearly in the doctrine of the Trinity. Here the God who is numerically and not merely specifically one when compared with any other form of being, now appears to have within himself a distinction of specific and numerical existence. We speak of the essence of God in contrast to the three persons of the Godhead. *We speak of God*

---

29. Van Til, *Christian Apologetics*, 25.

30. Van Til, *An Introduction to Systematic Theology*, 33.

31. Ibid., 296.

32. Cornelius Van Til, 'Common Grace: Third Article,' *Westminster Theological Journal* 9, no. 1 (Nov. 1946): 53.

*as a person; yet we speak also of three persons in the Godhead.* As we say that each of the attributes of God is to be identified with the being of God, while yet we are justified in making a distinction between them, so we say that each of the persons of the Trinity is exhaustive of divinity itself, while yet there is a genuine distinction between the persons. Unity and plurality are equally ultimate in the Godhead. The persons of the Godhead are mutually exhaustive of one another and therefore of the essence of the Godhead. God is a one-conscious being, and yet he is also a tri-conscious being.[33]

The traditional language, as found in the ancient creeds and in the Reformed confessions, speaks of God in terms of *three persons* and *one substance* (e.g., WCF, II.3) or *three persons* and *one essence* (Belgic Confession, Art. 8). Van Til does not deny that in the unity of the Godhead there are 'three persons,' but he also asserts that God is 'one absolute person.'[34] It is this assertion that has created controversy.

Lane Tipton argues that Van Til's Trinitarian theology 'represents the integration of the Old Princeton (English Puritan) and Old Amsterdam (Continental Dutch) expressions of Trinitarian dogma.'[35] He argues that Van Til appropriated the idea from A. A. Hodge of 'a common consciousness and a common personality' in the Godhead.[36] Hodge understood these ideas, according to Tipton, to be implications of the divine unity and simplicity.[37] From Herman Bavinck, Van Til appropriated the concept of God as an 'absolute personality' as a means of denying that God is some kind of 'unconscious force.'[38] According to Tipton, it is the combination of these two streams of Trinitarian thought in Van Til's mind that led him to assert that God is one person.

---

33. Van Til, *An Introduction to Systematic Theology*, 348. Emphasis mine.

34. Ibid., 362. Several Van Tillian scholars have offered explanations and defenses of Van Til's one person/three person formula. See for example, Frame, *Cornelius Van Til: An Analysis of His Thought*, 65-71; cf. also Tipton, *The Trinitarian Theology of Cornelius Van Til*, 79-86.

35. Tipton, *The Trinitarian Theology of Cornelius Van Til*, 57.

36. Ibid., 71.

37. Ibid.

38. Ibid., 76. Whether or not Hodge or Bavinck influenced Van Til's formulation of the doctrine of the Trinity, neither, to my knowledge, expressed it in terms of 'one person' and 'three persons.'

In an attempt to explain what he means by asserting that God is one person and three persons, Van Til begins by drawing a parallel between the manner in which the divine attributes relate to the Godhead and the manner in which the persons relate to the Godhead.

> We do assert that God, that is, the whole Godhead, is one person. We have noted how each attribute is coextensive with the being of God. We are compelled to maintain this in order to avoid the notion of an uninterpreted being of some sort. In other words, we are bound to maintain the identity of the attributes of God with the being of God in order to avoid the specter of brute fact. In a similar manner we have noted how theologians insist that each of the persons of the Godhead is coterminous with the being of the Godhead. But all this is not to say that the distinctions of the attributes are merely nominal. Nor is it to say that the distinctions of the persons are merely nominal. We need both the absolute cotermineity of each attribute and each person with the whole being of God, and the genuine significance of the distinctions of the attributes and the persons.[39]

Because God is not composed of parts (divine simplicity), each divine attribute is affirmed to be coextensive with the being of the Godhead. Each attribute is, in other words, identical with the being of God. Likewise, Van Til argues, each of the three persons of the Trinity is coterminous with the one being of the Godhead. In an application of the doctrine of *perichoresis*, Van Til then argues, following Bavinck, that if each person is coterminous with the being of God, and if there is only one God, then each person is also coinherent with the other persons.[40] If this is the case, then it is appropriate, according to Van Til, to speak of one absolute person as well as three persons.

Van Til says that when he speaks of God as 'one person' he is attempting to communicate the idea that God is a personal being as opposed to some kind of impersonal force. He clarifies this idea saying, 'It were quite legitimate and true to say that the foundation of all personal activity among men must be based upon the personality of one ultimate person, namely, the person of God, if only it be understood that this ultimate personality of God is a triune personality.'[41] In other

---

39. Van Til, *An Introduction to Systematic Theology*, 363-364 .

40. Ibid., 364.

41. Cornelius Van Til, *Survey of Christian Epistemology*, Vol. 2 of *In Defense of the Faith/ Biblical Christianity* (Nutley, NJ: Presbyterian and Reformed, 1969), 78.

words, when we speak of the *personality* of the one person of God, we assert that this *personality* is a triune personality.

Finally, it is important to note with regard to the theme of knowledge that Van Til also argues that the doctrine of the Trinity provides a solution to the philosophical problem of the one and the many. This problem involves explaining both our knowledge of particulars and our knowledge of abstract universals. We observe particular things all around us, but we also speak in terms of universals. We see all kinds of different dogs, but we also speak of 'dogs' in general. No one has ever seen the universal 'canine nature,' so how do we make sense of this language?

According to Van Til, non-Christian epistemologies cannot make sense of the 'one and the many' regardless of whether those epistemologies are realist or nominalist. Van Til rejects the strong realist view of Plato, which claims that the universals exist in some impersonal world of forms.[42] He also rejects the nominalist claim that there are no universals. According to Van Til, universals exist, and the solution to the problem of the one and the many is found in the doctrine of the Triune God. Van Til explains:

> The Christian conception of God implies that 'whatsoever comes to pass' in the created universe has been preinterpreted by God's plan. God's logic precedes history. God makes and sustains the facts and the laws of the scientists. The particulars and universals of the created universe are adapted to one another by God. They have their coherence and admit of interpretation by man because back of them is the absolute coherence of God.[43]

In other words, universals do not exist in some impersonal world of forms. The universals and the particulars both exist in the mind of the tri-personal God. Van Til notes the connection with the doctrine of the Trinity: 'In the ontological trinity there is complete harmony between an equally ultimate one and many.'[44]

---

42. Van Til, *An Introduction to Systematic Theology*, 96

43. Cornelius Van Til, review of *De Noodzakelijkeheid eener Christelijke Logica*, by D. H. Th. Vollenhoven, *The Calvin Forum* 1/6 (Jan 1936) in Cornelius Van Til and Eric H. Sigward, *Reviews by Cornelius Van Til*, Electronic ed. (Labels Army Company: New York, 1997).

44. Cornelius Van Til, *Common Grace and the Gospel*, 2nd ed. (Phillipsburg: P&R Publishing, 2015), 13.

The relation between the one unified decree of God and the many decreed facts within it is also grounded in the nature of the Trinity. As Frame explains it, God is the solution. 'His plan is perfectly unified,' and that unity has content – the particular details of the plan. His plan 'is a personal one and many, because his nature is one and many.'[45] For Van Til, both universals and the particular facts within the creation reflect their Triune Creator, and the Trinity provides the one ultimate reference point for the knowledge and interpretation of the creation. This is part of the reason why Van Til will argue that the Triune God of Scripture must be presupposed in order for there to be any meaningful predication.[46]

## The Divine Decree

The doctrine of the Triune God is the foundational starting point for everything Van Til teaches, but if we are to fully understand how it serves as a foundation, it is also necessary to examine what he says regarding the doctrine of the divine decree. It is necessary because the divine decree is included in God's perfect knowledge. The Westminster Confession of Faith expresses the doctrine in the following words: 'God, from all eternity, did, by the most wise and holy counsel of his own will, freely, and unchangeably ordain whatsoever comes to pass: yet so, as thereby neither is God the author of sin, nor is violence offered to the will of the creatures; nor is the liberty or contingency of second causes taken away, but rather established' (3.1). The key doctrinal point that Van Til repeatedly emphasizes in his writings about the decree is that God has eternally *planned* 'whatsoever comes to pass' and thus eternally *knows* 'whatsoever comes to pass.'

The first thing we must observe about Van Til's thought regarding the divine decree is that it encompasses all facts ('whatsoever comes to pass'). For Van Til, a 'fact' is the 'object of knowledge.'[47] Because God's decree or plan encompasses all facts, the meaning of all decreed facts is *necessarily* related to the God who decreed them. As Van Til

---

45. Frame, *Cornelius Van Til: An Analysis of His Thought*, 75.

46. Van Til, *Christian Apologetics*, 39. To 'predicate' is to affirm or deny something in a proposition. If I say, 'The car is red,' I am predicating 'redness' of the car.

47. Cornelius Van Til, *Survey of Christian Epistemology* (Nutley, NJ: Presbyterian and Reformed, 1969), 116. These may be material facts, spiritual facts, psychological facts, mathematical facts, etc. (pp. 116-17).

explains, 'God is the ultimate subject of every predicate.'[48] He observes: 'It is the plan of God that gives any fact meaning in terms of the plan of God. The whole meaning of any fact is exhausted by its position in and relation to the plan of God.'[49] According to Van Til, 'the absolute meaning that God has for himself implies that the meaning of every fact in the universe must be related to God.'[50] Every *thing* and every *event* in creation is, accordingly, a God-decreed *thing* or *event* and 'accomplishes what it does accomplish by virtue of the plan or purpose of God.'[51]

The second thing we must observe about Van Til's thought on this point is that because every fact is related to the God who decreed it, every fact is also related to every other fact within God's unified divine decree. Van Til explains:

> The whole meaning of any fact is exhausted by its position in and relation to the plan of God. This implies that every fact is related to every other fact. God's plan is a unit. And it is this unity of the plan of God, founded as it is in the very being of God, that gives the unity that we look for between all the finite facts. If one should maintain that one fact can be fully understood *without reference to all other facts*, he is as much antitheistic as when he should maintain that one fact can be understood without reference to God.[52]

As Van Til explains here, the relationship of all decreed facts to God and to one another indicates that God's plan is 'a unit,' a holistic system. It is also important to note Van Til's claim that the unitary nature of God's plan means that one cannot fully understand any one fact without reference to every other fact. Facts are truly understood or known only when they are known in relation to God and to all other facts in the plan of God.

The third thing we must note about Van Til's thought on this point is directly related to the previous two. Because all decreed facts are related to the God who decreed them and because all decreed facts are also related to each other within God's unified divine decree, there

---

48. Ibid., 158.

49. Ibid., 6.

50. Van Til, *An Introduction to Systematic Theology*, 58.

51. Cornelius Van Til, *Christian Theistic Evidences*, 2nd ed. (Phillipsburg: P&R Publishing, 2016), 92.

52. Van Til, *Survey of Christian Epistemology*, 6. Emphasis mine.

are no and can be no 'brute facts.' Van Til explains, 'Scripture teaches that every fact in the universe exists and operates by virtue of the plan of God. There are *no brute facts* for God.'[53] If a brute fact existed, it would be a non-decreed fact. According to Van Til, the assumption that brute facts exist is a denial of the most basic truths about God and his all-encompassing decree.[54]

Instead of being brute facts, the facts that God decrees are already interpreted facts. This point is vitally important for understanding Van Til's entire system of thought. For Van Til, 'facts and interpretation of facts cannot be separated. It is impossible even to discuss any particular fact except in relation to some principle of interpretation.'[55] What this means is that there is 'a necessary connection between the facts and the observer or interpreter of facts.'[56] This is true even in eternity 'before' God creates any facts 'outside' of himself and 'before' God creates any other interpreters of facts.

Because God is omniscient, God fully knows all of the facts he has eternally decreed and fully knows the relation of every fact to himself and to every other fact. This means that in eternity, all decreed facts are already 'God-interpreted' facts.[57] Furthermore, since God's eternal plan is a unitary whole, God's exhaustive interpretation of this unitary whole (including his interpretation of every fact within this unitary system) is the one perfectly true interpretive system, the one perfectly true system of knowledge. God, therefore, is the ultimate principle of interpretation of all facts.

## Conclusion

When we examine Van Til's doctrine of God, several key elements stand out. Each must be grasped if we are to understand the system of thought that Van Til builds upon this doctrine of God. In the first place, the fact that Van Til is working within the framework of confessional

---

53. Van Til, *Christian Theistic Evidences*, 92.

54. Ibid., 151-52.

55. Ibid., 2.

56. Ibid., 67.

57. Cornelius Van Til, 'Facts,' *The Banner* 75/2232 (16 Feb 1940): 150, in Cornelius Van Til and Eric H. Sigward, *The Articles of Cornelius Van Til*, Electronic ed. (Labels Army Company: New York, 1997).

Reformed theology is significant. Only Reformed theology, for example, emphasizes the doctrine of the divine decree. Given his view that all facts are God-decreed facts, and given his view that all God-decreed facts are God-interpreted facts, we are now better able to understand why Van Til argues *this* God, and no other, is the final reference point for all predication.[58] Only the God described in the Reformed confessions has eternally and unconditionally decreed whatsoever comes to pass. Only this God has already pre-interpreted all facts.

Second, the affirmation of God's attribute of independence and the corresponding denial of any form of correlativism is fundamental to Van Til's system. God does not depend on anything in creation. Everything in creation depends on God. When considered in relation to the crucial Van Tillian question of epistemology, Van Til affirms that God does not depend on anything for his knowledge. God perfectly, eternally, and immutably knows himself and all that he has freely decreed. God's knowledge, as a result, is the one perfectly true system of knowledge, which means that God is the final reference point of predication, the ultimate principle of interpretation.

Third, the doctrine of the Trinity stands out in Van Til's system of thought. It is crucial for Van Til because of Van Til's concern with the problem of the one and the many in epistemology. For Van Til, the Trinity provides the only real solution because in the Trinity, both the one and the many are equally ultimate. Furthermore, the Trinity provides Van Til with an eternal absolute personality, apart from which he believes a solution to the problem of knowledge is impossible.

Finally, nothing in Van Til's apologetic system ultimately makes sense unless understood in light of his doctrine of the divine decree. For Van Til, it is absolutely vital to understand that God not only decreed all facts but that he eternally knows and interprets all facts. This is because, for Van Til, facts and the interpretation of facts cannot be separated, so the true meaning of any fact is determined by its place in the plan of God. In the plan of God every fact is related to God as well as to every other fact. The plan of God is also a unified whole, and because it is a unified whole, no fact can be truly known apart from a

---

58. Cornelius Van Til, *A Christian Theory of Knowledge*, ed. K. Scott Oliphint (Glenside: Westminster Seminary Press, 2023), 33.

full understanding of its relation to God and its relation to every other fact in that unified whole. God alone has such infinite knowledge. God alone eternally and fully understands himself as well as understanding every fact in relation to himself and in relation to every other fact. This is the starting point in Van Til's system of apologetic thought.

# CHAPTER 2

# Creation and Revelation

From all eternity, God *decreed* the heavens and the earth, and in the beginning, God *created* the heavens and the earth (Gen. 1:1). As the Westminster Confession of Faith expresses it: 'It pleased God the Father, Son, and Holy Ghost, for the manifestation of the glory of his eternal power, wisdom, and goodness, in the beginning, to create, or make of nothing, the world, and all things therein whether visible or invisible, in the space of six days; and all very good' (4.1). Herman Bavinck explains the importance of this doctrine: 'The realization of the counsel [decree] of God begins with creation. Creation is the initial act and foundation of all divine revelation and therefore the foundation of all religious and ethical life as well.'[1]

Bavinck provides further explanation regarding what it means to attribute the work of creation to the Trinity. In the first place, it means that there were no intermediary beings involved in the work of creation.[2] Second, it testifies to the fact that all the external works of God are undivided.[3] The work of creation is not the work of only one Person of the Trinity. As the Westminster Confession states, it is the

---

1. Bavinck, *Reformed Dogmatics*, vol. 2, *God and Creation*, 407. By 'counsel,' Bavinck means the divine decree. Cf. Van Til, *An Introduction to Systematic Theology*, 120-21.

2. Ibid., 420. Bavinck refers here specifically to those Jews who believed that Genesis 1:26 speaks of angels, to Gnostics who believed in a series of intermediate creative 'aeons,' and to Arians who believed the Son to be an intermediate being between God and creation.

3. Ibid., 422.

work of the Father, Son, and Holy Spirit (4.1). More importantly, for our purposes, is the relation between the one and the many in God and the one and the many in creation. Bavinck explains, 'Just as God is one in essence and distinct in persons, so also the work of creation is one and undivided, while in its unity it is still rich in diversity.'[4] The unity and diversity in creation reflect the unity and plurality of the Triune Creator.

Regarding the creation of the first human beings, the Westminster Confession goes on to state: 'After God had made all other creatures, he created man, male and female, with reasonable and immortal souls, endued with knowledge, righteousness, and true holiness, after his own image; having the law of God written in their hearts, and power to fulfill it: and yet under a possibility of transgressing, being left to the liberty of their own will, which was subject unto change. Beside this law written in their hearts, they received a command, not to eat of the tree of the knowledge of good and evil; which while they kept, they were happy in their communion with God, and had dominion over the creatures.' (4.2). Again, Bavinck provides a helpful explanation of the importance of this doctrine of revelation:

> The essence of human nature is its being [created in] the image of God. The entire world is a revelation of God, a mirror of his attributes and perfections. Every creature in its own way and degree is the embodiment of a divine thought. But among creatures, only man is the image of God, God's highest and richest self-revelation and consequently the head and crown of the whole creation, the *imago Dei* and the epitome of nature, both *mikrotheos* (microgod) and *mikrokosmos* (microcosm).[5]

It is not merely that human beings *have* the image of God; human beings *are* the image of God.[6] According to Bavinck, this means that the image 'extends to the whole person. Nothing in a human being is excluded from the image of God.'[7] Given their importance, it is necessary that we examine the way in which the doctrines of creation and revelation fit into Van Til's system of thought.

---

4. Ibid.

5. Ibid., 530-31.

6. Ibid., 554.

7. Ibid., 555.

## The Creator-Creature Distinction

Anyone who has studied Van Til for any length of time is familiar with his diagram consisting of two separate circles, a larger circle above a smaller circle. This diagram was used by Van Til in the classroom to illustrate the crucial distinction in the Christian worldview between the being of the Creator and the being of creatures. As we saw in the previous chapter, Van Til emphasizes in his teaching the doctrine that God, from all eternity, decreed whatsoever comes to pass. The facts that God creates are the facts that God decreed to create. Van Til explains, 'As Christians we believe that God has made the facts of this world and the laws of this world. He has made the facts and the laws for one another. Moreover, he continues to support both facts and laws.'[8] God has created these facts according to his eternal plan, thus 'every fact in the universe exists and operates by virtue of the plan of God.'[9] For Van Til, every God-created fact was first an eternally God-decreed fact and, as such, is an eternally God-interpreted fact.

Because every created fact is a God-created fact, every created fact has a kind of being that is distinct from God's uncreated being. Van Til explains the fundamental point: 'God has one kind of being, being that is infinite, eternal, and unchangeable and full of holy attributes. The universe has another sort of being, being that has been produced and is sustained by God.'[10] This metaphysical distinction between God and his creatures is all-important for Van Til, and it applies to his human creatures as much as it applies to any other creature. As Van Til puts it, 'In Protestantism man is really taken to be the creature of God. Man is not thought of as participant with God in some principle of being that is above and exemplified in both.'[11] There is no chain of being.

Human beings have been uniquely created in the image of God. To be created in the image of God means, according to Van Til, that God's

---

8. Van Til, *Christian Theistic Evidences*, 152.

9. Ibid., 92.

10. Van Til, *Christian Apologetics*, 30.

11. Cornelius Van Til, *The Intellectual Challenge of the Gospel* (London: Tyndale Press, 1950) in Cornelius Van Til and Eric H. Sigward, *The Pamphlets, Tracts, and Offprints of Cornelius Van Til*, Electronic ed. (Labels Army Company: New York, 1997).

'rationality' is 'stamped' upon all mankind.[12] However, although God's rationality has been stamped upon man, man remains a finite creature, which means that his knowledge is finite.[13] Van Til explains, 'The *Adamic consciousness*, or, the reason of man as it existed before the fall of man .... was derivative. Its knowledge was, in the nature of the case, true, though not exhaustive. This reason was in covenant with God, instead of at enmity against God.'[14] Van Til also explains that because human beings are created in God's image, they have an 'ineradicable sense of deity within them.'[15] Man's nature itself, as a created being, is revelatory of God. As soon as man is aware of himself, therefore, he 'knows that he is the creature of God and responsible to God.'[16]

## Revelation

Because every fact is a God-decreed fact as well as a God-created fact, every fact necessarily reveals its Creator. Not only human beings themselves, but the world in which God placed them, is revelatory of God since it too was created by God.[17] The revelatory nature of God-created facts introduces us to Van Til's doctrine of general revelation (or natural revelation). The term 'general revelation' emphasizes 'the fact that this revelation is accessible to all men and valid for all men ...'[18] The doctrine of general revelation teaches that all created facts are 'exhaustively revelational' of God.[19] Van Til explains:

> We may characterize this whole situation by saying that the creation of God is a revelation of God. God revealed himself in nature and God also revealed himself in the mind of man. Thus it is impossible for the mind of

---

12. Cornelius Van Til, 'A Christian Theistic Theory of Knowledge,' *The Banner* 66/1809 (6 Nov 1931), in Cornelius Van Til and Eric H. Sigward, *The Articles of Cornelius Van Til*, Electronic ed. (Labels Army Company: New York, 1997).

13. Van Til, *An Introduction to Systematic Theology*, 61.

14. Ibid., 62.

15. Cornelius Van Til, 'Presuppositionalism, Part 2,' *The Bible Today* 42, no. 9 (June/Sept 1949), in Cornelius Van Til and Eric H. Sigward, *The Articles of Cornelius Van Til*, Electronic ed. (Labels Army Company: New York, 1997).

16. Van Til, *Christian Apologetics*, 119.

17. Cornelius Van Til, *The Protestant Doctrine of Scripture* (Philadelphia: The Presbyterian and Reformed Publishing Company, 1967), 67.

18. Van Til, *An Introduction to Systematic Theology*, 138.

19. Van Til, *Common Grace and the Gospel*, 181, 193.

man to function except in an atmosphere of revelation. And every thought of man when it functioned normally in this atmosphere of revelation would express the truth as laid in the creation by God. We may therefore call a Christian epistemology a *revelational epistemology*.[20]

The implication is that, 'Everything in the created universe therefore displays the fact that it is controlled by God, that it is what it is by virtue of the place that it occupies in the plan of God.'[21] In other words, everything in the universe reveals God, and everything also reveals that it is a part of the interrelated and unified system of truth that is eternally and exhaustively known by the Triune God.

According to Van Til, God's general revelation to man was never intended to stand alone and apart from special revelation.[22] 'There was superadded to God's revelation in nature another revelation, a supernaturally communicated positive revelation.'[23] This supernatural revelation is covenantal revelation. General revelation, in other words, 'was from the outset incorporated into the idea of a covenantal relationship of God with man. Thus every dimension of created existence, even the lowest, was enveloped in a form of exhaustively personal relationship between God and man.'[24] Every aspect of creation, then, was covenantal.

According to Van Til, just as God's special revelation has the attributes of necessity, authority, sufficiency, and perspicuity, God's general revelation in nature has the same four attributes.[25] Van Til explains the necessity of general revelation by way of the command not to eat of the tree of the knowledge of good and evil. In order to achieve its purpose, the command had to appear arbitrary, and this could be the case only if the tree was 'naturally like other trees.'[26] Additionally, according to Van Til, this prohibition was given not merely to teach

---

20. Van Til, *Survey of Christian Epistemology*, 1.

21. Van Til, 'Presuppositionalism, Part 2.'

22. On this point, Van Til appears to be following Herman Bavinck. See Bavinck, *Reformed Dogmatics*, 4 vols. ed John Bolt, trans. John Vriend (Grand Rapids: Baker Academic, 2003–2008), 1:310.

23. Cornelius Van Til, 'Nature and Scripture' in *The Infallible Word: A Symposium by the Faculty of Westminster Theological Seminary*, eds. Ned B. Stonehouse and Paul Woolley, (Philadelphia: Presbyterian Guardian Publishing Corporation, 1946), 267.

24. Ibid.

25. Ibid., 264.

26. Ibid., 269.

Adam what to do with regard to this one tree. It was also given to teach him 'to be self-consciously obedient in all that he did with respect to all things and throughout all time.'[27]

The key point with regard to the authority of general revelation is the fact that in general revelation, just as in special revelation, the same authoritative God is the Revealer. Just as God gave the command concerning the tree through an act of special revelation, 'in and through the things of nature, there spoke the self-same voice of God's command.'[28] In other words, in both special revelation and general revelation, the Revealer is the same. The authority of God's revelation is the same regardless of the form that revelation takes. Adam was given the command to take dominion and rule over God's creation, but, 'The mark of God's ownership was from the beginning writ large upon all the facts of the universe.'[29] Adam was always subordinate to the revelation of God.

Van Til's explanation of the sufficiency of general revelation is a bit more complicated. As we have seen, according to Van Til, general revelation was never intended to function apart from special revelation. In that sense it was insufficient. It was, however, sufficient in the sense that it served as 'the presupposition of historical action on the part of man as covenant personality with respect to supernaturally conveyed communication.'[30] In other words, it was sufficient as a 'limiting notion.'[31]

When Van Til turns to the perspicuity of general revelation, he grants the fact that because general revelation was always meant to function together with special revelation some might understand this to mean that general revelation itself is not perspicuous.[32] He also says

---

27. Ibid., 270.

28. Ibid., 272.

29. Ibid., 273.

30. Ibid., 275. In the works of the Reformed theologians of the sixteenth and seventeenth centuries, the insufficiency of general (or natural) revelation is typically discussed in terms of its insufficiency with regard to the saving knowledge of God. See, for example, Francis Turretin, *Institutes of Elenctic Theology*, ed. James T. Dennison, Jr., trans. George Musgrave Giger (Phillipsburg: P&R Publishing Company, 1992–1997), 1:56.

31. Ibid. In Van Til's thought, a limiting notion or limiting concept is a concept 'that needs another [concept] if it is to be properly understood.' See William Edgar, notes to Cornelius Van Til, *An Introduction to Systematic Theology*, 136, n. 51.

32. Van Til, 'Nature and Scripture,' 277.

that because the incomprehensible God stands behind both general and special revelation, this too might seem to undermine the idea that general revelation is perspicuous.[33] For Van Til, however, the truth is precisely the opposite.

> … these very facts themselves are the best guarantee of the genuine perspicuity of natural revelation. The perspicuity of God's revelation in nature depends for its very meaning upon the fact that it is an aspect of the total and totally voluntary revelation of a God who is self-contained. God's incomprehensibility to man is due to the fact that he is exhaustively comprehensible to himself. God is light and in him is no darkness at all. As such he cannot deny himself. This God naturally has an all-comprehensive plan for the created universe. He has planned all the relationships between all the aspects of created being. He has planned the end from the beginning. All created reality therefore actually displays this plan. It is, in consequence, inherently rational.[34]

This does not mean that finite human beings can understand general revelation exhaustively. Human beings are not omniscient. Their knowledge of that which is revealed in general revelation, although not exhaustive, is not false on this account. The perspicuity of general revelation means, 'Created man may see clearly what is revealed clearly even if he cannot see exhaustively.'[35]

As we have seen, God's general revelation to Adam was accompanied by special revelation from the first moment of creation.[36] Van Til explains, 'The revelation of God in the facts of nature has always required and been accompanied by revelation in propositional form given by supernatural positive communication. Natural and supernatural revelation are limiting concepts the one of the other.'[37] Because of this, it was true even before the fall, that 'as man studies any of the factual revelation of either nature or Scripture he is required to do so in subordination to

---

33. Ibid.

34. Ibid.

35. Ibid.

36. Van Til, *The Intellectual Challenge of the Gospel* in Cornelius Van Til and Eric H. Sigward, *The Pamphlets, Tracts, and Offprints of Cornelius Van Til*, Electronic ed. (Labels Army Company: New York, 1997).

37. Van Til, introduction to B. B. Warfield, *The Inspiration and Authority of the Bible*, 30.

and in conformity with the propositional revelation given him in the way of direct communication by God.'[38]

The content of God's special revelation to man at creation was in the form of a covenant. In the chapter on creation, the Westminster Confession of Faith speaks of Adam and Eve 'having the law of God written in their hearts, and power to fulfill it,' but then it adds that they also received from God 'a command, not to eat of the tree of the knowledge of good and evil' (4.2). The Confession explains this covenant more fully in chapter 7 where we read that, 'The first covenant made with man was a covenant of works, wherein life was promised to Adam; and in him to his posterity, upon condition of perfect and personal obedience' (7.2).

Bavinck explains that the covenant of works was early on called a covenant of nature because 'the foundation on which the covenant rested, that is, the moral law, was known to man by nature, and because it was made with man in his original state and could be kept by man with the powers bestowed on him in the creation, without the assistance of supernatural grace.'[39] It was called the covenant of works because it was conditioned on perfect and personal obedience to God's law, which, before the fall, Adam and Eve had the power to fulfill (WCF, 4.2; WLC, Q. 17). Because the threat of death and the implicit promise of life in the covenant of works was made to Adam 'and in him to his posterity,' if Adam obeyed, he and his posterity would be covenant-keepers, but if he disobeyed, he and his posterity would be covenant-breakers.

## God's Knowledge and Man's Knowledge

The importance of the Creator-creature distinction to Van Til's apologetic thought becomes more apparent when we examine the implications of this distinction for his understanding of the relationship between God's knowledge and man's knowledge. We recall that Van Til affirms that God is omniscient. God knows himself in one eternal act of knowing. God also fully knows all the facts he has eternally decreed and fully knows the relation of each fact both to himself and to every other fact. Because God is independent, God's knowledge of all decreed

---

38. Ibid.

39. Bavinck, *Reformed Dogmatics*, vol. 2, *God and Creation*, 567.

facts precedes the creation of any of these facts. Van Til explains the significance of this point: 'There was coherence in God's plan before there was any space-time fact to which his knowledge might correspond, or which might correspond to his knowledge.'[40]

What this means for Van Til is that every created fact is what it is because it is part of the one all-encompassing system that God eternally decreed.[41] In other words, every fact is a part of the eternal plan of God.[42] Within that eternal plan, God exhaustively knows all the facts, and 'he sets these facts in relation to one another.'[43] Therefore, each individual fact that God knows is part of God's act of knowing all things as a unit.[44] Given all of this, the meaning of every fact is necessarily related to the God who decreed it and created it. Van Til explains:

> What is true with respect to the existence of the whole space-time world is equally true with respect to the *meaning* of it. As the absolute and independent existence of God determines the derivative existence of the universe, so the absolute meaning that God has for himself implies that the meaning of every fact in the universe must be related to God. Scripture says constantly that the world has its whole meaning in the fact that it was created for the glory of God.[45]

This means that a fact is known truly only if it is known in its relation to God. If a fact is not known in its relation to God, it is not known truly.[46] God, therefore, is the necessary final reference point of true knowledge.

Van Til argues that if God is not understood as the final reference point, man would have to be the final reference point and then man would have to know everything. He writes:

> *If one does not make human knowledge wholly dependent upon the original self-knowledge and consequent revelation of God to man, then man will have to seek knowledge within himself as the final reference point. Then he will have to seek an exhaustive understanding of reality. Then he will have to*

---

40. Van Til, *Survey of Christian Epistemology*, 3.

41. Van Til, *Christian Apologetics*, 193-94.

42. Van Til, *Christian Theistic Evidences*, 92.

43. Van Til, *A Christian Theory of Knowledge*, 20.

44. Van Til, *An Introduction to Systematic Theology*, 270.

45. Ibid., 58.

46. Van Til, *Survey of Christian Epistemology*, 4.

hold that if he cannot attain to such an exhaustive understanding of reality, he has no *true* knowledge of anything at all. Either man must then know everything or he knows nothing. This is the dilemma that confronts every form of non-Christian epistemology.[47]

But why would man have to know everything in order to have true knowledge of anything? Why would a human being have to either know everything or nothing? Because, as we observed in the previous chapter, true knowledge of anything requires knowledge of everything. As Van Til explains: 'All knowledge is inter-related. The created world is expressive of the nature of God. If one knows "nature" truly, one also knows nature's God truly. Then, too, the mind of man is a unit. It cannot know one thing truly without knowing all things truly.'[48]

All facts require an ultimate principle of interpretation or a final reference point if there is to be true knowledge of those facts. Van Til explains, 'It is impossible even to discuss any particular fact except in relation to some principle of interpretation. The real question about facts is, therefore, what kind of universal can give the best account of the facts.'[49] There are only two possible answers: God or man. The Christian view, according to Van Til, is that God is the final reference point for the interpretation of facts because God eternally decreed and eternally knows all facts.

Given that true knowledge of anything requires true knowledge of all things, Van Til teaches that someone must know everything in order for there to be any knowledge of anything.[50] Since man is a finite creature and cannot possibly know everything, God's knowledge of everything is necessary in order for there to be true knowledge of anything.[51] Significantly, Van Til adds that human beings themselves do not need to know everything as long as God knows everything.[52] Using the knowledge of a cow as an illustration, Van Til explains:

---

47. Van Til, *A Christian Theory of Knowledge*, 8. Emphasis in original.

48. Van Til, *An Introduction to Systematic Theology.*, 64.

49. Van Til, *Christian Theistic Evidences*, 2.

50. Van Til, 'A Christian Theistic Theory of Knowledge,' in Cornelius Van Til and Eric H. Sigward, *The Articles of Cornelius Van Til*, Electronic ed. (Labels Army Company: New York, 1997).

51. Ibid.

52. Ibid.

Complete knowledge of what a cow is can be had only by an absolute intelligence, i.e., by one who has, so to speak, the blueprint of the whole universe. But it does not follow from this that the knowledge of the cow that I have is not true as far as it goes. It is true if it corresponds to the knowledge that God has of the cow.[53]

God, then, exhaustively knows the cow in relation to his divine decree. He knows the cow in its relation to himself as the one who decreed the cow, and he knows the cow in relation to every other decreed fact and in relation the whole system of decreed facts. Man's knowledge of the cow is necessarily finite, and as such, if that knowledge is to be true, it must be grounded in exhaustive knowledge somewhere.[54] God alone has such exhaustive knowledge, so man's knowledge will be true only to the extent that it corresponds to God's perfect knowledge.[55]

Once we grasp Van Til's claim that God rather than man or anything else is the final reference point, and once we grasp what he means by that claim, we are in a better position to understand what Van Til means when he says that man's knowledge is analogical to God's knowledge. Van Til explains that the idea of man's knowledge as analogical to God's knowledge is rooted in the doctrine of man's creation in the image of God.[56] God is the original 'knower,' and God's system of knowledge is the original system of knowledge. As Van Til observes, 'God has absolute self-contained system within himself. What comes to pass in history happens in accord with that system or plan by which he orders the universe.'[57]

God's system of knowledge includes his exhaustive knowledge of himself and everything he decreed. Because God has decreed whatsoever comes to pass and knows all the facts that he has decreed, everything in creation 'has been preinterpreted by God's plan.'[58] Van Til continues:

---

53. Van Til, *Survey of Christian Epistemology*, 1-2.

54. Van Til, 'A Christian Theistic Theory of Knowledge;' cf. also Van Til, *A Christian Theory of Knowledge*, 6.

55. Van Til, *Survey of Christian Epistemology*, 2.

56. Cornelius Van Til, 'The Christian Scholar,' *Westminster Theological Journal* 21/2 (May 1959): 172.

57. Van Til, *A Christian Theory of Knowledge*, 7.

58. Cornelius Van Til, review of *De Noodzakelijkeheid eener Christelijke Logica*, by D. H. Th. Vollenhoven, *The Calvin Forum* 1/6 (Jan 1936): 142.

God's logic precedes history. God makes and sustains the facts and the laws of the scientists. The particulars and universals of the created universe are adapted to one another by God. They have their coherence and admit of interpretation by man because back of them is the absolute coherence of God.[59]

As the one who decreed all things, then, God is the original interpreter of all things. 'It follows from this that any human interpreters would have to be *derivative* interpreters or reinterpreters.'[60]

According to Van Til, because human beings are created 'knowers,' they are analogical knowers. As such, their knowledge cannot be exhaustive. It can, however, be true.[61] In order for it to be true knowledge, man's knowledge must correspond to God's knowledge: 'True human knowledge corresponds to the knowledge which God has of himself and his world.'[62] There is coherence in human knowledge only when it corresponds to God's knowledge. Van Til writes: 'If all of our thoughts about the facts of the universe are in correspondence with God's ideas of these facts, there will naturally be coherence in our thinking because there is a complete coherence in God's thinking.'[63] God's full comprehension, Van Til argues, 'gives validity to our partial comprehension.'[64]

Van Til's explanation of what correspondence does and does not mean introduces one of the more complex and difficult elements of his thought. Van Til claims that man's knowledge and God's knowledge coincide at every point in one sense and at no point in another sense. Van Til explains:

> In the first place, it is possible in this way to see that the knowledge of God and the knowledge of man coincide at *every* point in the sense that always and everywhere man confronts that which is already fully known or interpreted by God. *The point of reference cannot but be the same for man as for God.* There is no fact that man meets in any of his investigation [*sic*] where the face of God does not confront him. On the other hand, in this way it is possible to see that the knowledge of God and the knowledge of

---

59. Ibid.

60. Van Til, *An Introduction to Systematic Theology*, 60.

61. Ibid., 61.

62. Van Til, *Survey of Christian Epistemology*, 1.

63. Ibid., 2.

64. Van Til, *An Introduction to Systematic Theology*, 61.

man coincide at no point in the sense that, in his awareness of meaning of anything, in his mental grasp or understanding of anything, man is at each point dependent upon a prior act of unchangeable understanding and revelation on the part of God.[65]

If by 'God's knowledge,' we mean the 'point of reference,' then God's knowledge and man's knowledge coincide at every point. The 'point of reference,' is that which is already known by God. The 'point of reference,' then, is the object of knowledge.[66] The 'objects of knowledge' are the same for God and man. If by 'God's knowledge,' however, we mean God's 'awareness,' or his 'mental grasp,' then man's knowledge and God's knowledge coincide at no point. A human *act* of knowledge is never the same as God's *act* of knowledge, but a *fact* of knowledge that God has decreed and created is the same *fact* of knowledge that man encounters in the world.

The first point is what leads to Van Til's claim that there is no 'identity of content' between God's mind and man's mind.[67] For Van Til, to claim that there is identity of content is to deny the incomprehensibility of God.[68] Why is this the case? Because for Van Til, when we speak of the 'content' of God's knowledge this 'content' includes the 'mode' of God's knowledge (the *act* of knowledge).[69] Van Til states that the distinction between the content and the mode of knowledge is a 'false distinction.'[70] In short, as Van Til states, 'There could and would be an identity of content only if the mind of man were identical with the mind of God.'[71] According to Van Til, man never has the same 'thought content' in his mind that God has in his mind.[72] This is the case, according to Van Til,

---

65. Ibid., 270.

66. See K. Scott Oliphint, 'The Consistency of Van Til's Methodology,' *Westminster Theological Journal* 52, no. 1 (Spr. 1990): 38, n. 40.

67. Van Til, *An Introduction to Systematic Theology*, 270-71.

68. Ibid. This claim about the relation between God's knowledge and man's knowledge was at the heart of the so-called 'Clark-Van Til Controversy.' For a helpful overview of the details of this controversy, see Douma, *The Presbyterian Philosopher*, 75-164, 251-66. See also Frame, *Cornelius Van Til: An Analysis of His Thought*, 97-113.

69. See Bahnsen, *Van Til's Apologetic: Readings and Analysis*, 227, n. 152.

70. Van Til, *An Introduction to Systematic Theology*, 272.

71. Ibid., 271.

72. Ibid., 295.

because 'Man can never experience the experience of God.'[73] Man's *act* of knowledge, according to Van Til, can never correspond to God's *act* of knowledge.

We also have to take care when we discuss the *facts* of knowledge. The *fact* '2+2=4' is the same 'point of reference' for both man and God. It is the same object of knowledge. That fact of knowledge, however, can also be considered as part of a unified whole (a system of inter-related *facts*). God's system of knowledge contains all facts and all relations between all facts. Man's system of knowledge (while containing some individual facts of knowledge and some relations) can correspond to God's system of knowledge if those facts are reinterpreted in their proper relation to God as the final reference point. Man's system of knowledge, however, cannot ever fully replicate God's system of knowledge.[74]

Full replication of God's system of knowledge would require that man know every fact about God. Man would have to fully comprehend God. It would also require that man know every fact in the divine decree. Man would have to know everything about every physical thing God has created, down to the last sub-atomic particle. Man would have to know every event in God's decree – past, present, and future. This would include visible events as well as invisible actions such as human thoughts and choices. In short, full replication of God's system of knowledge is impossible for any finite mind. It is impossible because of the Creator-creature distinction. God's mind is infinite. Man's mind is finite. Human knowledge, therefore, can only be analogical. It can only be a finite reflection of the infinite original. This finite human knowledge will be true knowledge, however, if it corresponds to God's perfect unified system of knowledge. It corresponds to God's perfect system of knowledge only when it makes God the ultimate principle of interpretation.

## Conclusion

Van Til's doctrines of creation and revelation are rooted in his doctrine of God and are a crucial part of his larger apologetic system. The doctrine of God's creation of the heavens and earth and all that is within them introduces the all-important Creator-creature distinction, without

---

73. Ibid., 297.

74. Van Til, *A Christian Theory of Knowledge*, 7.

which Van Til's system of thought would make no sense. There is a fundamental metaphysical distinction between the being of the Triune Creator and the being of creatures. As we observed in the previous chapter, God's being is independent, immutable, infinite, and simple. Creaturely being is, by definition, dependent, mutable, finite, and composite. God is also omniscient. His knowledge is infinite. Creaturely knowledge, where it exists, is finite.

God's created works are all revelatory of their Creator. This teaching stands at the heart of Van Til's doctrine of general revelation. As soon as the first human being was created, he was confronted by the general revelation of God in everything he encountered. He was also confronted by general revelation in his own constitution as a creature of God. But general revelation never existed apart from God's special revelation. The first human being was created in a covenantal context with the covenantal requirements revealed by God. This placed man in a necessarily ethical relation to God. Adam could remain a covenant-keeper or become a covenant-breaker. To remain a covenant-keeper, he would have to maintain correspondence of his finite system of knowledge to God's perfect system of knowledge. He would have to maintain God as the final reference point.

Van Til explains that since human beings are creatures, man's knowledge could only be analogical to God's knowledge. The metaphysical distinction between the being of the Creator and the being of creatures results in a corresponding epistemological distinction. God knows himself and all facts that he has freely decreed in one eternal and incomprehensible act of knowledge. Because God's decree is a unified system, God exhaustively knows every fact he decreed in relation to himself and in relation to every other decreed fact. Since this is what is necessary if there is to be true knowledge, God's omniscience undergirds the very possibility of the existence of true human knowledge. God is the ultimate principle of interpretation. He fully preinterprets all facts as a part of his one unified system of divine knowledge. Man's knowledge is also a system, but man's knowledge is analogical because human beings are created re-interpreters. Human beings do not have God's mind and thus do not know in the same manner that God knows. Even human knowledge of facts is true as far as it goes only if it corresponds to God's knowledge. Human knowledge of facts is never exhaustive knowledge.

# CHAPTER 3

# Man's Fall and God's Grace

Thus far in our overview of Van Til's thought, we have observed that the foundation of his apologetic system of thought is his doctrine of God. From all eternity, God perfectly and immutably knows himself. God also eternally decreed all facts, and he eternally knows and interprets those facts. For Van Til, facts and the interpretation of facts cannot be separated, so the true meaning of any fact is determined by its place in the eternal decree or plan of God who eternally interprets those facts. The decree of God is a unified whole, and in this plan, every fact is related to God and to every other fact. Because God's plan is a unified whole, no fact can be truly known if it is not known in its relation to God and in its relation to every other fact in that unified whole. God alone has this infinite knowledge. God alone perfectly knows every fact in relation to himself and in relation to every other fact. There are, therefore, no 'brute facts.'

God's creation of all things introduces a metaphysical distinction between two kinds of being: the Being of God and the being of his creatures. In other words, it introduces the Creator-creature distinction. Among God's creatures were Adam and Eve, human beings created in the image of God. Adam and Eve were created as rational beings capable of knowledge, but as creatures their knowledge could not possibly be exhaustive. In short, corresponding to the metaphysical distinction between the Creator and the creature is an epistemological distinction. Creaturely knowledge is necessarily finite. Only the Creator is omniscient.

The world into which the first human beings were placed by God, according to Van Til, was exhaustively revelatory of its Creator. This general revelation declared the glory of God from its first moment of existence. Every created fact pointed not only to the existence of God but also to the God-decreed unified system of truth of which it was a part. In addition to general revelation, human beings were also given special revelation. They were, from the moment of creation, placed in a covenantal context in relation to their Creator. They were required to interpret all facts, including themselves, in terms of God as the final reference point, the one who decreed and pre-interpreted all facts. This means that there is an ethical component to human knowledge.

Van Til explains that because man is a creature, his knowledge is to be analogical to God's knowledge. God has perfect and infinite knowledge of himself and his all-encompassing decree. Man's knowledge is derivative of God's knowledge. Man's knowledge cannot be a perfect replica of God's knowledge because God's knowledge includes God's infinite knowledge of himself and every fact in his decree. Man is finite. Man must, therefore, have a system of knowledge that corresponds to God's knowledge to the extent that God has revealed it to him. Man's knowledge, therefore, can be only analogical. This means that God has preinterpreted every fact, and man must reinterpret every fact in light of God's preinterpretation. If that human reinterpretation corresponds to God's preinterpretation, then that derivative human knowledge is true knowledge even though it is not exhaustive knowledge. It is a finite reflection of God's perfect system of knowledge. This was the state of affairs before the fall.

# The Fall of Man

In the covenant of works, life was promised to man on the condition of perfect and personal obedience (WCF, 7.2). Adam and Eve, however, did not continue in obedience. They, 'being seduced by the subtlety and temptation of Satan, sinned, in eating the forbidden fruit' (WCF, 6.1). The Confession continues: 'By this sin they fell from their original righteousness and communion with God, and so became dead in sin, and wholly defiled in all the parts and faculties of soul and body' (6.2). The guilt of this sin and corrupted nature was then 'conveyed to all their posterity' (6.3). Understanding the fall and its impact on human knowledge is the next step in understanding Van Til's apologetic system of thought.

Van Til explains the nature of man's first sin as his act of making himself rather than God the final reference point for the interpretation of all facts.[1] God had given man a command saying that if he ate of the fruit of the tree of the knowledge of good and evil, he would die (Gen. 2:17). Satan came in the form of a serpent and suggested a different interpretation of the facts. Satan said that man would *not* die if he ate of this tree (Gen. 3:4). Adam and Eve chose to eat. Van Til explains:

> Here then is the heart of the matter: through the fall of Adam man has set aside the law of his Creator and therewith has become a law to himself. He will be subject to none but himself. He seeks to be autonomous.[2]

Adam, in other words, set himself up as judge over God's Word. When presented with God's interpretation of the facts and Satan's interpretation of the facts, Adam acted as if he himself could be the authoritative judge. Adam, according to Van Til, chose autonomy and made himself the final reference point of predication.[3] The result of this sinful human choice was catastrophic.

## The Effects of the Fall

The Canons of Dordt explain the effects of the fall on human nature as follows: 'Man was originally formed after the image of God. His understanding was adorned with a true and saving knowledge of his Creator and of spiritual things; his heart and will were upright; all his affections pure; and the whole man was holy; but revolting from God by the instigation of the devil, and abusing the freedom of his own will, he forfeited these excellent gifts; and on the contrary entailed on himself blindness of mind, horrible darkness, vanity and perverseness of judgment, became wicked, rebellious, and obdurate in heart and will, and impure in his affections' (3rd and 4th Heads of Doctrine, Art. 1).

---

1. Van Til, *Christian Apologetics*, 98.

2. Van Til, *A Christian Theory of Knowledge*, 34. The word 'autonomy' is based etymologically on a combination of two Greek words: *autos* (meaning 'self') and *nomos* (meaning 'law'). In this context, Van Til is using the word to communicate the idea that Adam and Eve rejected God's law and chose to determine good and evil for themselves – to be a law unto themselves.

3. Ibid.

In other words, the result of man's sin is total depravity. Total depravity means that man has been corrupted in every aspect of his being. As the Westminster Confession states, fallen man is 'wholly defiled in all the parts and faculties of soul and body' (6.2).

Van Til observes that fallen man's sensory faculties, those senses through which human beings know nature, have been impacted by the fall. 'Man's eye and ear and all his senses have been greatly weakened through the effects of sin.'[4] More importantly, as a result of sin, man's mind became 'ethically depraved.'[5] It has to be understood as 'abnormal.'[6] However, although sin has corrupted man's mind, it has not completely destroyed its ability to function. Van Til observes: 'According to Scripture, sin has not destroyed the psychological make-up of human beings. The laws of the human mind and heart work now as they worked from the beginning.'[7] Fallen man, as Van Til says, 'has not lost his rationality, his sense of moral responsibility and ability to will freely according to his nature.'[8]

What does it mean then to say that the minds of human beings are abnormal after the fall? One of the faculties of the human mind is the rational faculty. According to Van Til, 'sin has blinded the intellect of man.'[9] Thus although the rational faculty of man was not destroyed, it was corrupted. Similarly, the volitional faculty of human beings was also corrupted by the fall when Adam and Eve used it to choose autonomy instead of submission to the law of God. Van Til explains the meaning of this corruption of man's will:

> This is often spoken of as the hardening of man's heart. Paul says that the natural man is at enmity against God. The natural man cannot will to do God's will. He cannot even know what the good is. The sinner worships

4. Van Til, *An Introduction to Systematic Theology*, 163.

5. Ibid., 61.

6. Ibid., 168.

7. Cornelius Van Til, *Psychology of Religion* (The Presbyterian and Reformed Publishing Company: Phillipsburg, NJ, 1971), 3.

8. Cornelius Van Til, 'Common Grace and Witness-Bearing,' *Torch and Trumpet* 4/5 (Dec 1954–Jan 1955), in Cornelius Van Til and Eric H. Sigward, *The Articles of Cornelius Van Til*, Electronic ed. (Labels Army Company: New York, 1997).

9. Cornelius Van Til, *Christian Theistic Ethics* (The Presbyterian and Reformed Publishing Company: Phillipsburg, NJ, 1980), 22.

the creature rather than the Creator. He has set all the moral standards topsy-turvy.[10]

Fallen human beings are now, as a result, sinners. They are covenant-breakers and objects of the wrath of God. Fallen man now stands in what Van Til calls an *'absolute ethical antithesis'* to God.[11] The corrupted mind of man is now under the curse of God, and most important for our purposes, it cannot interpret reality correctly.[12] In that sense, it is abnormal.

As a result of the corruption of his mind, fallen man now both knows God in one sense and does not know God in another sense.[13] Van Til says, 'All men know not merely that *a* God exists, but they know that God, the *true* God, the *only* God, exists. They cannot be conscious of themselves, says Calvin, except they be at the same time conscious of God as their creator.'[14] Van Til elaborates further:

> The picture of fallen man as given in Scripture is that he knows God but does not want to recognize him as God (Rom. 1). That he knows God is due to the fact that all things in the universe about him and within him speak clearly of God. It is as 'knowing God' that man rebels against God.[15]

Fallen man knows God because he cannot escape the general revelation of God. God objectively impresses this knowledge on him.

In another sense, however, fallen man does not know God. Part of the explanation of this is the fact that there is an ethical element to knowledge. As Van Til explains, 'It is indeed possible to have theoretically correct knowledge about God without loving God.'[16] True knowledge of God involves loving God. All other knowledge of God, Van Til explains, is false.[17] Because fallen man does not love God and is, in fact, hostile toward God, he suppresses the knowledge

---

10. Ibid.

11. Van Til, *An Introduction to Systematic Theology*, 64.

12. Ibid., 164.

13. Cornelius Van Til, *Common Grace and Witness-Bearing* (Phillipsburg, NJ: Lewis J. Grotenhuis, 1955), 9.

14. Ibid., 8.

15. Van Til, *A Christian Theory of Knowledge*, 34.

16. Van Til, *Christian Apologetics*, 48.

17. Ibid.

of God that God has impressed upon him.[18] Van Til emphasizes this point:

> Though it is of the greatest possible importance to keep in mind that man knows God in this original sense it is of equally great importance to remember that he is now, since the fall, a sinner without *true* knowledge of God. He is spiritually blind. He will not see things as he, in another sense, knows that they are. He hates to see them that way because if he admits that they are what they really are, then he therewith condemns himself as a covenant-breaker. He therefore cannot see the truth till he at the same time repents.[19]

This suppression of the knowledge of God is a sinful act. In short, the point about fallen man, as Van Til explains, is that 'ethically he does not know God.'[20]

Not only does fallen man not know God because he suppresses that knowledge, but fallen man also knows nothing else truly because he rejects its God-decreed and God-created nature. Van Til explains:

> It is this point on which many theologians are vague. They maintain, to be sure, that the natural man cannot truly know God, but they will not maintain that the natural man cannot truly know the flowers of the field. Now it may seem as though it is straining at a gnat to insist on the point that the natural man does not even know the flowers truly, as long as it is maintained that he does not know God truly. The point is, however, that unless we maintain that the natural man does not know the flowers truly, we cannot logically maintain that he does not know God truly.[21]

But why is it the case that fallen man cannot know the flowers truly? For Van Til, this assertion is based on his definition of true knowledge as a unity in which knowledge of all things is necessary for a true knowledge of anything. And given this definition of true knowledge, if we are

---

18. It is worth noting that the translation of the word *katecho* as 'suppress' in Romans 1:18 is debatable. Prior to the twentieth century, English versions translated the word in the sense of holding something that is fully known. See David Noe, 'Suppress or Retain? Theodore Beza, Natural Theology, and the Translation of Romans 1:18,' in *Theodore Beza at 500: New Perspectives on an Old Reformer*, ed. Kirk Summers and Scott M. Manetsch (Göttingen: Vandenhoeck & Ruprecht, 2020), 139-56. Thanks are due to J. V. Fesko for bringing Noe's chapter to my attention.

19. Van Til, *A Christian Theory of Knowledge*, 37.

20. Ibid., 249.

21. Van Til, *An Introduction to Systematic Theology*, 64.

to know anything we have to know it in relation to God. As Van Til explains: 'All knowledge is inter-related. The created world is expressive of the nature of God. If one knows "nature" truly, one also knows nature's God truly. Then, too, the mind of man is a unit. It cannot know one thing truly without knowing all things truly.'[22]

It is vitally important to understand this definition of knowledge if we are to understand what Van Til teaches. He elaborates on this understanding of knowledge in many places. In his *Survey of Christian Epistemology*, for example, he writes:

> For the Christian system, knowledge consists in understanding the relation of any fact to God as revealed in Scripture. I know a fact truly to the extent that I understand the *exact* relation such a fact sustains to the plan of God. It is the plan of God that gives any fact meaning in terms of the plan of God. The whole meaning of any fact is exhausted by its position in and relation to the plan of God. This implies that every fact is related to every other fact. God's plan is a unit. And it is this unity of the plan of God, founded as it is in the very being of God, that gives the unity that we look for between all the finite facts. *If one should maintain that one fact can be fully understood without reference to all other facts, he is as much antitheistic as when he should maintain that one fact can be understood without reference to God.*[23]

In other words, if man is to truly know any fact, that fact must be understood in reference to the God who decreed all facts, and it must be understood in reference to all other facts. All facts are part of a unified system of truth and must be known as a part of that system.[24]

When man sinned, he made himself rather than God the final principle of interpretation.[25] Fallen man now tries to interpret the facts of creation apart from any relation to their Creator.[26] Given what Van Til says about the necessity of interpreting all facts in relation to God and every other fact if those facts are to be known truly, the implication would seem to be that fallen man cannot have any knowledge of anything. Van Til, however, says that fallen man does sometimes know

22. Ibid.
23. Van Til, *Survey of Christian Epistemology*, 6. Emphasis mine.
24. Van Til, *Christian Apologetics*, 193-94.
25. Van Til, *A Christian Theory of Knowledge*, 34.
26. Van Til, *The Protestant Doctrine of Scripture*, 48.

things in a certain sense despite his attempt to interpret facts apart from God.

Part of Van Til's explanation of fallen man's knowledge is God's restraint of fallen man's sin, which prevents him from fully applying his false principle of interpretation. We will address this divine restraint below. Here we note another part of Van Til's explanation, namely, the fact that fallen man is not always fully self-conscious of his interpretive principle. Van Til uses the illustration of the world as God's 'estate' in which every fact on that estate is what it is in relation to the owner of the estate. He explains:

> You will only know the facts 'truly' in such a case insofar as you have not thought out ultimate relations. However, if this ultimate relation is denied and/or supplanted by some other ultimate relation, the whole 'system' of facts and laws is misconceived and therefore <u>ultimately false</u>. You may indeed represent one section of the estate correctly, but this is <u>in spite of</u> your misconception of the ultimate relation, and indeed, 'true' only when considered separate from such ultimate postulates.[27]

In other words, if fallen man is not self-conscious about the ultimate interpretive principle, he can know facts in a certain limited sense. However, if fallen man self-consciously denies God as the ultimate interpretive principle or self-consciously makes something else the ultimate interpretive principle, then his entire system is false. He does not truly know any facts in that system. Van Til also says that fallen man's interpretive principle *often* lies 'dormant' thereby allowing him to have knowledge.[28]

Van Til describes the entire history of philosophy as the story of fallen man's attempts to self-consciously create a system of knowledge based on autonomous human thought. 'From the ancient Greeks to the present time, philosophy in general has worked upon the assumption that the mind of man can act independently of God.'[29] For Van Til, the entire history of unbelieving philosophical thought manifests two basic starting points. The metaphysical starting point of fallen thought is the

---

27. Ibid.

28. See Cornelius Van Til, 'Reply to Professor J. Vanden Bosch,' *The Banner* 75/2246 (24 May 1940), in Cornelius Van Til and Eric H. Sigward, *The Articles of Cornelius Van Til*, Electronic ed. (Labels Army Company: New York, 1997).

29. Van Til, *Psychology of Religion*, 11.

idea of brute factuality, and the epistemological starting point of fallen thought is autonomy.[30] This describes all non-Christian philosophical views from ancient times to the modern day.[31] All unbelieving philosophers think that facts are not pre-interpreted by God, and they all think that man is the final reference point for predication. This explains why all unbelieving philosophy has failed to solve the problem of human knowledge.

## The Impossibility of Natural Theology

Natural theology may be defined as 'the knowledge of God that is available to reason through the revelation of God in the natural order.'[32] Given Van Til's understanding of the nature of knowledge and the effects of the fall, it is not difficult to understand his position with regard to natural theology. In the first place, man's sin resulted in a curse on creation. Van Til writes: 'According to Scripture the moral evil of man has brought a curse upon "nature" so that it does not really reveal itself in all the glory that it might. In fact, the curse of God rests upon all the facts of the universe.'[33] Van Til has already pointed out that no fact can be truly known apart from its relation to God. Here he is explaining that 'a part of the qualification of finite "facts" is that evil is found in them.'[34] So, the first problem with natural theology is that the natural order is under the curse of God, and therefore the general revelation found in it is not as clear as it was before the fall. After the fall, 'darkness covers the "facts" or objects of knowledge.'[35]

Not only has a 'veil' been cast over nature, but the mind of fallen humanity is now corrupt.[36] Van Til explains: 'After sin has entered the world, no one of himself knows nature aright, and no one knows the soul of man aright. How then could man reason from nature to nature's God

30. Van Til, *The Protestant Doctrine of Scripture*, 14; cf. Van Til, *Christian Apologetics*, 192-93.

31. E. R. Geehan, ed. *Jerusalem and Athens: Critical Discussions on the Philosophy and Apologetics of Cornelius Van Til* (Phillipsburg: P&R Publishing Company, 1971), 90.

32. Richard A. Muller, *Dictionary of Latin and Greek Theological Terms*, 2nd ed. (Grand Rapids: Baker Academic, 2017), 362.

33. Van Til, *Survey of Christian Epistemology*, 122.

34. Ibid., 123.

35. Ibid.

36. Van Til, *An Introduction to Systematic Theology*, 164.

and get anything but a distorted notion of God?'[37] Fallen man no longer reasons analogically. Fallen man reasons 'univocally,' presuming himself to be autonomous.[38] Because 'they reason univocally about nature, they conclude that no god exists or that a god exists but never that the true God exists.'[39] In short, for Van Til, 'Natural theology is the result of the interpretative reaction that sinful man has given to the revelation of God to him in the created world.'[40]

Note that Van Til says that fallen humanity cannot even establish the existence of God through natural theology.[41] Why is this the case? Why can fallen man not observe God's general revelation in the created world and through the use of his rational faculties come to some knowledge of God? Why is natural theology impossible? One part of the answer, according to Van Til, is found in the curse that rests on creation. General revelation is not as clear as it was. Another part of the answer is found in the corruption of man's fallen mind. Man is actively and sinfully suppressing the knowledge of God that is impressed on him.[42]

---

37. Ibid., 133.

38. It should be observed that Van Til has departed here from the traditional theological use of the terms 'analogical' and 'univocal.' Traditionally, theologians spoke of three kinds of predication: univocal, equivocal, and analogical. Predication is 'univocal' if the predicate means exactly the same thing when applied to separate things. If I say, 'Rover is a dog' and I also say, 'Fido is a dog,' I am predicating 'dog-ness' to Rover and Fido in the same sense. Predication is 'equivocal' if the predicate means something wholly different when applied to separate things. If I point to the shore of a river, and say, 'That is the bank' and I also point to a building in my town and say, 'That is the bank,' I am predicating 'bank-ness' of the land next to the river and of the building in completely different senses. Predication is 'analogical' if the predicate means something similar when applied to separate things. If I say, 'That sandwich is a good sandwich' and I say, 'My friend Larry is a good man,' I am predicating 'goodness' to the sandwich and to my friend in a similar, but not identical, sense. The issue often arises in connection with discussions of the communicable attributes of God. When I say that my friend is a 'good' man and I say that God is 'good,' I am speaking analogously because God's goodness is infinitely greater than any creaturely goodness.

39. Van Til, *An Introduction to Systematic Theology*, 178.

40. Van Til, *The Protestant Doctrine of Scripture*, 56.

41. Van Til, *An Introduction to Systematic Theology*, 178.

42. Greg L. Bahnsen examines, from a Van Tillian perspective, the self-deception involved in the thought of fallen man in his 'A Conditional Resolution of the Apparent Paradox of Self-Deception,' PhD diss (University of Southern California, 1978). For a more concise presentation of the thesis, see his 'The Crucial Concept of Self-Deception in Presuppositional Apologetics,' *Westminster Theological Journal* 57, no. 1 (Spring 1995): 1-31.

A final part of the answer is found in Van Til's understanding of the nature of true knowledge: true knowledge of the unified whole is necessary for true knowledge of any of the parts. According to Van Til, God has that infinite knowledge. Man's knowledge, he argues, has to correspond with God's knowledge to be true knowledge, but since fallen man suppresses the knowledge of God, he distorts all knowledge. Distorted knowledge does not correspond to God's knowledge and is not true knowledge. Traditional natural theology, on the other hand, assumes that man can have true knowledge of a fact without having to have a knowledge of all facts. It says that by starting with such knowledge of any fact in the natural order, human beings can reach some limited knowledge of God. Natural theology is rejected because, according to Van Til, it has an incorrect definition of true knowledge.

## God's Response to the Fall

God responded to man's sin with grace: both special and common. Van Til explains: 'Both types of grace, special and common, presuppose total depravity. The difference between the two must be indicated by the different effect they accomplish upon the totally depraved.'[43] Special grace after the fall involved the special revelation of the covenant of grace.[44] Special revelation is necessary because fallen man is 'a criminal who has committed high treason.'[45] Fallen man needs the gospel of Christ, and that Gospel is not part of the content of general revelation. As Van Til explains, 'Men are lost without Christ – and he is not revealed in nature.'[46] All are 'under the condemnation of God' and 'in general revelation there is no remedy for this condition.'[47] Special revelation is necessary, according to Van Til, not only if man is to receive the Gospel,

---

43. Van Til, *Common Grace and the Gospel*, 22.

44. The Westminster Confession of Faith explains that 'Man, by his fall, having made himself incapable of life by that covenant [of works], the Lord was pleased to make a second, commonly called the covenant of grace; wherein he freely offereth unto sinners life and salvation by Jesus Christ; requiring of them faith in him, that they may be saved, and promising to give unto all those that are ordained unto eternal life his Holy Spirit, to make them willing, and able to believe' (7.3).

45. Van Til, *An Introduction to Systematic Theology*, 192.

46. Ibid.

47. Ibid.

but if he is to know the facts of creation rightly.[48] In other words, there is both a soteriological dimension and an epistemological dimension to postlapsarian special revelation in the thought of Van Til.

Apart from God's special revelation, fallen man cannot understand nature or general revelation correctly. Van Til writes: 'Man *ought*, to be sure, from nature to know God as creator, seeing that nature clearly displays the creator. But since man has become a sinner, he has become a willing slave of sin (*ethelodoulos*). He therefore never reads the "book of nature" aright even with respect to "natural" things.'[49] Special revelation is necessary because it provides man with the divine system of truth to which his interpretation of all facts must correspond if his own knowledge is to be true. As Van Til puts it, without 'the word of the self-attesting Christ we would know no fact for what it is, i.e., as set in the only framework in which it can have meaning.'[50]

The facts of nature cannot be understood apart from special revelation, but special revelation cannot be understood apart from the regenerating work of the Holy Spirit, which means that ultimately only the regenerate will be able to understand anything rightly. God has, however, also manifested a kind of grace to all without distinction. This is God's common grace. Generally speaking, common grace may be defined as 'a nonsaving, universal grace according to which God in his goodness bestows his favor upon all creation in the general blessings of physical sustenance and moral influence for the good. Thus rain falls on the just and the unjust, and all persons have the law engraved on their hearts.'[51] It is, therefore contrasted with God's special grace, which is given only to the elect.

Louis Berkhof, under whom Van Til studied for a time, provides a helpful explanation of the concept of common grace. He explains first that the term 'common' is meant to express the idea that this grace extends universally to all fallen human beings rather than to the elect alone. He adds, however, that some Reformed theologians have distinguished among three types of common grace: '(1) Universal Common Grace, a

---

48. Ibid., 194.

49. Ibid.

50. Van Til, *Survey of Christian Epistemology*, 123.

51. Muller, *Dictionary of Latin and Greek Theological Terms*, 142.

grace that extends to all creatures; (2) General Common Grace, that is a grace which applies to mankind in general and to every member of the human race; and (3) Covenant Common Grace, a grace that is common to all those who live in the sphere of the covenant, whether they belong to the elect or not.'[52] In distinction from the first two types, Covenant Common Grace is not universal among all of humanity.

Berkhof explains that the doctrine of common grace originated as Christians sought to explain the existence of goodness, truth, and beauty in this fallen world.[53] John Calvin began the exploration of the doctrine in the Reformed tradition, but the Dutch theologians Abraham Kuyper and Herman Bavinck 'did more than anyone else for the development of the doctrine.'[54] Berkhof provides us with a helpful summary of the doctrine:

> In general it may be said that, when we speak of 'common grace,' we have in mind, either (a) *those general operations of the Holy Spirit whereby He, without renewing the heart, exercises such a moral influence on man through His general or special revelation, that sin is restrained, order is maintained in social life, and civil righteousness is promoted*; or, (b) *those general blessings, such as rain and sunshine, food and drink, clothing and shelter, which God imparts to all men indiscriminately where and in what measure it seems good to Him.*[55]

While Van Til agrees with this general understanding of the doctrine, his emphasis is on common grace's restraining of sin. Kuyper emphasized the same idea, but for Kuyper, the primary focus is on the fact that God's restraint of sin makes fallen human *society* possible. For Van Til, the primary focus is on the fact that God's restraint of sin makes fallen human *knowledge* possible.

## Common Grace and Fallen Human Knowledge

Because fallen man rejects the one true God and sets himself up as the final reference point of interpretation, he can, in principle, know

---

52. Louis Berkhof, *Systematic Theology*, New Combined Ed. (Grand Rapids: William B. Eerdmans Publishing Company, 1996), 434-435.

53. Ibid., 432.

54. Ibid., 434. For more on the views of Kuyper and Bavinck on the doctrine of common grace, see Cory C. Brock and N. Gray Sutanto, *Neo-Calvinism: A Theological Introduction* (Bellingham, WA: Lexham Academic, 2022), 212-49.

55. Ibid., 436; cf. Bavinck, *Reformed Dogmatics*, vol. 2, *God and Creation*, 16-18.

nothing as it really is. Van Til explains that 'the natural man is as blind as a mole with respect to natural things as well as with respect to spiritual things.'[56] In principle, fallen man 'interprets all things without God. In *principle* he is hostile to God.'[57] In principle, fallen man seeks 'to be a law unto himself.'[58] In principle, 'he is set against God.'[59] It is the idea of interpreting all things without God that is of central importance here. This is an epistemological principle which rejects God as the ultimate reference point of interpretation and replaces God with man. As a result of this principle, fallen man can know nothing truly.

However, although fallen man attempts to carry this principle through, he is not able to do so fully. As Van Til explains, 'Fallen man does *in principle* seek to be a law unto himself. But he cannot carry out his own principle to its full degree. He is restrained from doing so. God himself restrains him.'[60] This restraint is due to God's common grace.[61] Because of this grace, 'God has restrained the powers of darkness as they seek to control the souls of men.'[62]

As a result of God's common grace and restraint of sin, fallen man, who in one sense is able to know nothing, is in another sense able to have true knowledge. Van Til elaborates on what this means:

> Thus it comes to pass that they of whom Scripture says that their minds are darkened can yet discover much truth. But this discovery of truth on their part is effected *in spite of* the fact that *in principle* they are wholly evil. Their discovery of truth is adventitious so far as their own principle is concerned. They are not *partly* evil, they are not just sick; they are *wholly* evil, they are spiritually *dead*. But in spite of being dead in sins, they can, because of God's common grace, discover truth. The universe is what the Scripture says it is, and man is what the Scripture says he is. On both of these points it says the opposite of what fallen man says. Fallen man knows

---

56. Van Til, *An Introduction to Systematic Theology*, 148.

57. Van Til, *A Christian Theory of Knowledge*, 13.

58. Ibid., 35.

59. Ibid., 36.

60. Ibid., 35.

61. Ibid.

62. Cornelius Van Til, *Christianity in Conflict* (Philadelphia: Westminster Theological Seminary, 1962–1964). Syllabi in Cornelius Van Til and Eric H. Sigward, *The Pamphlets, Tracts, and Offprints of Cornelius Van Til*, Electronic ed. (Labels Army Company: New York, 1997).

truth and does 'morally good' things in spite of the fact that *in principle* he is set against God.[63]

Fallen man, then, can come to a knowledge of truth and can do good. Fallen man is able to do so in spite of his ultimate interpretive principle because God, in his common grace, restrains him from carrying out that principle to the fullest degree.

Fallen man's knowledge, therefore, is a complicated issue. Human beings have adopted an epistemological principle that replaces God with man as the ultimate reference point of interpretation. Given Van Til's definition of true knowledge, the fact that this adoption of a false principle leads to fallen man's inability to know anything truly is not difficult to understand. However, as Van Til, observes, common grace complicates the issue:

> So far as he [fallen man] lives from this principle he will not because he cannot, and he cannot because he will not, accept the overtures of the grace of God unless by the regenerating power of the Holy Spirit he is made alive from the dead. But he does not live fully from his principle. Therefore he does not react in the exclusively negative way that we would expect him to, if we look at the principle that ultimately controls him. Like the prodigal of the scriptural parable he cannot forget the father's voice and the father's house. He knows that the father has been good and is good in urging him to return. Yet his principle drives him on to the swine trough. On the one hand he will do the good, in the sense of that which externally at least is in accord with the will of God. He will live a 'good' moral life. He will be anxious to promote the welfare of his fellow men. In all this he is not a hypocrite. He is not sufficiently self-conscious to be a hypocrite. It is therefore of the utmost importance to distinguish between what the natural man is by virtue of his adopted principle and what he still is because of the knowledge of God as his creator that he has within him and because of the non-saving grace by which he is kept from working out his principle to the full and by which he is therefore also able to do the 'morally good.'[64]

What this means is that when a fallen human being is consistent with his ultimate principle of knowledge, he can have no true knowledge. Due to common grace, however, fallen man is often not consistent with his own principle and does attain true knowledge.

---

63. Van Til, *A Christian Theory of Knowledge*, 36.

64. Ibid., 229.

## Conclusion

Van Til's doctrine of the effects of the fall on man and the response of God to the fall is an important element in his overall system of thought. Man had been created as a rational and volitional creature in a covenant relationship with God. He was required by God to interpret all facts, including himself, in terms of God as the final reference point, the one who decreed and created all facts. Because he was a finite creature, his knowledge could never be exhaustive, but it could be true if it corresponded to God's exhaustive knowledge.

When the serpent presented Adam and Eve with an interpretation of the facts that differed from God's revealed interpretation of the facts, Adam and Eve assumed they could be the authoritative judges. Man chose autonomy and made himself rather than God the ultimate principle of interpretation. Because facts are truly known only in relation to God, once God was removed as the final reference point of interpretation, the possibility of true knowledge was, in principle, lost for fallen man. The entire history of human philosophy since the fall has been a futile attempt to solve the human problem of knowledge apart from the true God.

According to Van Til, despite fallen man's effort to work out this autonomous interpretive principle consistently, he is restrained from doing so by God. Because of God's common grace, fallen man is able to achieve some measure of knowledge in spite of himself. Man is able to come to a knowledge of facts about the natural world. Man is able to do outwardly good works. Fallen man is, therefore, a complicated being. In one sense he does not know God, and in another sense he does know God. In one sense he does not know anything, and in another sense he does know some things. God's redemptive work will add another layer of complexity to the picture.

CHAPTER 4

# Redemption and the Antithesis

Cornelius Van Til taught that the fall has placed man in dire straits. Fallen man is now a totally depraved covenant-breaker who is hostile to God and is, therefore, under the wrath of God. Every faculty of man's nature, including his reason and will, has been corrupted. Man has rejected God as the final reference point of interpretation and replaced God with himself. The result is that man cannot, in principle, know anything truly. Through common grace, however, God restrains fallen man from taking his autonomous hermeneutical principle to its consistent end, but this common grace cannot save him from the wages of sin. Unless God does something else, fallen man is without hope in this world or the next.

Thanks be to God, he has done something else, and he does not leave fallen man in ruin. As the Westminster Confession of Faith expresses the biblical teaching: 'Man, by his fall, having made himself incapable of life by that covenant [of works], the Lord was pleased to make a second, commonly called the covenant of grace; wherein he freely offereth unto sinners life and salvation by Jesus Christ; requiring of them faith in him, that they may be saved, and promising to give unto all those that are ordained unto eternal life his Holy Spirit, to make them willing, and able to believe' (7.3). The Lord Jesus has been eternally ordained to be the Mediator, and God gave him 'a people, to be his seed, and to be by him in time redeemed, called, justified, sanctified, and glorified' (8.1).

The Confession explains further: 'The Lord Jesus, by his perfect obedience, and sacrifice of himself, which he, through the eternal Spirit, once offered up unto God, hath fully satisfied the justice of his Father; and purchased, not only reconciliation, but an everlasting inheritance in the kingdom of heaven, for all those whom the Father hath given unto him' (8.5). Furthermore, 'All those whom God hath predestinated unto life, and those only, he is pleased, in his appointed and accepted time, effectually to call, by his Word and Spirit, out of that state of sin and death, in which they are by nature, to grace and salvation, by Jesus Christ; enlightening their minds spiritually and savingly to understand the things of God, taking away their heart of stone, and giving unto them a heart of flesh; renewing their wills, and, by his almighty power, determining them to that which is good, and effectually drawing them to Jesus Christ: yet so, as they come most freely, being made willing by his grace' (10.1).

## The Effects of Redemption on Human Knowledge

According to Van Til, the fall had a dramatic impact on human knowledge. In fact, prior to regeneration, fallen man has no true knowledge. As Van Til says, 'No sinner knows anything truly except he knows Christ, and no one knows Christ truly unless the Holy Ghost, the Spirit sent by the Father and the Son, regenerates him.'[1] Remember that for Van Til, no fact can be truly known unless it is known in relation to God and to every other fact in God's unified plan. The unbeliever makes such knowledge impossible in principle by rejecting God as the final reference point for the interpretation of all facts. The unbeliever interprets all facts within a false system with himself as the final point of reference. But what does Van Til say are the effects of redemption on those who are regenerated, those who are called by God out of the state of sin and death?

We look first at what Van Til says the effects of redemption are *not*. Regenerate human beings do not receive new rational faculties. 'When a man is born again he does not get a new set of brains with which to think. He has all the gifts of nature in common with his friend the unbeliever.'[2] Nor is it the case that regenerate human beings receive new reasoning capabilities. Van Til explains:

---

1. Van Til, *Survey of Christian Epistemology*, 5.
2. Van Til, *The Protestant Doctrine of Scripture*, 46.

The regeneration of the Spirit has not given them new and different powers of logical reasoning. All that has happened is that while as sinners they stood on their heads, now they have been set up on their feet. They now see all the data of experience in the light of the data of revelation. And this makes all the difference.[3]

The noetic effects of regeneration, then, do not elevate redeemed man to some new level of being. Redeemed man remains human, but he is given a new perspective, as it were. He now sees all facts in the light of God's revelation.

This is necessary because man cannot know anything truly unless his knowledge corresponds to God's knowledge. Man must interpret any fact in its relation to God in order to know that fact truly. As Van Til argues:

The contention of Christianity is exactly that there is not one fact that can be known without God. Hence if anyone avers that there is even *one* fact that can be known without God, he reasons like a non-Christian. It follows then that such a person in effect rejects the whole of the Christian position, the final conclusions as well as the starting point.[4]

Since no fact can be known without God, God's special revelation is necessary for true human knowledge to exist. Van Til explains, 'Without the Scripture as the word of the self-attesting Christ we would know no fact for what it is, i.e., as set in the only framework in which it can have meaning.'[5] That 'framework' is God's unified system of truth in which all facts are preinterpreted by God. We cannot even know scientific facts without God's special revelation: 'Even in the study of zoology or botany the Bible is involved. The Bible sheds its indispensable light on everything we as Christians study.'[6]

God's special revelation, therefore, is necessary to truly know any fact, but only those who are regenerate can know God's special revelation rightly. As Van Til observes:

---

3. Van Til, *Christianity in Conflict*, in Cornelius Van Til and Eric H. Sigward, *The Pamphlets, Tracts, and Offprints of Cornelius Van Til*, Electronic ed. (Labels Army Company: New York, 1997).

4. Van Til, *Survey of Christian Epistemology*, 5-6.

5. Ibid., 123.

6. Van Til, *An Introduction to Systematic Theology*, 37.

... no one can see Scripture for what it is unless he is given the ability to do so by the regenerating power of the Holy Spirit. Only those who are taught of God see the Scriptures for what they are and therefore see the revelation of God in nature for what it is. To be taught of God is a 'singular privilege' which God bestows only on his 'elect whom he distinguishes from the human race as a whole.' As taught of God, the elect both understand the Bible as the Word of God, and interpret natural revelation through the Bible.[7]

This has important implications for knowledge. As Van Til explains, 'Even the world of natural and historical fact with which science deals cannot be truly interpreted by anyone who is not a Christian.'[8]

In short, only a person with a right knowledge of Scripture is able to truly know any facts, including scientific facts, and only a regenerate Christian is able to know the Scriptures rightly. Only Christians, therefore, can truly know any facts. It is important to note at this point, however, that although Christians *can* know facts, regeneration does not guarantee that they *do* know any facts. Van Til clarifies the point he wants to make:

> ... the claim is not that the believer by being a believer is transformed 'into an expert botanist or physicist.' To become an expert botanist or physicist one must study botany or physics. But to be an intelligent botanist or physicist there should be an intelligible science of botany or physics. And no such intelligible science exists except on a Christian basis.[9]

This is an important clarification because some readers of Van Til might be tempted to make an incorrect inference based on what he has taught. He does teach that only Christians *can* have true knowledge of any facts because only regenerate Christians can interpret all facts in light of Scripture, but he does not say that being a Christian guarantees that a Christian knows any facts, much less all facts. Being a Christian does not make one an expert on every topic. If a Christian wishes to know facts, the Christian must do the work of learning those facts.

---

7. Cornelius Van Til, *The Reformed Pastor and the Defense of Christianity & My Credo* (Phillipsburg: The Presbyterian and Reformed Publishing Company, 1980), 11.

8. Ibid., 8.

9. Van Til, *The Defense of the Faith*, 280.

## The Antithesis

As a result of God's redemptive work, there are now both believers and unbelievers on earth. There is now a distinction between covenant-breakers and covenant-keepers. Van Til refers to this distinction as the 'antithesis.' In his doctrine of the antithesis, Van Til builds on the work of Abraham Kuyper, who in his *Encyclopedia of Sacred Theology* begins to explore the implications of 'the antithesis between falsehood and truth.'[10] Van Til uses the concept of antithesis to speak of the two kinds of people that now exist in the world. He explains: 'There are two and only two classes of men. There are those who worship and serve the creature and there are those who worship and serve the Creator. There are covenant breakers and there are covenant keepers.'[11]

Before we proceed to examine what Van Til teaches with regard to the differences between believers and unbelievers, it is important first to clear away possible misunderstandings. Van Til does this by insisting that the antithesis does not mean that the facts are different for believers and unbelievers. He observes, 'we can profitably begin from the point that the facts and the laws of created existence are indeed in a fundamental sense the same for Christians and non-Christians alike. They are objectively or revelationally the same whatever one's attitude to them may be.'[12]

Although the facts are 'objectively' and 'revelationally' the same for both Christians and non-Christians, Van Til also notes that there remains a sense in which Christians and non-Christians have all facts in common and no facts in common. He writes:

> We conclude then that when both parties, the believer and the non-believer, are epistemologically self-conscious and as such engaged in the interpretative enterprise, they cannot be said to have any fact in common. On the other hand, it must be asserted that they have every fact in common. Both deal with the same God and with the same universe created by God. Both are made in the image of God. In short, they have the metaphysical situation

---

10. Abraham Kuyper, *Encyclopedia of Sacred Theology*, trans. J. Hendrik de Vries (New York: Charles Scribner's Sons, 1898), 117.

11. Van Til, *Christian Apologetics*, 62.

12. Cornelius Van Til, 'Reply to Professor J. Vanden Bosch,' *The Banner* 75/2246 (24 May 1940), in Cornelius Van Til and Eric H. Sigward, *The Articles of Cornelius Van Til*, Electronic ed. (Labels Army Company: New York, 1997).

in common. Metaphysically, both parties have all things in common, while epistemologically they have nothing in common.[13]

Metaphysically, in terms of their objective being, the facts are the same for the Christian and the non-Christian. Epistemologically, in terms of the human interpretation of those facts, they are completely different for the Christian and the non-Christian.

The antithesis, therefore, does not mean that the facts are objectively different, but it does mean that the human interpreters are objectively different in the way they approach the facts. As Van Til puts it, 'there are only two kinds of people in the world, non-Christians and Christians; covenant breakers and covenant keepers; these two kinds of people have mutually exclusive beliefs about everything.'[14] As we will see, understanding how Christians and non-Christians are different is absolutely crucial to having a clear understanding of Van Til's claims about proper apologetic methodology.

Van Til teaches that there have been three kinds of human consciousness since creation. The first type of consciousness was the original Adamic consciousness. This was 'the reason of man as it existed before the fall of man. This reason was derivative. Its knowledge was, in the nature of the case, true, though not exhaustive. This reason was in covenant with God, instead of at enmity against God.'[15] The non-regenerate consciousness describes man after the fall. The non-regenerate consciousness is characterized by the desire of fallen man 'to be "as God,"' himself the judge of good and evil, himself the standard of truth.'[16] Redemption results in the third type of consciousness, the regenerate consciousness. The regenerate consciousness, as Van Til explains, 'is the Adamic consciousness *restored* and *supplemented*, but restored and supplemented in principle or standing only.'[17]

To say that the regenerate consciousness is the Adamic consciousness 'restored' indicates that the antithesis is not between two metaphysically

---

13. Van Til, *Common Grace and the Gospel*, 9.

14. Cornelius Van Til, 'What I Believe Today,' *Journal of Christian Reconstruction* 8/2 (Winter 1982), in Cornelius Van Til and Eric H. Sigward, *The Articles of Cornelius Van Til*, Electronic ed. (Labels Army Company: New York, 1997).

15. Van Til, *An Introduction to Systematic Theology*, 62.

16. Ibid., 63.

17. Ibid., 66-67.

distinct human faculties, one fallen and one redeemed. The believer, as we have already seen, is not given a different kind of human brain. The antithesis concerns the different *use* of the rational faculties. The antithesis results in two types of *reasoning*. This is true, according to Van Til, because the faculty of reason is an instrument of the individual person, and that person is either a Christian or a non-Christian. Van Til uses the imagery of a table saw to illustrate his point:

> To use once again the illustration of the saw: the saw is in itself but a tool. Whether it will move at all and whether it will cut in the right direction depends upon the man operating it. So also reason, or intellect, is always the instrument of a person. And the person employing it is always either a believer or an unbeliever. If he is a believer, his reason has already been changed in its set, as Hodge has told us, by regeneration. It cannot then be the judge; it is now a part of the regenerated person, gladly subject to the authority of God. It has by God's grace permitted itself to be interpreted by God's revelation. If, on the other hand, the person using his reason is an unbeliever, then this person, using his reason, will certainly assume the position of judge with respect to the credibility and evidence of revelation, but he will also certainly find the Christian religion incredible because impossible and the evidence for it always inadequate.[18]

The saw blade (the rational faculty) is the same for both the believer and the unbeliever, but the unbeliever uses the saw incorrectly because the unbeliever has the saw set at the wrong angle. As a result, 'Reason employed by a Christian always comes to other conclusions than reason employed by a non-Christian.'[19]

Because unbelievers have the saw set incorrectly, Christians and non-Christians come to different conclusions even though they use the same rational faculties. Van Til explains: 'The distinguishing characteristic between the very non-Christian theory of knowledge on the one hand, and the Christian concept of knowledge on the other hand, is, therefore, that in all non-Christian theories men reason *univocally*, while in Christianity men reason *analogically*.'[20] What this means is that Christians and non-Christians presuppose a different final reference point for the interpretation of facts.

---

18. Van Til, *Christian Apologetics*, 104.

19. Van Til, introduction to B. B. Warfield, *The Inspiration and Authority of the Bible*, 25.

20. Van Til, *An Introduction to Systematic Theology*, 31.

Recall that for Van Til, God is omniscient. God knows himself perfectly, and God knows all of the facts he has eternally decreed in their relation to himself as the one who decreed them and in their relation to every other fact in his unified plan. God, therefore, has preinterpreted all facts. He is the final reference point for the interpretation of all things. Man's knowledge is to be reinterpretive. Man's knowledge is true knowledge if it corresponds with God's knowledge, and it cannot do that if man assumes anyone or anything other than God as the final reference point for interpretation. Van Til explains that Christians and non-Christians do, in fact, presuppose different final reference points:

> As you know, I have constantly maintained that there are basically only two philosophies of life. One of these views is that which is based on the triune God of Scripture as the final reference point for all predication. This is my position. The other is that which assumes that man, fallen and apostate man, is the final reference point in predication.[21]

To reason univocally, then, is to presuppose fallen man as the final reference point of interpretation. To reason analogically is to presuppose God as the final reference point of interpretation. Because the unbeliever is a covenant breaker and desires autonomy, the unbeliever makes man the final reference point.[22]

As a result of the two different types of reasoning, there are two types of knowledge. Van Til explains that, 'epistemologically believers and non-believers have nothing in common.'[23] Believers and unbelievers are looking at reality from different perspectives. Van Til uses colored glasses to illustrate the point he is making: 'What the more particularly do I mean by saying that epistemologically the believer and the non-believer have nothing in common? I mean that every sinner looks through colored glasses. And these colored glasses are cemented to his face.'[24]

The 'colored glasses' causing fallen man to see everything incorrectly are illustrative of the false interpretive principle that leads to univocal reasoning. Because fallen man presupposes himself as the final reference

---

21. E. R. Geehan, ed., *Jerusalem and Athens*, 300.

22. Van Til, *A Christian Theory of Knowledge*, 34.

23. Van Til, 'Presuppositionalism, Part 2,' in Cornelius Van Til and Eric H. Sigward, *The Articles of Cornelius Van Til*, Electronic ed. (Labels Army Company: New York, 1997).

24. Ibid.

point of interpretation, fallen man is, in principle, wrong about everything. Van Til explains:

> The natural man, who assumes that he himself and the facts about him are not created, therefore assumes what is basically false. Everything he says about himself and the universe will be colored by this assumption. It is therefore impossible to grant that he is right, basically right, in what he says about any fact.[25]

As we have seen, Van Til does qualify what he says about the knowledge of unbelievers. For example, while it is true that the unbeliever does not know God in one sense, he does know God in another sense.[26] The unbeliever knows God through God's general revelation in himself and in the world around him, but the unbeliever always attempts to suppress that knowledge.

Similarly, Van Til qualifies his statements when he asserts that although the unbeliever's principle of interpretation, if applied consistently, would render knowledge of any creaturely fact impossible, unbelievers do in fact have some knowledge of earthly things. The knowledge that unbelievers do have of earthly things is due in part to God's common grace restraint. Furthermore, unbelievers can have knowledge of earthly things because they are often not self-conscious of their false interpretive principle. In other words, sometimes the unbeliever does not reason consistently with his principle of interpretation.

Van Til, therefore, emphasizes that the antithesis is absolute *in principle*. There can be no compromise between covenant-keepers and covenant-breakers. He explains, 'There can be no appeasement between those who presuppose in all their thought the sovereign God and those who presuppose in all their thought the would-be sovereign man.'[27] The conflict between the two can only be considered as 'an all-out global war.'[28] He explains that 'the battle is between *two mutually exclusive*

25. Cornelius Van Til, 'Defending the Faith' *Torch and Trumpet* 1/1 (Apr–May 1951), in Cornelius Van Til and Eric H. Sigward, *The Articles of Cornelius Van Til*, Electronic ed. (Labels Army Company: New York, 1997).

26. Van Til, *Common Grace and Witness-Bearing*, 9.

27. Van Til, *The Intellectual Challenge of the Gospel*, in Cornelius Van Til and Eric H. Sigward, *The Pamphlets, Tracts, and Offprints of Cornelius Van Til*, Electronic ed. (Labels Army Company: New York, 1997).

28. Van Til, introduction to B. B. Warfield, *The Inspiration and Authority of the Bible*, 24.

*totality views of life.*[29] This means that neutrality is impossible.[30] In striking language, Van Til asserts that the only possible point of contact between the two is a 'head on collision.'[31]

The reason there can be no appeasement and no neutrality is because the antithesis involves two totally different systems of thought. Van Til refers to them as 'two totality views of man and his environment.'[32] They are two whole systems based on two different principles of interpretation.[33] God's perfect and infinite knowledge of himself and of all decreed facts in relation to himself and to every other fact is the foundational system of truth. If there were no omniscient God, true knowledge would be impossible because true knowledge involves a knowledge of each fact in relation to every other fact, and only God has such infinite knowledge. If man presupposes God as the final reference point for interpretation, his finite system of knowledge corresponds with God's infinite knowledge and is true as far as it goes. The unbeliever's system of knowledge makes fallen man the final reference point of interpretation, thereby rendering the entire system of knowledge false.

It is important to distinguish the different terms to which Van Til applies the concept of the antithesis. If we fail to do this, much of what he says on the subject will be confusing. First, the antithesis *between the regenerate and the unregenerate*, according to Van Til, is absolute. There is no commonality between covenant-keepers and covenant-breakers, between the children of God and the children of the devil. Second, the antithesis *between the two principles of interpretation* is also absolute. Analogical reasoning and univocal reasoning are entirely different methods of reasoning, which lead to completely different systems of knowledge. We have to note a qualification to the concept of antithesis, however, because neither the Christian nor the non-Christian is completely consistent with his or her respective interpretive principle. This introduces a level of complexity into the concept of the antithesis as it exists in this present age before the final judgment and final separation of the sheep and the goats.

---

29. Van Til, *A Christian Theory of Knowledge*, 349.

30. Van Til, *Survey of Christian Epistemology*, 19.

31. Van Til, *A Christian Theory of Knowledge*, 348.

32. Ibid.

33. Ibid., 6, 41.

Van Til explains that no individual person 'fully exemplifies either system perfectly.'[34] As a result, there are 'many gradations of self-consciousness with which men fall into either of these two classes.'[35] As we have already seen, Van Til discusses what this looks like for the unbeliever in his doctrine of God's common grace. Through common grace, God restrains the unbeliever from following through completely with the autonomous interpretive principle.[36] As a result, the unbeliever does know God in one sense.[37] The unbeliever can also come to some true knowledge of scientific truths.[38] As Van Til says, the unbeliever has 'a great deal of knowledge about this world which is true as far as it goes.'[39] This is a significant qualification.

All of this means that the unbeliever is a complex creature.[40] Recognizing this reality is crucial for Van Til, 'It is therefore of the utmost importance to distinguish between what the natural man is by virtue of his adopted principle and what he still is because of the knowledge of God as his creator that he has within him and because of the non-saving grace by which he is kept from working out his principle to the full and by which he is therefore also able to do the "morally good."'[41] Common grace has complicated the picture as far as our understanding of fallen human knowledge is concerned. The antithesis between the believer and unbeliever is absolute in principle. The antithesis between the two different *principles* of interpretation is also absolute. But due to God's common grace the line is blurry during the present age when we look at *actual individual fallen human beings*.

The situation for the believer is also more complicated than it would seem based on what Van Til has said about the antithesis between the believer and unbeliever. Just as the unbeliever does not apply the false principle of interpretation consistently, neither does the believer apply the true principle of interpretation consistently. The unbeliever

---

34. Van Til, introduction to B. B. Warfield, *The Inspiration and Authority of the Bible*, 24.

35. Van Til, *Christian Apologetics*, 62.

36. Van Til, *A Christian Theory of Knowledge*, 13-14.

37. Van Til, *An Introduction to Systematic Theology*, 65.

38. Van Til, *Christian Theistic Evidences*, 113.

39. Van Til, *An Introduction to Systematic Theology*, 63.

40. Van Til, *A Christian Theory of Knowledge*, 229.

41. Ibid.

is restrained from full consistency by God because of common grace. The believer is kept from full consistency by the remnants of sin within. The antithesis is, therefore, complex in the case of both believers and unbelievers in the present age.

Van Til provides a helpful explanation of the complicated situation that now exists using Paul's imagery of an 'old man' and a 'new man' in reference to both Christians and non-Christians.

> To illustrate this point we may refer to Paul's teaching on the new man and the old man in the Christian. It is the new man in Christ Jesus who is the true man. But this new man in every concrete instance finds that he has an old man within him which wars within his members and represses the working out of the principles of his true new man. Similarly it may be said that the non-believer has his new man. It is that man which in the fall declared independence of God, seeking to be his own reference point. As such this new man is a covenant breaker. He is a covenant breaker always and everywhere. He is as much a covenant breaker when he is engaged in the work of the laboratory as he is when he is engaged in worshiping gods of wood or stone. But as in the new man of the Christian the new man of the unbeliever finds within himself an old man warring in his members against his will. It is the sense of deity, the knowledge of creaturehood and of responsibility to his Creator and Judge which, as did *Conscience* in Bunyan's *Holy War*, keeps speaking of King Shaddai to whom man really belongs. Now the covenant breaker never fully succeeds in this life in suppressing the old man that he has within him. He is never a finished product. That is the reason for his doing the relatively good though in his heart, in his new man, he is wholly evil. So then the situation is always mixed. In any one's statement of personal philosophy there will be remnants of his old man. In the case of the Christian this keeps him from being consistently Christian in his philosophy of life and in his practice. In the case of the non-believer this keeps him from being fully Satanic in his opposition to God. But however true it is that non-Christians are always much better in their statements of philosophy and in their lives than their own principle would lead us to expect and however true it is that Christians are always much worse in the statement of their philosophy and in their lives than their principle would lead us to expect, it is none the less also true that in principle there are two mutually exclusive systems, based upon two mutually exclusive principles of interpretation.[42]

---

42. Van Til, introduction to B. B. Warfield, *The Inspiration and Authority of the Bible*, 24-25.

This means that 'we have the "relative good" in the "absolutely evil" and the "relatively evil" in the "absolutely good."'[43] As Van Til further explains: 'the ideas of common wrath and common grace must both be kept as constitutive factors in measuring the present historical situation by the Word of God.'[44] In short, during the present age, the antithesis is absolute *in principle*, but it is qualified *in practice*.

## Conclusion

Van Til's doctrine of redemption and the resulting antithesis sets the stage for his doctrine of apologetic methodology. Without an understanding of the former, we will have little hope of understanding the latter. For Van Til, Christians, as a result of God's work of regeneration, are now able to see all facts as they truly are. Believers have renounced their autonomous claim to be the final reference point of interpretation. Believers are now able to see that God is the ultimate interpretive principle, and by reasoning analogically, they see all facts as the God-decreed and God-created facts they are. Believers now interpret all facts in light of Scripture. They are now able to have true knowledge because they are now able to have knowledge that corresponds to God's unified and exhaustive system of knowledge.

As a result of God's work of redemption, there are now two kinds of human beings in the world, believers and non-believers. These two kinds of people reason differently. Unbelievers reason univocally by autonomously making themselves the final reference point for interpretation. Believers, on the other hand, reason analogically by recognizing that God alone is the final reference point for interpretation. Because there are two types of reasoning among human beings, there are also two antithetical systems of knowledge. Because unbelievers assume themselves to be the final reference point of interpretation, in principle, they know nothing truly. Believers, however, can know facts truly insofar as their system of knowledge corresponds to God's system of knowledge.

Although the antithesis between the regenerate and the unregenerate and the antithesis between the two principles of interpretation is

---

43. Van Til, 'Common Grace: Third Article,' 81.
44. Ibid., 73

absolute in principle, the concrete situation prior to the final judgment is complicated. Neither the regenerate nor the unregenerate are completely consistent with their antithetical principles of interpretation. God's common grace restrains the unbeliever from being completely consistent, and the remnants of sin prevent the believer from being completely consistent. As a result, unbelievers who, in principle, can know nothing truly, have a certain amount of true knowledge. Believers, too, can be inconsistent, and introduce elements of autonomy and falsehood into their systems of knowledge. The implications of the antithesis for Van Til's apologetic methodology will be explored in the following chapter.

# CHAPTER 5

# The Apologetic Implications
# of the Antithesis

When Cornelius Van Til began making a public case for his apologetic methodology in the 1930s, few of those who heard or read him were fully aware of the way in which his methodology was shaped by his epistemology, by his theory of knowledge. Few had read more than a handful of his writings. As a result, few were fully aware that his theory of knowledge was a significant thread that connected his doctrine of God, the eternal decree, creation, the resulting Creator-creature distinction, the fall of humanity, the effects of sin, the redemption of humanity, and the resulting antithesis between believers and unbelievers. It appears that this lack of understanding of Van Til's theological building blocks inevitably led to much of the confusion and misunderstanding among some when his apologetic was studied.

Having examined Van Til's doctrines of God, humanity, the fall, redemption, and the antithesis in some detail, and having looked at the way he develops his epistemology throughout his discussion of each of these doctrines, we are now in a better position to look carefully at the implications these doctrines have for his apologetic methodology and hopefully avoid misunderstanding in the process. We have observed that the key theme running through Van Til's discussion of each of these doctrines is knowledge. Keeping in mind all that Van Til has said about knowledge thus far is necessary because his understanding of God's knowledge, the believer's knowledge, and the unbeliever's knowledge is assumed in everything he says about apologetic methodology.

## Defining Apologetics

Van Til defines apologetics as 'the vindication of Christian theism against any form of non-theistic and non-Christian thought.'[1] It is important to remember, however, that Van Til is not interested in defending Christian theism in general. As we have seen, he was seeking to develop a specifically Reformed apologetic, an apologetic that would be consistent with Reformed theology. He explains, 'The present writer holds with the late B. B. Warfield that the Reformed Faith is the most consistent expression of Christianity. *Christian* apologetics is therefore considered identical with *Reformed* apologetics.'[2] For Van Til, 'A Protestant theology requires a Protestant apologetic.'[3]

Given Van Til's definition of apologetics, it is not difficult to understand why he sided with Kuyper against Warfield on the relationship between systematic theology and apologetics. In systematic theology, 'we have the system of truth that we are to defend.'[4] Van Til explains the difference between Warfield and Kuyper on this point:

> The point of difference concerns chiefly the nature of apologetics. Warfield says that apologetics as a theological discipline has to establish the presuppositions of systematic theology such as the existence of God, the religious nature of man, and the truth of the historical revelation of God given us in the Scriptures. In contrast to this, Kuyper says that apologetics must seek only to defend that which is given it in systematics. Warfield argues that if we were to follow Kuyper's method we would first be explicating the Christian system and afterwards we would be asking ourselves whether perchance we had been dealing with facts or with fancies. Kuyper argues that if we allow apologetics to establish the presuppositions of theology we have virtually attributed to the natural man the ability to understand the truth of Christianity and have thus denied the doctrine of total depravity.[5]

---

1. Van Til, *Christian Theistic Evidences*, 1; cf. also Van Til, *Christian Apologetics*, 17.

2. Van Til, *A Christian Theory of Knowledge*, xxxv.

3. Van Til, *Christian Apologetics*, 86.

4. Ibid., 23.

5. Van Til, *An Introduction to Systematic Theology*, 17-18.

In classic Reformed theology, God is said to be the *principium essendi* ('principle of being') of theology, and God's revelation is the *principium cognoscendi externum* ('external principle of knowledge') of theology.[6] Systematic theology, therefore, presupposes God. Because apologetics is, for Van Til, an element of systematic theology, he argues that it too must presuppose the whole of that theology, and it too must presuppose God.[7]

## The Origins and Development of Traditional Apologetics

Van Til sets his apologetic methodology in stark contrast with what he usually refers to as 'traditional apologetics.' Traditional apologetics, he argues, has its origins in attempts to blend the Christian system of thought with autonomous Greek systems of thought. Given that systems of thought are, for Van Til, mutually exclusive unified wholes with every part related to every other part, we can understand why such blending would be a serious problem for him. Van Til associates this kind of syncretism with the Roman Catholic Church. According to Van Til, 'Rome has been consistently inconsistent in the confusion of non-Christian with Christian elements of teaching along the entire gamut of doctrinal expression.'[8] The result is that the theism of Rome is 'a theism in which the God of Christianity and the God of Greek philosophy, particularly the Unmoved Mover of Aristotle, are ground together into a common mixture.'[9]

Van Til explains that Roman Catholic theologians and apologists attempted to harmonize Aristotle and Christianity by means of the doctrine of the analogy of being (*analogia entis*).[10] According to Van Til, Thomas Aquinas is largely responsible for setting the trajectory of late medieval Roman Catholic theology on this question. He explains:

> The position of the Roman Catholic church on this point may at once be noted. While claiming to hold to the Christian theory of reality Thomas Aquinas and his modern followers in effect follow Aristotle in speaking

---

6. Muller, *Dictionary of Latin and Greek Theological Terms*, 288-89.

7. Van Til, *An Introduction to Systematic Theology*, 19.

8. Van Til, *Christian Apologetics*, 90.

9. Van Til, 'Defending the Faith,' in Cornelius Van Til and Eric H. Sigward, *The Articles of Cornelius Van Til*, Electronic ed. (Labels Army Company: New York, 1997).

10. Van Til, 'Nature and Scripture,' 287-88.

first of being in general and in introducing the distinction between divine being and created being afterwards. The consequences are fatal both for systematic theology and for apologetics.[11]

The result of Aquinas' adoption of the analogy of being is medieval scholasticism, and this is important because the epistemology of scholasticism 'is still the official epistemology of the Roman Church.'[12]

It is important to observe that when Van Til uses the term 'scholasticism' he means 'synthesis thinking.' He defines the principle of scholasticism as 'commingling Aristotelianism with Christian principles.'[13] In another place, he explains, 'The scholastic idea is based on the conviction that the method of finding truth advocated by Aristotle and the method of finding truth advocated by Christianity can be brought into a synthesis.'[14] What does scholasticism attempt to synthesize? Van Til explains: 'Scholasticism thinks it is intelligible to synthesize (a.) the Christian and the non-Christian view of man (b.) the Christian and the non-Christian view of the principle of unity (logic) and (c.) the Christian and the non-Christian view of diversity by which man must interpret God, himself and the world.'[15] In its attempt to synthesize Christian and non-Christian views, scholasticism directly attacks the doctrine of the antithesis. It attempts to combine mutually exclusive worldviews.

According to Van Til, John Calvin was the first theologian to truly break free from the synthesis thinking of scholasticism. Calvin 'alone of all the Reformers could rid himself of the last remnants of Platonic reasoning.'[16] Calvin did not do so perfectly, however, because even he 'did not bring out with sufficient clearness at all times that the natural man is as blind as a mole with respect to natural things as well as with respect to spiritual things.'[17] Calvin did, however, make more progress

---

11. Van Til, *Christian Apologetics*, 31.

12. Van Til, *Survey of Christian Epistemology*, 56.

13. Van Til, *An Introduction to Systematic Theology*, 94.

14. Van Til, *The Defense of the Faith*, 286.

15. Cornelius Van Til, 'Herman Dooyeweerd and Reformed Apologetics,' Philadelphia: Westminster Theological Seminary, 1974, in Cornelius Van Til and Eric H. Sigward, *The Pamphlets, Tracts, and Offprints of Cornelius Van Til*, Electronic ed. (Labels Army Company: New York, 1997).

16. Van Til, *Survey of Christian Epistemology*, 96.

17. Van Til, *An Introduction to Systematic Theology*, 148.

than anyone else up to that point in history. Unfortunately, according to Van Til, the generation of theologians following Calvin returned the Reformed church to synthesis thinking. Van Til explains:

> The entire enterprise of Luther and Calvin was to destroy this scholastic monstrosity by the ideas of *solus Christus*, *sola scriptura* and *sola fide*. But after Calvin the everlasting temptation besetting all Christians, especially sophisticated Christians, to make friends with those that are of Cain's lineage proved too much for many Lutheran and even Reformed theologians and so Lutheran and Reformed Scholasticism were begotten and born.[18]

In other words, the efforts of Calvin (and Luther) to free believers from the errors of synthesis thinking and syncretism was undermined by the Reformed and Lutheran scholastic theologians.

Post-reformation apologetics, according to Van Til, has effectively followed in the footsteps of Thomas Aquinas and has adopted scholastic synthesis thinking. Van Til observes:

> The great textbook of Evangelical apologetics is Bishop Butler's famous *Analogy*. It is not our purpose here to deal with its argument fully. Suffice it to point out that its argument is closely similar to that which is found, for instance, in the *Summa Contra Gentiles* of Thomas Aquinas.[19]

Joseph Butler (1692–1752) was the author of *The Analogy of Religion*, published in 1736.[20] According to Van Til, Butler is largely responsible for bringing Aquinas' doctrine of analogy into Protestant apologetics.[21] The bigger problem, as Van Til sees it, is that this corrupt apologetic methodology has also infiltrated the Reformed churches.[22]

## The Failure of Traditional Apologetics

Van Til determined that it would be necessary to completely rethink Reformed apologetics after reading the works of Princetonians such as

---

18. Van Til, 'Herman Dooyeweerd and Reformed Apologetics,' in Cornelius Van Til and Eric H. Sigward, *The Pamphlets, Tracts, and Offprints of Cornelius Van Til*, Electronic ed. (Labels Army Company: New York, 1997).

19. Van Til, *Christian Apologetics*, 100.

20. For a good contemporary edition, see Joseph Butler, *The Analogy of Religion*, ed. David McNaughton (Oxford: Oxford University Press, 2021).

21. Van Til, *The Protestant Doctrine of Scripture*, 20.

22. Van Til, *The Defense of the Faith*, 204–205.

B. B. Warfield (1851–1921) and William Brenton Greene (1854–1928). Van Til explains:

> Deciding, therefore, to follow the Reformers in theology, it was natural that I attempt also to do so in apologetics. I turned to such Reformed apologists as Warfield, Greene, and others. What did I find? I found the theologians of the 'self-attesting Christ,' defending their faith with a method which denied precisely that point![23]

In other words, Van Til believed that traditional Reformed apologetics was inconsistent with Reformed theology. Not only was it inconsistent with Reformed theology, it was in direct contradiction with it. It was necessary, therefore, to reject traditional apologetics.

Van Til argued that traditional apologetics 'had always been unbiblical and therefore inadequate.'[24] To begin with, traditional apologetics had a wrong view of natural theology. As Van Til explains: 'The natural theology of Rome is little else than Platonico-Aristotelian philosophy in theological garb. It is this "natural theology" as taken over by not a few Protestants, even by some Reformed theologians, that still lurks in our apologetical and systematic literature.'[25] Recall that for Van Til, natural theology is impossible because fallen human beings do not know any created fact correctly. They cannot, therefore, reason from any created fact to the Creator.

Because it has a wrong view of natural theology, traditional apologetics has a wrong view of the theistic proofs, the traditional arguments for the existence of God. Van Til explains:

> Accordingly, we would not say that these arguments, as they have been historically formulated even by non-Christians, are valid to a point. We do not hesitate to affirm that they are invalid. If they were valid, Christianity would not be true. Accordingly, too, we would not say that, though they are weak as proofs, they are strong as witnesses. If they were strong as witnesses, they would be strong to witness that Christianity is not true.[26]

---

23. Van Til, 'My Credo,' in E. R. Geehan, ed. *Jerusalem and Athens*, 10.

24. Van Til, *Survey of Christian Epistemology*, iii.

25. Cornelius Van Til, 'Plato,' in *Proceedings of the Calvinistic Philosophy Club*, edited by Jacob T. Hoogstra (Englewood, NJ, 1939), in Cornelius Van Til and Eric H. Sigward, *The Articles of Cornelius Van Til*, Electronic ed. (Labels Army Company: New York, 1997).

26. Van Til, *An Introduction to Systematic Theology*, 317.

One reason these proofs are weak is that all they claim to prove is a bare theism rather than Christian theism.[27] Furthermore, at best, all they can offer are probabilistic arguments for God.[28] For Van Til, if man reasons about any fact within a system of thought that lacks God as the final reference point of interpretation for all facts, it is impossible to come to the true conclusion of Christian theism. In other words, it is impossible to reason oneself from within a non-Christian worldview into the Christian worldview because the two systems of thought are mutually exclusive at every point.

According to Van Til, the natural theology of traditional apologetics 'starts with man as autonomous.'[29] This assumption of human autonomy and the assumption of the existence of 'brute facts' is another reason traditional apologetics must be rejected. Recall that autonomy and the assertion of brute factuality are the starting points of the worldview of fallen and sinful humanity. Van Til explains:

> … the weakness of the method of defense of Christianity as advocated by Butler appears most clearly. It was based upon the assumption of brute facts and man's ability, apart from God, to explain at least some of them. If one grants this much one cannot present any argument against modern science on the question of creation. The assumption of brute fact is itself the most basic denial of the creation doctrine. And the assumption that man can of himself interpret brute facts is itself the denial of God as creator. We need therefore to challenge the very idea of brute fact. We need to challenge man's ability to interpret any fact unless that fact be created by God and unless man himself is created by God.[30]

Note the close relation between what Van Til has already taught concerning knowledge and what he teaches here concerning the problems with traditional apologetics. Traditional apologetics, as Van Til understands it, contradicts the Christian theory of knowledge.

Because of its faulty epistemology, traditional apologetics also has a wrong view of the 'common ground' between the believer and the

---

27. Van Til, introduction to B. B. Warfield, *The Inspiration and Authority of the Bible*, 20.

28. Van Til, *The Defense of the Faith*, 340-41.

29. Cornelius Van Til, *The Case for Calvinism* (Philadelphia: The Presbyterian and Reformed Publishing Company, 1963), 109.

30. Van Til, *Christian Theistic Evidences*, 151-52.

unbeliever and a corresponding wrong view of the point of contact between the two. Traditional apologetics, according to Van Til, wrongly believes that the believer and the unbeliever have some kind of epistemological common ground. Traditional apologetics wrongly claims that at least some facts and laws are epistemologically the same for both.[31] Traditional apologetics fails to grasp the nature of the antithesis and the all-out war between the believer's worldview and the unbeliever's worldview and therefore sees this 'common ground' as the believer's point of contact with the unbeliever.

Because of its wrong views on all of these points, traditional apologetics is in a state of 'compromise with unbelief at every point.'[32] Van Til provides an extensive list of the ways in which traditional apologetics compromises every important Reformed doctrine.

> The traditional method was constructed by Roman Catholics and Arminians. It was, so to speak, made to fit Romanist or Evangelical theology. And since Roman Catholic and Evangelical theology compromises the Protestant doctrines of Scripture, of God, of man, of sin and of redemption so the traditional method of Apologetics compromises Christianity in order to win men to an acceptance of it.
>
> The traditional method compromises the Biblical doctrine of God in not clearly distinguishing his self-existence from his relation to the world. The traditional method compromises the Biblical doctrine of God and his relation to his revelation to man by not clearly insisting that man must not seek to determine the nature of God, otherwise than from his revelation.
>
> The traditional method compromises the Biblical doctrine of the counsel of God by not taking it as the only all-inclusive ultimate cause of whatsoever comes to pass.
>
> The traditional method therefore compromises the clarity of God's revelation to man, whether this revelation comes through general or through special revelation. Created facts are not taken to be clearly revelational of God; all the facts of nature and of man are said to indicate no more than that a god probably exists.
>
> The traditional method compromises the necessity of supernatural revelation in relation to natural revelation. It does so in failing to do justice

---

31. Van Til, introduction to B. B. Warfield, *The Inspiration and Authority of the Bible*, 39.

32. Cornelius Van Til, 'Wanted – A Reformed Testimony,' *Presbyterian Guardian* 20/7 (16 July 1951), in Cornelius Van Til and Eric H. Sigward, *The Articles of Cornelius Van Til*, Electronic ed. (Labels Army Company: New York, 1997).

to the fact that even in paradise man had to interpret natural revelation in the light of the covenantal obligations placed upon him by God through supernatural communication. In consequence the traditional method fails to recognize the necessity of redemptive supernatural revelation as concomitant to natural revelation after the fall of man.

The traditional method compromises the sufficiency of redemptive supernatural revelation in Scripture inasmuch as it allows for wholly new facts to appear in Reality, new for God as well as for man.

The traditional method compromises the authority of Scripture by not taking it as self-attesting in the full sense of the term.

The traditional method compromises the Biblical doctrine of man's creation in the image of God by thinking of him as being 'free' or ultimate rather than as analogical.

The traditional method compromises the Biblical doctrine of the covenant by not making Adam's representative action determinative for the future.

The traditional method compromises the Biblical doctrine of sin, in not thinking of it as an ethical break with God which is complete in principle even though not in practice.

In spite of these things, this traditional method has been employed by Reformed theologians. This fact has stood in the way of the development of a distinctly Reformed apologetic.[33]

Given that traditional apologetics involves the compromise of every important Reformed doctrine, traditional apologetics must be discarded and replaced with a consistently Reformed apologetic.

## The Consistently Reformed Method of Apologetics

In contrast to what he believes is an apologetic methodology that is inconsistent with Reformed theology, Van Til offers an alternative that he believes is consistent. This is the method of implication or presupposition. Van Til explains what this means: 'To argue by presupposition is to indicate what are the epistemological and metaphysical principles that underlie and control one's method.'[34] Van Til continues:

The method of reasoning by presupposition may be said to be indirect rather than direct. The issue between believers and non-believers in Christian theism

---

33. Van Til, *The Defense of the Faith*, 340-41.

34. Van Til, *Christian Apologetics*, 128.

cannot be settled by a direct appeal to 'facts' or 'laws' whose nature and significance is already agreed upon by both parties to debate. The question is rather as to what is the final reference-point required to make the 'facts' and 'laws' intelligible. The question is as to what the 'facts' and 'laws' really are.[35]

Recall that the question of the 'final reference point' is, for Van Til, absolutely fundamental to his doctrine of human knowledge. One's choice of the 'final reference point' determines whether one knows anything truly or not, and this idea of the 'final reference point' is key to understanding his apologetic methodology.

Van Til is clear that his apologetic methodology is directly connected to his theory of knowledge. He writes: 'Which method fits with a certain system of thought depends upon the idea of knowledge a system has. For the Christian system, knowledge consists in understanding the relation of any fact to God as revealed in Scripture. I know a fact truly to the extent that I understand the exact relation such a fact sustains to the plan of God.'[36] As a result, 'the only possible way for the Christian to reason with the non-believer is by way of presupposition. He must say to the unbeliever that unless he will accept the presuppositions and with them the interpretations of Christianity there is no coherence in human experience.'[37] In other words, the Christian reasons with the unbeliever by telling him that he must acknowledge God as the final reference point of all interpretation if he is to have true knowledge of anything.

Because the method of presupposition rests on Van Til's understanding of the difference between the believer's knowledge and the unbeliever's knowledge, which itself assumes the absolute antithesis between two principles of interpretation, the method of presupposition is a 'whole system' vs. 'whole system' method of apologetics. To put it another way, it is a worldview vs. worldview method. Christian theism is, as Van Til explains, 'an organic whole.'[38] We cannot simply present isolated facts to the unbeliever because there is no such thing as an isolated fact. Van Til writes:

---

35. Ibid., 129.

36. Van Til, *Survey of Christian Epistemology*, 6.

37. Van Til, *Christian Apologetics*, 197.

38. Cornelius Van Til, 'Seeking for Similarities,' *The Banner* 72/2076 (22 Jan 1937) in Cornelius Van Til and Eric H. Sigward, *The Articles of Cornelius Van Til*, Electronic ed. (Labels Army Company: New York, 1997).

> ... there is one system of reality of which all that exists forms a part. And any individual fact of this system is what it is primarily because of its relation to this system. It is therefore a contradiction in terms to speak of presenting certain facts to men unless one presents them as parts of this system.[39]

According to Van Til, when we realize that the Christian system of knowledge is absolutely antithetical to the non-Christian system of knowledge, we are forced to realize that 'the battle is between *two mutually exclusive totality views of life.*'[40] There is, therefore, no possibility of neutrality.[41] Each system of knowledge is an all or nothing affair.

Because the Christian system of knowledge is completely antithetical to the non-Christian system of knowledge, believers and unbelievers have no facts or laws in common. How then should the believer reason with the unbeliever? According to Van Til, the believer and unbeliever 'will have to place themselves upon one another's positions for the sake of argument.'[42] Van Til explains what this means:

> The Christian apologist must place himself upon the position of his opponent, assuming the correctness of his method merely for argument's sake, in order to show him that on such a position the 'facts' are not facts and the 'laws' are not laws. He must also ask the non-Christian to place himself upon the Christian position for argument's sake in order that he may be shown that only upon such a basis do 'facts' and 'laws' appear intelligible.[43]

According to this method of apologetics, the Christian will seek to demonstrate the impossibility of the non-Christian system of knowledge and then demonstrate that only the Christian system makes sense of anything – including the non-Christian's arguments against Christianity.

When the Christian assumes the position of the unbeliever 'for the sake of argument,' his goal is to demonstrate 'the impossibility of the contrary' to Christianity. Van Til explains:

> It is this that we ought to mean when we say that *we must meet our enemy on their own ground.* It is this that we ought to mean when we say that we reason

---

39. Van Til, *Christian Apologetics*, 193-94.

40. Van Til, *A Christian Theory of Knowledge*, 349.

41. Van Til, *Survey of Christian Epistemology*, 19.

42. Van Til, introduction to B. B. Warfield, *The Inspiration and Authority of the Bible*, 39.

43. Van Til, *Christian Apologetics*, 129.

*from the impossibility of the contrary.* The contrary is impossible only if it is self-contradictory when operating on the basis of its own assumptions. It is this too that we should mean when we say that we are arguing *ad hominem*. We do not really argue *ad hominem* unless we show that someone's position involves self-contradiction, and there is no self-contradiction unless one's reasoning is shown to be directly contradictory of or to lead to conclusions which are contradictory of one's own assumptions.[44]

In other words, in his critique of the non-Christian view, the Christian seeks to demonstrate that the non-Christian system is internally self-contradictory. The goal, as Van Til explains, is 'to reduce our opponent's position to an absurdity.'[45] The Christian accomplishes this goal by stepping into the non-Christian's system of knowledge and showing him that it is self-contradictory.

According to Van Til's method of presupposition, the Christian apologist should next ask the non-believer to assume the Christian position 'for the sake of argument.' He should ask the non-Christian to step into the Christian system of knowledge. The Christian's goal is to 'show that human predication at any point is unintelligible unless it be in terms of the self-identifying Christ of Scripture.'[46] Van Til explains this point in more detail:

> He must say to the unbeliever that unless he will accept the presuppositions and with them the interpretations of Christianity there is no coherence in human experience. That is to say, the argument must be such as to show that unless one accept the Bible for what true Protestantism says it is, as the authoritative interpretation of human life and experience as a whole, it will be impossible to find meaning in anything, it is only when this presupposition is constantly kept in mind that a fruitful discussion of

---

44. Van Til, *Survey of Christian Epistemology*, 205.

45. Ibid. It should be observed that reducing an opponent's position to absurdity is not original to Van Til. Many significant Christian apologists through the centuries have pointed out the internal contradictions and absurdities of various non-Christian views. This includes the two most influential theologians of the pre-Reformation church. Augustine reduces pagan idolatry to utter absurdity in Books 6–10 of *The City of God*. Thomas Aquinas discusses the 'demonstration to contradiction' in his *Commentary on Aristotle's Physics* (Book I, Lecture 3). This 'demonstration to contradiction' is intended to show how an adversary's assumptions involve self-contradiction. Aristotle's own use of this method of argument is found in Book IV of his *Metaphysics*.

46. Van Til, preface to *The Protestant Doctrine of Scripture*, n.p.

problems pertaining to the phenomena of Scripture and what it teaches about God in his relation to man can be discussed.[47]

In other words, as Van Til explains, 'The point I am interested in is to show that all the knowledge non-Christians have – whether as simple folk by common sense, or as scientists exploring the hidden depths of the created universe – they have because Christianity is true.'[48]

According to Van Til, the apologetic method of presupposition, in contrast to traditional apologetics, has a correct view of the theistic proofs. He says, 'The better theologians of the church have constantly sensed the fact that the theistic argument must not be used univocally. They have sensed something of the fact that all the theistic arguments should really be taken together and reduced to the one argument of the possibility of human predication.'[49] Van Til adds to this idea, arguing that Calvin had a correct view of the theistic proofs. Calvin argues, according to Van Til,

> ... that men ought to believe in God, because there is, and has been from the beginning of time, an abundance of evidence of His existence and of His character. There is objective evidence in abundance and it is sufficiently clear. Men ought, if only they reasoned rightly, to come to the conclusion that God exists. That is to say, if the theistic proof is constructed as it ought to be constructed, it is objectively valid, whatever the attitude of those to whom it comes may be.[50]

In this sense, according to Van Til, 'the theistic proofs are absolutely valid.'[51] As Van Til explains, the theistic proofs properly understood 'are but the restatement of the revelation of God.'[52]

According to Van Til, the presuppositional method of apologetics also has a correct view of the common ground between believers and unbelievers and a correct view of the point of contact between the two. With regard to common ground, the presuppositional method affirms that: 'Metaphysically, both parties have all things in common, while

---

47. Van Til, *Christian Apologetics*, 197.

48. Van Til, *The Defense of the Faith*, 282.

49. Van Til, *An Introduction to Systematic Theology*, 180.

50. Van Til, 'Common Grace: Second Article,' 192.

51. Van Til, *Common Grace and the Gospel*, 209.

52. Ibid.

epistemologically they have nothing in common.'[53] In other words, the presuppositional method has a proper understanding of the antithesis. In terms of metaphysics, the believer and the unbeliever occupy the same universe and share the same human nature. In that sense, everything in creation is common ground. Epistemologically, however, their principles of interpretation lead them to see all facts in creation differently.

With regard to the point of contact between the believer and the unbeliever, Van Til affirms that we 'find the point of contact for the presentation of the Gospel to non-Christians in the fact that they are made in the image of God and as such have ineradicable sense of deity within them.'[54] He explains, 'The point of contact for the Gospel, then, must be sought within the natural man. Deep down in his mind every man knows that he is the creature of God and responsible to God.'[55] The apologist, therefore, is to make his appeal to that which the unbeliever suppresses, knowing that only the Holy Spirit can give the unbeliever the ability to accept the truth.[56]

In his short work 'My Credo,' Van Til provides a brief summary of what he believes a consistently Reformed apologetic methodology should look like. In this summary, we can observe the way in which the threads of Van Til's teaching come together. Van Til writes:

My proposal, therefore, for a consistently Christian methodology of apologetics is this:

1. That we use the same principle in apologetics that we use in theology: the self-attesting, self-explanatory Christ of Scripture.

2. That we no longer make an appeal to 'common notions' which Christian and non-Christian agree on, but to the 'common ground' which they actually have because man and his world are what Scripture says they are.

3. That we appeal to man as man, God's image. We do so only if we set the non-Christian principle of the rational autonomy of man against

---

53. Ibid., 9.

54. Van Til, 'Presuppositionalism, Part 2,' in Cornelius Van Til and Eric H. Sigward, *The Articles of Cornelius Van Til*, Electronic ed. (Labels Army Company: New York, 1997).

55. Van Til, *Christian Apologetics*, 119.

56. Van Til, introduction to B. B. Warfield, *The Inspiration and Authority of the Bible*, 39.

the Christian principle of the dependence of man's knowledge on God's knowledge as revealed in the person and by the Spirit of Christ.

4. That we claim, therefore, that Christianity alone is reasonable for men to hold. It is wholly irrational to hold any other position than that of Christianity. Christianity alone does not slay reason on the altar of 'chance.'

5. That we argue, therefore, by 'presupposition.' The Christian, as did Tertullian, must contest the very principles of his opponent's position. The only 'proof' of the Christian position is that unless its truth is presupposed there is no possibility of 'proving' anything at all. The actual state of affairs as preached by Christianity is the necessary foundation of 'proof' itself.

6. That we preach with the understanding that the acceptance of the Christ of Scripture by sinners who, being alienated from God, seek to flee his face, comes about when the Holy Spirit, in the presence of inescapably clear evidence, opens their eyes so that they see things as they truly are.

7. That we present the message and evidence for the Christian position as clearly as possible, knowing that because man is what the Christian says he is, the non-Christian will be able to understand in an intellectual sense the issues involved. In so doing, we shall, to a large extent, be telling him what he 'already knows' but seeks to suppress. This 'reminding' process provides a fertile ground for the Holy Spirit, who in sovereign grace may grant the non-Christian repentance so that he may know him who is life eternal.[57]

Here we see, in a concise form, the basic contours of Van Til's apologetic system of thought. It is based on an attempt to be consistent with confessional Reformed theology, and it is driven by Van Til's theory of knowledge.

## Conclusion

In the first five chapters, we have observed that Van Til's presuppositional method of apologetics depends upon his theory of knowledge, which can be best understood by tracing it through his discussions of the doctrine of God, creation, humanity, the fall, redemption, and the antithesis. We have observed that, for Van Til, everything he teaches rests on his doctrine of the Triune God. The Triune God has perfect, infinite, and

---

57. Van Til, 'My Credo,' in E. R. Geehan, ed., *Jerusalem and Athens*, 20-21.

eternal self-knowledge as well as perfect, infinite, and eternal knowledge of all that he has freely decreed. God, therefore, knows all facts in relation to himself and to every other fact within his unified plan. Because he perfectly knows all facts in every relation, he has preinterpreted all facts.

Human beings are finite creatures, so even before the fall, man's knowledge could not possibly be an exact replica of God's infinite knowledge. Man's knowledge, instead, was to be analogical to God's knowledge. As Van Til explains, man was to reinterpret all facts in light of God's revelation. If he does so, his knowledge corresponds to God's knowledge and is true as far as it goes. When man sinned, he set himself up as the final interpretive principle. He assumed his own autonomy and treated all facts as 'brute facts' instead of facts that were already preinterpreted by God. All fallen human beings since then have followed Adam and Eve in their presumed autonomy. As a result, fallen man has lost the ability to know any fact for what it truly is, namely a God-decreed and God-interpreted fact.

When God redeemed the first fallen human being, the result was an antithesis between two kinds of people, believers and unbelievers. Unbelievers continued to maintain their autonomous principle of interpretation, but believers reasserted the true principle of interpretation and were able to have true knowledge again. As covenant-keepers, they made God, rather than themselves, the final reference point for all knowledge and predication. The antithesis between these two principles of interpretation is absolute. However, according to Van Til, the situation among actual human beings in this age is more complicated because God restrains fallen man from taking his interpretive principle to its consistent end and because the remnants of sin prevent believers from taking their interpretive principle to its consistent end.

Van Til argues that the implications of the absolute antithesis between the two principles of interpretation used by believers and unbelievers requires an apologetic method that recognizes this situation for what it is. The method of traditional apologetics, he argues, is not adequate because it fails to recognize the absolute nature of the antithesis and allows that unbelievers can have some true knowledge. It allows that the apologist can find common ground with the unbeliever on the basis of this knowledge and, using that as a starting point, argue for the existence of God. Van Til claims that a consistently Reformed method of apologetics, on the other hand, must follow the method of presupposition. By means of this method, the Christian apologist begins by demonstrating the self-contradictory nature of the unbeliever's system of knowledge and continues by demonstrating that the unbeliever cannot explain any facet of human knowledge or experience without presupposing the existence of the Triune God revealed in Scripture.

Many Reformed Christians will wonder at this point what all the fuss is about. Why, they might ask, would Van Til's apologetic teachings have caused an often bitter, decades long debate in various Reformed denominations and churches? Furthermore, why would any confessionally Reformed Christian not embrace Van Til's apologetic system? Isn't what he taught simply the implication of Reformed theology for apologetics? What possible concerns could a Reformed Christian have with any of this? I hope to provide answers to such questions in the following chapters.

# PART TWO:

# Reconsidering The Thought of Cornelius Van Til

# CHAPTER 6

# Biblical Concerns

In the previous chapters, I have attempted to provide a relatively concise and understandable overview of Van Til's apologetic system of thought by looking at what he says about knowledge in connection with the doctrine of God, creation, humanity, the fall, and redemption. I have refrained from offering any substantive criticisms along the way in these chapters in order to avoid unnecessary distraction from my primary goal there of simply stating and explaining Van Til's own views. In this and the remaining chapters I will attempt to explain a variety of concerns related to Van Til's system of thought with the goal of helping readers better understand why some confessionally Reformed Christians do not embrace Van Tillian apologetics.

I will focus first on certain biblical concerns. I will then address, in the following chapters, several philosophical, theological, historical, and practical concerns with his thought. I remind readers that although I am describing some of the concerns that I, and other non-Van Tillians, have with Van Til's thought, this is intended as a contribution to an ongoing discussion among brothers in Christ about the teaching of another brother in Christ. My hope is that Van Tillians will treat such concerns of non-Van Tillians in the same way they ask that the concerns of Van Tillians be treated.

With such an emphasis on various concerns, however, it may appear as if I am suggesting that there is nothing good in Van Til's work. That is not the case. As I have already observed, Van Til subscribed to the Westminster Standards. There is abundant doctrinal agreement, therefore, among confessionally Reformed Van Tillians and confessionally Reformed non-Van Tillians, and there is much that is good in his writings when he is discussing these agreed upon confessional doctrines. If this book were an exhaustive analysis of Van Til's entire system of thought, significant space would be devoted to discussing these elements of his teaching. The focus of this book, however, is on Van Til's controversial attempt to develop a consistently Reformed apologetic method. We begin, then, with some of the biblical concerns of those who do not believe Van Til successfully achieved his goal.

## An Admitted Exegetical Defect

Given the fact that Cornelius Van Til subscribed to the Westminster Confession of Faith and Catechisms and believed that those standards contain the system of theology taught in Scripture, he and his confessionally Reformed critics agree on the biblical nature of the many doctrines contained in these standards. There is agreement, for example, on the clear biblical evidence for the independence, immutability, and omniscience of the Triune God, the divine decree, the Creator-creature distinction, total depravity, and much more. Confessionally Reformed non-Van Tillians have no concerns with respect to any biblically grounded confessional doctrines that Van Til faithfully proclaimed. Concerns arise only when elements of his apologetic system of thought create tensions or contradictions with those biblically grounded confessional doctrines.

A fundamental problem arises at precisely this point, however, because unlike the Reformed confessional standards, Van Til's apologetic system of thought is not biblically grounded. It has long been observed that his writings lack any detailed scriptural exegesis.[1] In a dissertation on Van Til's apologetic system, George Zemek, Jr., explains, 'Van Til and his followers have helped to break the apologetical shackles of humanistic philosophies by providing a Scriptural perspective for apologetics; however, their arguments are not exegetically corroborated.'[2] Van Til

---

1. This is *not* to say that Van Til's writings are devoid of scriptural references. He alludes to numerous biblical passages throughout his writings, and he mentions many texts explicitly. Mentioning a biblical text or alluding to a biblical text, however, is not the same as exegeting a biblical text and demonstrating that it teaches what one says it teaches.

2. George J. Zemek, Jr., 'Exegetical and Theological Bases for a Consistently Presuppositional Approach to Apologetics,' ThD diss, (Grace Theological Seminary, 1982), iv. Zemek does not seem to notice the irony of his claim that Van Til and his

himself admitted that the lack of exegesis was a 'defect' in his work, and he stated that he had no excuse for it.[3] While Van Til's honest acknowledgement of this lack of exegesis is certainly admirable, the acknowledgement of the lack does not eliminate all of the problems created by the lack.[4] Because of these problems, a number of Van Til's proponents have attempted to provide the missing exegetical foundation.

Zemek's entire dissertation, for example, was written 'to show that the validity of a consistently presuppositional approach to apologetics rests solidly upon exegetical and theological bases which permeate the totality of divine revelation.'[5] Greg Bahnsen wrote a biblical introduction to apologetics specifically intended to fill the exegetical gap, and that introduction is now included in his book *Always Ready*.[6] With regard to their book *Revelation and Reason*, the editors K. Scott Oliphint and Lane G. Tipton explain, 'At least part of the purpose of this collection of essays is to set in the foreground the necessity of exegetical and theological foundations for any Reformed, Christian apologetic.'[7] In short, many Van Tillians have recognized that if Van Til's system of thought is to be defended as a *biblical* system of thought, an exegetical case for that system must be made.

None of this means that Van Til did not believe his system of apologetic thought was rooted in the teaching of Scripture. He subscribed to the Westminster Standards and believed that those standards contained the system of theology taught in Scripture. He assumes the exegetical work underlying the Reformed confessions. His career is focused, however, on demonstrating that if we take that biblical Reformed theology as our starting point, it necessarily leads to the rejection of traditional apologetic methods and the adoption of the method of presupposition. He apparently did not see the need to restate the exegetical case for

---

followers have provided a 'Scriptural' apologetic while also acknowledging that they have not provided exegetical arguments for it.

3. Van Til, 'Response to G. C. Berkouwer,' in Geehan, *Jerusalem and Athens*, 203.

4. The lack of biblical exegesis is the reason there is no detailed discussion of any biblical text in the first five chapters of this book. Those chapters are my attempt to set forth what Van Til himself said, and he simply doesn't say much about the biblical texts.

5. Zemek, Jr., 'Exegetical and Theological Bases,' iv.

6. See Greg L. Bahnsen, *Always Ready*, 3-26.

7. K. Scott Oliphint and Lane G. Tipton, eds., *Revelation and Reason: New Essays in Reformed Apologetics* (Phillipsburg: P&R Publishing, 2007), 1.

the Reformed doctrines on which he and his critics agreed, but he also apparently did not see the need to state the exegetical case for his understanding of the doctrinal implications on which he and his critics strongly disagreed.

In this chapter I will explain some specifically biblical concerns with Van Til's system of apologetic thought. The lack of exegesis in his writings, however, means that I will have to approach this topic from a slightly different angle than might be the case had Van Til provided detailed exegesis in support of his view. It is obviously impossible to evaluate Van Til's exegesis of Scripture when that exegesis doesn't exist.[8] Therefore, in this chapter, I will instead focus first on some 'big picture' biblical issues before turning to a few key biblical passages.

## The Epistemological Assumptions of Scripture

According to Van Til, in order for there to be true knowledge of any fact, there has to be knowledge of that fact in relation to God, in relation to every other fact that God decreed, and in relation to the whole system of knowledge of which that fact is a part. As we have seen, Van Til explicitly repeats this view of knowledge dozens of times throughout his writings. As just one example out of many, he writes, 'we may say that we must know all about all things if we are to know anything about anything.'[9] This view of knowledge is at the heart of his concept of the antithesis. Because the unbeliever does not make God his final epistemological reference point but instead sees all facts as 'brute facts' that he is able to interpret autonomously, the unbeliever does not know any fact truly. It is the absolute antithesis between the worldview of the unbeliever and the worldview of the believer that then necessitates the presuppositional method of apologetics.

Reformed theology has always understood Scripture to be the *principium cognoscendi* of theology. In other words, Scripture is our rule of faith and life (WCF 1.2). Because Van Til's theory of knowledge is

8. It is also impossible in the space of one chapter to present a positive detailed exegetical case for another method of apologetics. A separate book would have to be written to provide a complete exegetical case for any alternative apologetic methodology. I will simply offer a few preliminary thoughts on the matter in the Conclusion.

9. Cornelius Van Til, 'A Christian Theistic Theory of Knowledge,' *The Banner* 66/1809 (6 Nov 1931), in Cornelius Van Til and Eric H. Sigward, *The Articles of Cornelius Van Til*, Electronic ed. (Labels Army Company: New York, 1997).

the most significant element in his apologetic system, the first question we have to ask, therefore, when examining Van Til's system is whether his theory of knowledge is biblical. We have to ask whether Van Til's theory of knowledge is shared by the authors of Scripture. In order to answer this question, we will have to look at what Scripture explicitly says as well as what it assumes with regard to human knowledge. We will have to pay particularly close attention to what Scripture reveals with regard to the knowledge of unbelievers.

When we compare Van Til's teaching and the teaching of Scripture on these subjects, what we find is that his theory of knowledge and its implications are contrary to Scripture. His theory of knowledge is not taken from the biblical text but read into it, and this causes him to distort the biblical text and its teaching. In other words, rather than starting with Scripture and exegetically demonstrating that it teaches his theory of knowledge, Van Til simply assumes his theory of knowledge to be true, calls it the Christian theory of knowledge, and then reads Scripture through that lens. Because everything in Van Til's apologetic system of thought is rooted in this theory of knowledge, its unbiblical nature results in an unbiblical apologetic system.

What then do the Scriptures actually teach about knowledge? If we begin with the widest angle lens by asking what the epistemological *assumptions* of Scripture are, the first thing we must observe is that the Scripture is God's written revelation to human beings. As such, the Bible itself is a form of communication between God and man. The Bible not only *is* a communication between God and man; it also *contains* the inspired accounts of many specific instances of communication between God and his rational creatures as well as many instances of communication among his rational creatures.

In Scripture, for example, we read of God communicating with both fallen and unfallen angels, and we read of these angels communicating with God (e.g., Job 1:6-12; Zech. 1:12-13). We read of angels communicating with human beings and of human beings communicating with angels (e.g., Luke 1:11-20, 26-38). We read of God communicating with unfallen human beings (Gen. 1:28-30; 2:15-17), with fallen human beings (e.g., Gen. 3:16-19; 4:6-7), and with redeemed human beings (e.g., Exod. 6:2, 33:9; 1 Sam. 3:1-15), and we read of human beings communicating with God (e.g., Exod. 3:11; Num. 22:10). Furthermore, we also read of human beings communicating with other human beings. We read of unbelievers communicating with other unbelievers (e.g., John 12:19), of believers communicating with other believers (e.g., Acts 15:6-21; Rom. 1:1-7; 1 Cor. 1:1-3), and of unbelievers and believers communicating with each other (e.g., Acts 2:38; Acts 16:29-32).

The many instances we find in Scripture of believers communicating with unbelievers are particularly important for our purposes. We read, for example, that Moses communicates with Pharaoh (Exod. 7:1–11:10). We read that Daniel communicates with Nebuchadnezzar (Dan. 1:18–4:37). We read that the prophets communicate oracles of judgment to the nations (e.g., Jonah 3:1-5; Amos 1:3–2:16; Isa. 13:1–20:6; Nah. 1:9–3:19; Zeph. 2:4-15; Hab. 2:6-20; Jer. 46:1–51:64; Obad. 1:1-21; Ezek. 25:1–32:32). We read that Jesus communicates with unbelieving Jews (e.g., Matt. 12:1-14; 16:1-4; 19:3-9; 23:1-39). We read that Peter communicates with unbelieving Jews (e.g., Acts 2:14-40) and with unbelieving Gentiles (e.g., Acts 10:34-43). We also read that Paul communicates with unbelieving Jews (e.g., Acts 13:16-41) and with unbelieving Gentiles (e.g., Acts 17:22-31). Such communication between believers and unbelievers occurs throughout the Bible.

Of course, Van Til does not deny that communication between God and man or between man and man takes place. Nor does he deny that communication between believers and unbelievers takes place. I am not arguing or implying that he denies these obvious biblical facts. The issue has to do with whether Van Til can account for these biblical facts given his theory of knowledge and his system of thought. In other words, can his theory of knowledge account for what we find in Scripture? The issue is the difference between the assumptions of Scripture concerning knowledge and the assumptions of Van Til's theory of knowledge. The problem we find is that the communication we see in Scripture rules out the absolute epistemological antithesis that is itself the foundation of Van Til's method of presuppositional apologetics.

The communication that we see in Scripture is important to consider because all communication between rational beings requires *a shared knowledge* of the language used to communicate. If two rational beings do not have a shared knowledge of the same language, communication cannot happen. As the Apostle Paul explains:

So with yourselves, if with your tongue you utter speech that is not intelligible, *how will anyone know what is said*? For you will be speaking into the air. There are doubtless many different languages in the world, and none is without meaning, but *if I do not know the meaning of the language*, I will be a foreigner to the speaker and the speaker a foreigner to me (1 Cor. 14:9-11).

If someone who knows only Mandarin Chinese speaks to someone who knows only English, communication cannot and will not occur. The Chinese speaker will be 'speaking into the air.' A speaker/writer and a hearer/reader must have a shared knowledge of the same language in order for any communication to occur. In other words, the kind of communication that the Bible is and the kind of communication that the Bible often describes *presupposes* a shared knowledge of language.[10]

Additionally, a shared knowledge of language implies a shared knowledge of something more than language. Notice that a knowledge of any language requires a shared knowledge of its grammar, syntax, and vocabulary, and a shared knowledge of a language's vocabulary requires a shared knowledge of the things signified by that vocabulary. In other words, a shared knowledge of language requires a shared knowledge of things in the external world. In short, the very nature of Scripture as divine communication *assumes* man's knowledge of both human language and of the world around him. God is not simply speaking into the air. His Word shall not return to him empty. It accomplishes its purpose (Isa. 55:11).

Regarding the assumed knowledge of things signified by a language's vocabulary, consider the vocabulary of Genesis 1. We read words such as heavens and earth, light and darkness, waters and dry land, vegetation, trees, fruit, living creatures, birds, livestock, fish, man, and more. Those words are not meaningless marks on a page. They signify real existing things in God's creation. God's word to man in Genesis 1 assumes that the hearer or reader already had a knowledge of the real things those words signify. It assumes that the readers or hearers of Genesis already knew what trees and fruit and birds and fish are, and it assumes that

---

10. I am aware that the issues involved in the philosophy of language are far more complex than this and the following few paragraphs can make completely clear. My point here is simply to elaborate on what Paul says in 1 Corinthians 14:9-11 in order to compare what he says to what we find in Van Til's system of thought.

they already knew the language by which they were able to communicate with other people about such things. They already had that knowledge prior to reading Genesis. If they had not already had that knowledge, they would not have been able to understand the words of Genesis on even the most basic level. They would not have been able to receive God's communication. The inspiration of Scripture in human language would have been pointless.

We have no biblical evidence that the original readers (or hearers) of Genesis gained their knowledge of the Hebrew language in any way other than the normal way all human beings gain such knowledge. Learning that language required the gradual acquisition of several other kinds of knowledge. It required the growing knowledge of the vocabulary, grammar, and syntax of the language, which they acquired from parents or from other fluent speakers of the language. It also required the growing knowledge of the things in the external world signified by the vocabulary of the language they were learning. That knowledge had to be gained through the use of their God-given sensory and rational faculties. What is true of the language of Genesis 1 is true of every word of Scripture.

When we turn to the biblical accounts of communication between rational creatures, the requirements of a shared knowledge of language and of the world do not change. Scripture records numerous acts of communication among human beings. Perhaps most significantly for our purposes, it includes numerous accounts of communication between believers and unbelievers. The most important act of communication between believers and unbelievers is the proclamation of the Gospel. However, regardless of what is being communicated, the existence of communication between believers and unbelievers requires a shared knowledge of a human language and a shared knowledge of things in the world that the vocabulary of that language signifies. Such communication requires a linguistic *common ground* with all that implies. If there is no linguistic common ground, there is no communication. If there is no common ground, the believer and unbeliever are speaking different languages, and the believer who is proclaiming the Gospel is speaking into the air.

The fact that the believer and the unbeliever must have a shared knowledge of a human language in order for the believer to proclaim the Gospel to the unbeliever does not imply that this linguistic common ground is religiously neutral ground. The very fact that it is *the Gospel* that is being proclaimed indicates a crucial religious difference. The Gospel promise is proclaimed 'together with the command to *repent and believe*' (Canons of Dordt, Second Head of Doctrine, Art. 5), but the fact that it is the Gospel that is being *proclaimed* indicates epistemological commonality with regard to the language being used to proclaim the Gospel.

If this shared knowledge of language exists, it requires a shared knowledge of vocabulary, and a shared knowledge of the real things the vocabulary signifies. In other words, the biblical assumption of the existence of communication indicates much more common ground between the believer and the unbeliever than Van Til's theory of knowledge allows. The biblical assumption rules out the *absolute* epistemological antithesis that grows out of Van Til's theory of knowledge. The biblical assumption of shared knowledge of language and of things in the world also removes the grounds for claiming that the method of presupposition is the *only* biblically faithful method of apologetics.

Some Van Tillians might respond at this point by saying that Van Til's doctrine of common grace qualifies the antithesis and that this qualification is what allows for communication to take place. Perhaps so, but according to Van Til, it is the absolute epistemological antithesis that necessitates the method of presupposition. Van Til argues that 'Since there is no fact and no law on which the two parties to the argument agree they will have to place themselves upon one another's positions for the sake of argument.' [11] However, if the very nature of communication requires that there are facts on which the two parties agree, they don't *have to* use this method of presupposition. The shared knowledge of the world that allows for the very possibility of communication may also be used as a starting point. In short, in order for Van Til to maintain consistency with Scripture, he has to qualify the antithesis, but a qualified antithesis does not necessitate the method of presupposition. If he is to maintain the absolute antithesis that necessitates the presuppositional method, he will be forced to maintain an idea that is completely inconsistent with what the Scriptures say about communication.

---

11. Van Til, introduction to *The Inspiration and Authority of the Bible*, 39.

## Express Statements of Scripture

Van Til's doctrine of the absolute antithesis, which necessitates the method of presupposition and is at the heart of his theory of knowledge, is not only contradicted by the Bible's *assumptions* regarding communication, it is also contradicted by many *express statements* of Scripture. The Scriptures regularly attribute knowledge to unbelievers. When God commands Abimelech to return Abraham's wife, he tells Abimelech, 'But if you do not return her, *know* that you shall surely die, you and all who are yours' (Gen. 20:7). One of the purposes of the Exodus is that the Egyptians 'shall *know* that I am the LORD' (Exod. 7:5). Moses tells the King of Edom that the king *knows* all the things Israel has been through (Num. 20:14-16).

The Sidonians *know* how to cut timber better than the Israelites (1 Kings 5:6; 2 Chron. 2:3-9). Jeremiah tells the unbelieving Israelites that they are to '*know* for certain that if you put me to death, you will bring innocent blood upon yourselves and upon this city and its inhabitants' (Jer. 26:15). Ezekiel repeatedly declares that God is sending judgment upon his people in order that 'they shall *know* that I am the LORD' (e.g., Ezek. 5:13). Jesus tells wicked men that they '*know* how to give good gifts to your children' (Matt. 7:11) and '*know* how to interpret the appearance of earth and sky' (Luke 12:56). Peter tells the Jews that they *know* about Jesus and the works he did (Acts 2:22). Paul says that the wicked '*know* God's righteous decree that those who practice such things deserve to die' (Rom. 1:32).

There is nothing in Scripture that treats fallen man's knowledge of things, events, and skills as unusual. They can learn these things through the teaching of others, through observation, and through experience. They can even learn things through nature. Nature teaches that certain sexual behaviors are immoral (Rom. 1:26). Nature teaches about the law (Rom. 2:12-16). Again, as we have seen, Van Til will grant that unbelievers have such knowledge because common grace qualifies the absolute epistemological antithesis. But that is precisely the problem. The absolute epistemological antithesis is the *raison d'être* for Van Til's apologetic system. If the state of human knowledge is as Scripture describes it, there are facts which both believers and unbelievers know, and if there are facts which both unbelievers and believers know, there is nothing requiring the method of presupposition.

## The Distorting Effects of Unbiblical Assumptions

The existence of communication in Scripture also reveals a difference in *focus* between the biblical authors and Van Til. The Bible, as we have seen, everywhere assumes that communication is occurring. It everywhere assumes that functional and intelligible human predication is occurring. The Bible assumes that there is a shared knowledge of language when communication takes place because such shared knowledge is an absolutely necessary prerequisite for communication to take place (1 Cor. 14:9-11). But notice that the Bible simply *assumes* all of this to be true. No biblical author ever makes a case for the existence of shared knowledge between a speaker and a hearer. No biblical author ever treats human predication or human communication as a problem in the way that Van Til does. In other words, the biblical authors are not consumed with the problem of knowledge. They do not even treat human knowledge as if it were a problem with which someone might or ought to be concerned.

On the other hand, for many post-Enlightenment philosophers, there has been no bigger problem than the problem of knowledge. The idealists Van Til studied discussed this problem endlessly. As we have seen, Van Til was also consumed with this problem, and Van Til considered the self-attesting Triune God of Scripture to be the solution to the problem. However, as a result of focusing so much of his energy on this problem, he has a tendency to read all of Scripture with that problem at the forefront of his mind. This distorts his reading of Scripture since the authors of Scripture do not treat human knowledge as if it were a pressing problem to be solved.

Consider, for example, what Van Til writes in one place regarding the message of God to man. He says: 'It is just because man cannot speak intelligently to himself without God and because the sinner has sent God out of his life that God in condescending grace comes back to him. *But he asks men to accept him at his word for what he is, the indispensable presupposition of all intelligent human predication.*'[12] This second sentence demonstrates the kind of distorting effect that Van Til's modernist obsession with the problem of knowledge has on his reading of Scripture.

---

12. Van Til, *A Christian Theory of Knowledge*, 231. Emphasis mine.

Scripture doesn't share this preoccupation with post-Enlightenment epistemological debates because the biblical authors don't share the false assumptions of post-Enlightenment epistemology. Scripture never says that God asks man to accept him as the indispensable presupposition of all intelligent human predication. It is never the message of any prophet or apostle in Scripture. Jesus never says, 'I am the way, the truth, and the indispensable presupposition of all intelligent human predication.' We find nothing like this expressly stated anywhere in the Bible, and it is not the good and necessary consequence of anything expressly stated in the Bible. The reason we find nothing like this in the Bible is because human predication is not treated as a problem by the biblical authors, much less as a significant problem. The significant human problem addressed in Scripture is man's sin and rebellion and the resulting wrath of God that rests upon him. The primary human problem is not what humanistic post-Enlightenment philosophers think it is. The primary human problem is not the presupposition of human predication.

This quote is merely one example of what happens when the Bible is read through humanistic post-Enlightenment philosophical lenses. Reading Scripture through such lenses distorts its message. The problem is that this is not the only example that could be cited. Even a surface-level reading of Van Til's works reveals that he reads *all* of Scripture through these lenses, with the problem of knowledge and the issue of intelligible human predication ever at the forefront of his mind. The problem is that what Van Til emphasizes in his message is not what the biblical authors emphasize in their message. Reading the Bible as if it is focused on providing the solution to the Enlightenment problem of human knowledge and predication can only result in a distorted reading of the biblical message.[13]

## The Bible and Natural Theology

In our survey of Van Til's thought in Part One, we observed that his system of theology entails the rejection of natural theology. Recall that

---

13. It should go without saying that I am not arguing that Van Til never proclaimed the biblical message of Jesus Christ and him crucified. He preached this message from the pulpit and even on the streets of New York City. What I am saying is that this biblical message often gets drowned out by other concerns because he is so intently focused on solving the epistemological problems endlessly discussed by Enlightenment philosophers and by the idealists of his own day. This is the issue that dominates all of his writings for decades.

natural theology is 'the knowledge of God that is available to reason through the revelation of God in the natural order.'[14] For Van Til, the unbeliever obviously cannot start with a knowledge of any created fact and then reason from that fact to God because the unbeliever does not know any created fact as it truly is. Furthermore, as we have seen, Van Til says that natural theology is impossible because the creation is under the curse of God.[15] Not only is creation under a curse that veils any true knowledge of God from man, but the mind of fallen humanity is also now corrupt.[16]

While it is certainly true that creation has been in bondage to corruption since the fall of man (Rom. 8:20-22), and while it is certainly true that as a result of the fall man 'became dead in sin, and wholly defiled in all the faculties and parts of soul and body' (WCF 6.2), this did not result in the impossibility of knowing something about God based on reflection on his general revelation in the works of his hands. In the following paragraphs we will look briefly at the two passages of Scripture most commonly cited by early Reformed theologians in support of their doctrine of natural theology.

## Psalm 19

In the first verse of Psalm 19, we read: 'The heavens declare the glory of God, and the sky above proclaims his handiwork.' The heavens were created by God in the beginning (Gen. 1:1). The Psalmist here tells us that this created work 'declares' or 'proclaims' something. What do the heavens declare? The glory of God. In other words, the Word of God is telling us that the heavens objectively do something. The heavens objectively reveal the glory of God. The heavens reveal something about the true and living God. In his commentary on the Psalms, Theodore Beza helpfully explains what the heavens reveal about God:

> This Psalm does teach us the sum of all true divinity, the end whereof is, that we have that knowledge both of God himself, and of the worship due unto him, whereby we may become partakers of everlasting life. Wherefore he says, that men are taught the glory and majesty of God, that is (as Paul

---

14. Richard A. Muller, *Dictionary of Latin and Greek Theological Terms*, 2nd ed. (Grand Rapids: Baker Academic, 2017), 362.

15. Van Til, *Survey of Christian Epistemology*, 122.

16. Van Til, *An Introduction to Systematic Theology*, 164.

interprets it, Rom. 1:10) his eternal power and godhead, by the beholding of the heavens, by the orderly changes of days and nights, but especially by the golden beauty of the Sun, which shines over the whole world with an unspeakable course, so that no man can pretend the ignorance thereof.[17]

Since the heavens are there for all to see, the implication is that all who see the heavens know something of the glory of God. If they know something of God based on God's general revelation, and if knowledge of God is theology, then by definition that something they know is natural theology. Now, in Psalm 19, the fact of general revelation is stated explicitly, while the resulting natural theology is only implied. In the book of Romans, Paul makes explicit what the Psalmist implies.

## Romans 1:18-22

Romans 1:18-22 is the *locus classicus* in Reformed discussions of natural theology. It is the beginning of a section of the letter (vv. 18-32) teaching that all human beings have sinned and that all human beings are responsible for their sin. The focus in verses 18-22 is on unbelieving Gentiles. The next section (2:1–3:8) is focused more on the Jews. The point of this entire section, however, is that all have sinned, whether Jew or Gentile. Verses 18-22 are significant for our purposes because of what they teach us concerning the knowledge of God unbelievers have through God's created works.

Paul opens this section by saying, 'For the wrath of God is revealed from heaven against all ungodliness and unrighteousness of men, who by their unrighteousness suppress the truth' (v. 18). This statement provides an answer to the implicit question raised by verses 16-17. In those verses, Paul wrote: 'For I am not ashamed of the gospel, for it is the power of God for salvation to everyone who believes, to the Jew first and also to the Greek. For in it the righteousness of God is revealed from faith for faith, as it is written, "The righteous shall live by faith."' But why has the righteousness of God been revealed in the Gospel, and why are the righteous to live by faith? Paul responds: Because of the wrath of God.

Paul says God's wrath is revealed against those who suppress the truth, but how can Paul assert that the unrighteous suppress the truth?

---

17. Theodore Beza, *The Psalms of David*, trans. Anthony Gilby (Richard Yardley & Peter Short, 1590), 29. I have modernized some of the spelling for the convenience of readers.

What truth do unbelievers have that they could suppress? Paul answers this question by pointing first to God's general revelation. He writes, 'what can be known about God is plain to them, because God has shown it to them' (v. 19). In short, there is an objective and clear general revelation of God to man. Paul then adds: 'For his invisible attributes, namely, his eternal power and divine nature, have been clearly perceived, ever since the creation of the world, in the things that have been made. So they are without excuse' (v. 20).

Here we begin to move from what God has objectively revealed (i.e., general revelation) to that which man has come to know from this revelation (i.e., natural theology). Paul indicates that God's invisible attributes have been 'clearly seen.' Those words tell us something about the human recipients of general revelation. They clearly saw God's invisible attributes 'in the things that have been made.' In other words, created facts revealed something about God, and the unrighteous did not miss that revelation. Furthermore, the unrighteous have had this knowledge of God 'ever since the creation of the world.' The fall destroyed neither the revelation nor the reception of it. Because of this, the unrighteous are 'without excuse.'

Paul explains why the unrighteous are without excuse in the next verse: 'For although they knew God, they did not honor him as God or give thanks to him, but they became futile in their thinking, and their foolish hearts were darkened' (v. 21). Paul's statement that 'they knew God' indicates that the unrighteous did not miss the general revelation of God's invisible attributes in the things that have been made. That general revelation resulted in their knowledge of God (i.e., natural theology). Given that knowledge, they should have honored God and given him thanks. Instead, they behaved foolishly.

Paul explains, 'Claiming to be wise, they became fools, and exchanged the glory of the immortal God for images resembling mortal man and birds and animals and creeping things' (vv. 22-23). Rather than worship the God who revealed his invisible attributes in the things that have been made, they worshipped the things that have been made (cf. Ps. 106:20). By doing so, they became foolish idolators (cf. Jer. 10:14). The point is that God clearly revealed himself in the things that have been made, the unrighteous clearly saw him in those created things, but the unrighteous rejected that knowledge they had.

## The Bible and Apologetic Method

Given what we have discovered with regard to the contrast between Van Til's theory of knowledge and the biblical teaching on that subject, we turn next to an examination of Van Til's claim that the apologetic method of presupposition alone is consistent with Scripture. We have already examined what the method of presupposition involves, so it is not necessary to repeat the details here. I simply remind the reader that this method involves two basic stages. In the first stage, the Christian steps into the shoes of the unbeliever for the sake of argument and attempts to demonstrate that the unbeliever's position reduces to absurdity. In the second stage, the Christian asks the unbeliever to step into his Christian shoes in order to demonstrate that only on Christian presuppositions do we have any hope for intelligible human predication about anything. It is a worldview vs. worldview method necessitated by the absolute antithesis between the knowledge of the believer and the unbeliever.

If this method of presupposition is the only consistently biblical method of addressing the unbeliever and defending the Christian faith, then it seems that it would be reasonable to expect that we would see prophets and apostles and other believers in the Bible using this method when they address unbelievers. In fact, however, we never read of anyone in Scripture arguing that the unbeliever's worldview cannot account for intelligible human predication and that only the Christian worldview can account for it. We never observe any believer in Scripture presenting an argument that even remotely resembles this. Of course, if we remember that the method of presupposition is founded upon Van Til's theory of knowledge, we can understand why this method is never observed in Scripture. It is never observed in Scripture because Van Til's theory of knowledge on which it rests is contrary to the biblical view of knowledge.

Van Til asserts that the presuppositional method of apologetics is the only biblically faithful method of apologetics, and he argues that Reformed Christians who use other methods are unfaithful to Scripture. That is a serious charge. In light of this, when we do not ever observe the method of presupposition being employed by anyone in Scripture, that fact alone should raise questions. When, in addition to this, we observe biblical prophets and apostles using strategies of communication condemned by Van Til as biblically unfaithful methods, it should cause us to question the truth of the assertion that the method of presupposition is the one exclusively biblical method. At this point, it will be instructive to examine a few biblical passages that raise serious questions about the claim that the method of presupposition is the only biblically faithful apologetic method.

## Exodus 4

In Exodus 3, God speaks to Moses from the burning bush and tells Moses that he is going to deliver the people of Israel from bondage and take them into the promised land (3:7-9). He then tells Moses that he is sending him to Egypt that he 'may bring my people, the children of Israel, out of Egypt' (3:10). Moses has a few questions, and the Lord responds to those questions, telling Moses exactly what he is to do and say (3:11-22). Then, Moses asks the question that is directly relevant to the issue of apologetic methodology. Moses expresses concern about what to do if the Israelites in Egypt do not believe he is speaking God's Word to them (4:1). God responds by promising to give evidence that will authenticate Moses's claim.

Why is this significant? It is significant because the Word that Moses is to speak to the Israelites is the Word of the self-attesting God of Scripture. Moses will be speaking God's very Word to them. There is no standard of authority higher than God by which his Word can be verified. There is no one greater by whom God can swear (Heb. 6:13). So, what is Moses to do, he wonders, if the Israelites ask, 'How do we know this is God's Word?' How does God respond to Moses?

He doesn't instruct Moses to use anything resembling the method of presupposition or a transcendental argument. He doesn't instruct Moses to tell the Israelites that unless they presuppose him and his word, all human predication is unintelligible and that they will be unable to know anything truly. Instead, even though there is no higher authority than God himself, God promises to provide Moses with corroborating evidence. This evidence does not give God's Word its authority, nor does it add to its authority or conflict with its authority. It simply gives evidence to the Israelites that what Moses is saying is, in fact, God's Word.

This is not the only place in Scripture where miracles or other corroborating evidence is provided to confirm that God's Word is, in fact, God's Word. The prophets' word from God is corroborated by

135

miracles (e.g., 1 Kings 17:24; cf. Deut. 18:21-22). The apostles' word from God is corroborated by various signs (2 Cor. 12:12). Neither God nor his faithful followers ever show any hesitation about using such corroborating evidence.

Van Til argues that this biblical phenomenon is explained by the fact that there is an 'organic relationship' among true prophecy, true theophany, and true miracle.[18] He explains:

> *All of this shows clearly that prophecy must be considered as a body.* Each individual prophecy must be interpreted in relation to the whole body of prophecy of which Christ is the center. This whole body of prophecy must then be taken into relation to the whole body of theophany and the whole body of miracle. If this is done, and only if this is done, can the meaning of any of these matters be fully understood. If this is done, and only if this is done, can the corroborative value of miracle in relation to prophecy and of prophecy in relation to miracle and the relation of both to theophany, be fully understood. All these are mutually corroborative. Their value as being mutually corroborative increases in proportion that it is seen that they are mutually dependent upon one another for their meaning. Prophecy without miracle is an abstraction, and miracle without prophecy is an abstraction, as both are abstractions unless related to theophany.'[19]

Note first the 'influence' of Van Til's theory of knowledge on this explanation. We can, according to this view, only know the parts if we know them in their organic interrelationship to every part within the whole.

Here again we have an example of unbiblical ideas distorting the biblical teaching. Let us assume for the sake of argument, however, that we are to treat prophecy, miracle, and theophany as a mutually corroborative organic whole. In whatever way Van Til means that to be understood, it does not change the fact that providing a miracle as verification of the authenticity of a prophecy is not a transcendental argument forcing the unbeliever to account for the necessary preconditions of knowledge. Prophecy itself, as an act of communication, *assumes* that the necessary preconditions for knowledge already exist. It *assumes* a shared knowledge of language and of the things that language signifies. Whenever an unbeliever in Scripture asks for verification of God's Word, neither God

---

18. Van Til, *An Introduction to Systematic Theology*, 216-17.

19. Ibid., 218-19.

nor his prophets ever respond with a transcendental argument. The prophets and apostles never respond to such challenges the way in which Van Til claims any godly man or woman must respond, namely, with the method of presupposition.

The reason God provides the kind of verification he does has to do with the fact that anybody can *claim* to be speaking the self-attesting and authoritative Word of God. God responds to this situation by authenticating his Word with evidence that cannot be easily duplicated by just anyone. Consider Jesus' words and actions in Matthew 9:1-8, for example:

> And getting into a boat he crossed over and came to his own city. And behold, some people brought to him a paralytic, lying on a bed. And when Jesus saw their faith, he said to the paralytic, 'Take heart, my son; your sins are forgiven.' And behold, some of the scribes said to themselves, 'This man is blaspheming.' But Jesus, knowing their thoughts, said, 'Why do you think evil in your hearts? For which is easier, to say, "Your sins are forgiven," or to say, "Rise and walk"? But *that you may know that the Son of Man has authority* on earth to forgive sins' – he then said to the paralytic – 'Rise, pick up your bed and go home.' And he rose and went home. When the crowds saw it, they were afraid, and they glorified God, who had given such authority to men.

Jesus is God incarnate and therefore speaks with the very authority of God. His Word carries that ultimate authority above which there is no higher standard. But Jesus knows that it is easier to say, 'Your sins are forgiven' than it is to say, 'Rise and walk.' He knows that any lying false prophet can say the first. Jesus therefore gives evidence that his Word is, in fact, God's Word by doing something that it is not so easy for a false prophet to do. He does this *so that they may know* that his Word actually is God's Word. The authority of God's Word is always 'self-attesting,' but knowledge of who is speaking God's Word is not always 'self-evident' to human beings. Corroborative evidence is given to help people distinguish between those who are truly speaking God's authoritative Word and those who are merely claiming to speak God's authoritative Word.

## Acts 17:16-34

Paul's first missionary journey is narrated in Acts 13–14. This first journey was followed by the Jerusalem council described in Acts 15.

137

Chapter 16 then narrates the first stages of his second journey concluding with Paul's time in a Philippian jail and the conversion of the jailer there. Chapter 17 then describes Paul's journey through Thessalonica, Berea, and Athens. Paul's interaction with various unbelievers throughout his journeys is instructive for understanding biblical apologetics.

One of the most instructive facts we observe in these interactions is that whether he is speaking to Jews (e.g., Acts 13:16-41) or to Gentiles (e.g., Acts 14:15-17; 17:16-34), there is nothing in Paul remotely resembling the method of presupposition. Nowhere do we find Paul talking about the necessary conditions for human predication. In spite of this fact, Acts 17 is believed by many to be crucial to the debate over Van Til's apologetic system. As Lane Tipton observes, for example, 'Paul's address to the Athenian philosophers on Mars Hill, recorded in Acts 17:16-34, presents us with the *locus classicus* for understanding the Pauline apologetic.'[20] An examination of Acts 17 is, therefore, necessary in any evaluation of Van Til's system of thought.[21]

When we look carefully at Acts 17, we note first the difference in Paul's approach when he is addressing Jews in the synagogues and when he is addressing the Greek philosophers in Athens. The Gospel message remains the same in both cases, but Paul has a different starting point depending on his audience. When he speaks to the Jews in the synagogue, 'he reasoned with them *from the Scriptures*, explaining and proving that it was necessary for the Christ to suffer and to rise from the dead, and saying, "This Jesus, whom I proclaim to you, is the Christ"' (Acts 17:2-3). Paul argues from the Old Testament Scriptures as well when he encounters the Jews in Berea (vv. 10-11). The Jews have the Old Testament and acknowledge it as the Word of God. Therefore, that is Paul's starting point when proclaiming the Gospel to the Jews.

Paul reasons with the Jews in Athens as well (v. 17), but for our purposes, it is particularly important to pay attention to his encounter with the pagan Greeks (vv. 18-34). The first thing we notice is that

---

20. Oliphint and Tipton, eds. *Revelation and Reason*, 42.

21. Van Til's *Paul at Athens* (Philadelphia: Presbyterian and Reformed, 1954) is perhaps the closest thing to an in-depth extended discussion of any single biblical passage that one finds in his apologetic works. But it isn't an example of biblical exegesis. In this work, Acts 17 serves more as a launching pad for Van Til to discuss the history of Greek philosophy and then to reassert his apologetic views.

Paul doesn't start with the Old Testament as he did when proclaiming the Gospel of Christ to the Jews. John Calvin explains that it would have been 'in vain should he have cited testimonies of Scripture.'[22] It would have been in vain because, unlike the Jews, these pagan Greeks did not acknowledge the divine authority of the Old Testament. Paul proclaims the same Gospel of 'Jesus and the resurrection' (v. 18; cf. 17:2-3), but when he is challenged, he doesn't defend his message by having his hearers search the Scriptures as he did with the Jews (vv. 2-3, 11). He can't present an argument from authority unless that authority is a mutually acknowledged authority. Acts 17 reveals that different audiences sometimes require different apologetic starting points.

Instead of going to the Old Testament, Paul begins by noting that the Greeks are very religious (v. 22). As proof of this claim, he mentions observing the objects of their worship as well as an altar to the unknown God (v. 23). He then proclaims to the Greeks what the Jews already knew about the one true God who created all things and who does not live in man-made temples (vv. 24-27). Tipton notes: 'The argument is designed to demonstrate that Paul presupposed *the entire redemptive-historical framework* in the presentation of the fact of the resurrection of Christ from the dead.'[23] Paul does, of course, argue as a biblically informed Christian when he presents the Gospel to these Athenians, and he does, of course, place his discussion of the resurrection into a larger understanding of redemptive history. He is summarizing for the Greeks the biblical storyline that he did not have to explain to the Jews who already knew it. In other words, Paul is proclaiming the same biblical Gospel to both Jews and Greeks. There is no substantive dispute on this point. The difference is that Paul could not appeal to the authority of Scripture with these Gentiles as he could with Jews for the truth of this story.

Paul then proceeds to provide support for his claim that God is not far from us. To do so, he quotes brief lines from two pagan Greek authors who said about God that 'In him we live and move and have our being' and 'we are indeed his offspring' (v. 28). Paul then discusses the implication of these statements: 'Being then God's offspring, we

---

22. John Calvin, commentary on Acts 17:24, in *Calvin's Commentaries* (Grand Rapids, Mich.: Baker, 1979), XIX/1, 157-58.

23. Oliphint and Tipton, eds. *Revelation and Reason*, 43.

ought not to think that the divine being is like gold or silver or stone, an image formed by the art and imagination of man' (v. 29). He then tells these Greeks that God has commanded all men to repent because he has appointed a man to judge the world and has raised this man from the dead (vv. 30-31). In other words, Paul has returned to the proclamation of Jesus and the resurrection. In the end, some of the Greeks mock him. Some want to hear more. Some believe the Gospel (vv. 32-34).

Although Paul proclaims the same Gospel of Jesus and the resurrection to both Jews and Greeks (vv. 3, 18, 31, 32; cf. 4:2), his response to the Jews and Greeks differs in its starting point. With the Jews, Paul starts on the common ground of their shared acknowledgment of the divine authority of the Old Testament. With the Athenian Greeks, Paul does not have a shared special revelation that he can use as a starting point.[24] What then does he do? He appeals to the comments of two pagan Greek poets his hearers might know, and he takes what these poets say as true in some sense.

Of course, Paul certainly does not believe that the writings of these pagan poets are inspired. Nor does Paul believe that the pagan theology within which those quotes find their original context is true. The god about whom those poets were writing is not the God of Scripture. However, nothing in this address makes any sense unless Paul is assuming these pagan poets had some element of true knowledge about the true God. He finds an isolated truth in their false system. But how can Paul treat their statements as true in any sense? Paul can treat them as true because Paul does not share Van Til's theory of knowledge in which any error about any fact in any system renders everything in the system false.

In classical Reformed theology, Acts 17 was understood in light of the Reformed doctrine of natural theology. Van Til, as we have seen, rejects this doctrine because of his theory of knowledge, but it was not rejected among the classical Reformed theologians. Calvin is, according to Van Til, the Reformed theologian who most completely freed himself from ideas like natural theology, and yet, Calvin, commenting on this passage in Acts says that Paul 'showeth *by natural arguments* who and

---

24. Paul and the pagan Athenians also have the common ground of a shared language and shared Greek vocabulary as well as a shared knowledge of what that vocabulary means. Paul could not even speak to the Athenians without that common ground.

what God is.'[25] Paul, he teaches, 'draweth proofs *from nature itself.*'[26] In other words, Paul's appeal to the statements of those pagan Greek poets as true statements indicates his understanding that they glimpsed something true about the real God through his general revelation even though they reject the full truth about the real God and worship the creature rather than the Creator (Acts 17:16, 29; cf. Rom. 1:18-25). If the statements Paul quotes in verse 28 are in any sense true statements about God (and Paul treats them as true), then Van Til's complete rejection of traditional Reformed natural theology is unwarranted.

## Conclusion

Van Til's lack of any detailed exegesis presents a problem when evaluating his system of thought. We are unable to evaluate that which does not exist. All we are able to do is determine whether Van Til's teaching is consistent with other exegetically grounded doctrines. Regarding those doctrines Van Til proclaims that are taught in the Reformed confessions, non-Van Tillians have no serious concerns. There are concerns, however, that arise when the doctrines specifically connected to his apologetic system of thought are considered. Because this entire system is tied together by his theory of knowledge, concerns arise about the implications of that theory. Van Til, however, never provides an exegetical case for this theory of knowledge. It is simply taken for granted that it is biblical although it is contradicted by everything we observe in Scripture.

Adding to the concern is the fact that the problems that drive Van Til are not the problems that drive the Divine Author and human authors of Scripture. They are not consumed with the so-called problem of human knowledge. They are not consumed with the principle of intelligible human predication. Van Til, on the other hand, was consumed with these issues because of his theory of knowledge, and he reads all of Scripture through these lenses. Whether he is reading about Adam, Moses, Paul, or Jesus, he reads everything in the Bible with those epistemological questions at the forefront of his mind, and he seems

---

25. John Calvin, commentary on Acts 17:22, in *Calvin's Commentaries* (Grand Rapids, Mich.: Baker, 1979), XIX/1, 154. Emphasis mine.

26. John Calvin, commentary on Acts 17:24, in *Calvin's Commentaries*, 157-58. Emphasis mine.

to assume that those epistemological questions are the fundamental questions Scripture is addressing. This distorts his reading of Scripture.

If one does not read Scripture already assuming Van Til's theory of knowledge to be true, one searches in vain for any biblical support of Van Til's apologetic system of thought. One can only find evidence for his apologetic system if one assumes the truth of his theory of knowledge. In short, one has to read his system of apologetic thought into Scripture before it can be found there. We looked briefly at several relevant passages of Scripture that are related to two important elements addressed in Van Til's system: natural theology and apologetic method. Van Til's system is consistent with none of these biblical texts. Traditional confessional Reformed theology is consistent with all of them. Van Til's theory of knowledge is simply not the same as the biblical doctrine of knowledge. This is why the Bible neither commands the use of the method of presupposition nor gives any examples of it in use.

Van Til's case for the method of presupposition often implies that fallen man's biggest need is to answer the question, 'How may I account for human predication?' The Bible teaches that fallen man's biggest need is to answer the question, 'How may I be saved from the wrath of a holy God?' The Bible also does not proclaim Jesus Christ as 'the indispensable presupposition of all intelligent human predication.' It proclaims Jesus Christ as God-incarnate and as the one who died as the once-for-all atoning sacrifice for our sins and as the one who was raised from the dead and who has ascended to the right hand of the Father.

The Bible does not teach that man's ultimate problem is ontological as Rome teaches. Nor does it teach that man's ultimate problem is epistemological as many post-Enlightenment philosophers assume. The Bible teaches that man's ultimate problem is sin and death as the wages of sin, and it teaches that the crucified and risen Jesus Christ is the solution to the problem of sin and death. Van Til certainly does not deny these biblical truths, but his theory of knowledge and the system of thought that grew from it creates an unnecessary tension and a misplaced focus due to its distortion of this biblical teaching.

# CHAPTER 7

# Philosophical Concerns

An examination of what Scripture both assumes and teaches about knowledge reveals that there is an inconsistency between the biblical doctrine of knowledge and Van Til's theory of knowledge. What we have seen thus far is that Scripture does not allow for an absolute epistemological antithesis and its claim that fallen man knows no fact as it truly is. What is not immediately evident from a search of Scripture is the underlying reason for the inconsistency between Scripture and Van Til. As we will discover in this chapter, the reason Van Til's theory of knowledge diverges from what Scripture assumes and teaches about knowledge is because he has incorporated into his system of thought philosophical elements that are foreign to Scripture.

Many Christians are unaware of the impact our metaphysical and epistemological assumptions have on our theology. Our metaphysical assumptions impact what we think and say about the being of God, the being of Jesus Christ, the being of creatures, and more. Our epistemological assumptions obviously impact what we think and say about knowledge, but our epistemological assumptions also impact what we say about the nature of truth. Historically, there have been correspondence theories of truth, coherence theories of truth, pragmatic theories of truth, and more, and each has been closely related to specific metaphysical and epistemological assumptions.

Furthermore, it is no coincidence that, as Reformed theologians began to adopt various Enlightenment philosophies in the latter half of the seventeenth century, Reformed theology suffered as a result. As Richard Muller has explained:

> The decline of Protestant orthodoxy, then, coincides with the decline of the interrelated intellectual phenomena of scholastic method and Christian Aristotelianism. Rationalist philosophy was ultimately incapable of becoming a suitable *ancilla* and, instead, demanded that it and not theology be considered queen of the sciences. Without a philosophical structure to complement its doctrines and to cohere with its scholastic method, Protestant orthodoxy came to an end.[1]

The Reformed theologians of the sixteenth and seventeenth centuries who developed and defended confessional Reformed theology did so with specific metaphysical and epistemological assumptions. Muller here refers to these philosophical assumptions as 'Christian Aristotelianism.'

The label is not terribly important. Some might prefer to speak of these assumptions in terms of 'Christian Aristotelianism.' Others might prefer to use the label 'Christian Platonism.' The main point is that the philosophy of the Reformed theologians of the sixteenth and seventeenth centuries was a generally realist philosophy. In terms of metaphysics, that means that the real world is what it is regardless of what humans think it is. In terms of epistemology, that means that humans are able to have true knowledge of this real world. In short, realism is the view that the real world is independent of our human minds. When those realist philosophical assumptions were rejected and replaced by various Enlightenment philosophies, it changed the theology. In short, philosophical concerns are not minor concerns. The philosophical views of Van Til, therefore, must be examined.

## Ambiguity at the Foundational Level

Before proceeding to a discussion of any specific philosophical concern, it is worth briefly discussing one general philosophical concern. Recall John Frame's observation that it is, 'very difficult to pin down precisely what Van Til believes on a given specific topic.'[2] As we have seen, there

---

1. Richard A. Muller, *Post-Reformation Reformed Dogmatics*. Vol. 1, *Prolegomena to Theology*, 2nd ed. (Grand Rapids: Baker Academic, 2003), 84.

2. Frame, *Cornelius Van Til: An Analysis of His Thought*, 34. It is interesting that Frame makes this point about the difficulty of pinning down 'precisely what Van Til believes on a given specific topic' not too many pages after he has criticized Van Til's 'debunkers' for always missing the obvious (p. 5). It is not clear why 'debunkers' should be criticized for

is nowhere that this is more clearly the case than in Van Til's discussions of knowledge. Van Til, for example, affirms that the knowledge of God and the knowledge of man coincide at *every* point and also affirms that they coincide at *no* point. He affirms that the unbeliever does not know anything truly and also affirms that the unbeliever does know some things truly. He affirms that true knowledge of anything requires exhaustive knowledge of everything and also affirms that non-exhaustive knowledge is true knowledge. It is difficult to believe that anyone reading those assertions for the first time wouldn't be at least a little bit puzzled. These are notoriously difficult elements of Van Til's thought.[3]

This kind of seemingly contradictory language about knowledge is without doubt at least part of the reason there has been so much misunderstanding of Van Til over the decades.[4] It's definitely at the root of the so-called Clark-Van Til controversy.[5] I do think we have to acknowledge (as I have already stated) that some of the misunderstanding has been due to a lack of careful and charitable reading on the part of

---

missing the obvious if it is very difficult to pin down what Van Til believes on any given topic. If what he believes on any given topic is 'very difficult to pin down,' then what he believes on any given topic is not 'obvious.'

3. This is acknowledged by many on both sides of the debate. K. Scott Oliphint, for example, observes that 'There is perhaps no greater controversy surrounding Van Til's thought than the question of knowledge.' See Van Til, *The Defense of the Faith*, 39, note 31.

4. In his *Cornelius Van Til: Reformed Apologist and Churchman*, John Muether observes that, 'While he was alive, it was often observed that Cornelius Van Til's readers could be divided into those who did not agree with him and those who did not understand him' (p. 15). In his 1979 biography of Van Til, William White, Jr. tells a story about a Westminster Seminary banquet at which the master of ceremonies was introducing Van Til to the audience. White recounts what happened: '"There is a controversy today as to who is the greatest intellect of this segment of the twentieth century," the m.c. said. "Probably most thinking people would vote for the learned Dr Einstein. Not me. I wish to put forth my candidate for the honor, Dr Cornelius Van Til." (Loud applause.) "My reason for doing so is this: Only eleven people in the world understand Albert Einstein .... Nobody – but *nobody* in the world – understands Cornelius Van Til"' (pp. 181-82). Obviously, this is hyperbole intended to be humorous, but it wouldn't be humorous if it didn't contain an element of truth. What Muether and White both reveal in their comments is that Van Til had a reputation for being difficult to understand.

5. For a helpful overview of the details of this controversy, see Douma, *The Presbyterian Philosopher*, 75-164, 251-66. See also Frame, *Cornelius Van Til: An Analysis of His Thought*, 97-113. If one reads the original Complaint, the original Answer, and the 15th OPC General Assembly Report, it appears that both sides were speaking past each other. One cannot help but wonder what might have happened had Clark and Van Til sat down and simply asked each other for clear definitions of the terms in the debate (e.g., 'contents of knowledge').

some of Van Til's critics. However, I think that if we are to be completely honest, we also must acknowledge that some of the responsibility for the misunderstandings lies with Van Til himself and is a direct result of his use of this kind of ambiguous language.[6]

John Frame is not an opponent of Van Til. He has long been one of Van Til's most enthusiastic supporters, so when one of Van Til's most enthusiastic supporters says that it is very difficult to pin down exactly what he believes on any topic, those who agree will have to grant that the blame for misunderstanding Van Til cannot be attributed *solely* to the incompetence or dishonesty of the critics. Of course, one could disagree with Frame and say that Van Til is easy to understand, but that does not seem to be a widespread view even among Van Tillians.

The reason this is important is because blaming the critics has, on occasion, become a way for some Van Tillians to avoid careful consideration of their concerns.[7] The critic is simply written off as someone who doesn't understand Van Til either because he cannot (due to some intellectual defect) or will not (due to some ethical defect), and then his concerns are dismissed without any serious consideration.[8] But

---

6. I have taught college students regularly for well over a decade. If one or two of them misunderstands me on occasion, I can likely place much of the blame on them. On the other hand, if I were to have large numbers of intelligent students misunderstanding me week after week and year after year, I would most likely be the one responsible for the misunderstanding. Such repeated and widespread misunderstanding would be evidence that I am not communicating effectively. I could not simply write all of those students off as ignorant, incompetent, or lazy.

7. It seems to be assumed by some Van Tillians (e.g., R. J. Rushdoony) that to understand Van Til is to agree with him and that if a person disagrees with him, that person obviously did not understand him. Either that, or the person is simply obstinate. In other words, one either understands Van Til and agrees with him, or one disagrees with Van Til because he is stupid or wicked.

8. Consider, for example, the words of the Van Tillian Rousas J. Rushdoony about Van Til's critics. He says, 'The difficulty most people experience is not with Van Til's writing but with his God; it is essentially He whom they find inacceptable and offensive' (Rushdoony, *By What Standard*, 98). Note what Rushdoony is asserting about Van Til's critics here: Their difficulty with Van Til is, in reality, a difficulty with God. They find God 'inacceptable and offensive.' That's not an argument. It's an implicit claim to be able to read human hearts. There is no way this discussion will ever move in a more constructive and God-honoring direction if faithful, confessionally Reformed brothers in Christ are treated as if they are God-hating reprobates. The debate between Van Tillians and non-Van Tillians is not the Fundamentalist-Modernist controversy. It is an intramural debate among brothers in Christ concerning what a consistently Reformed apologetic method should look like.

what if Frame's statement is true, as most Van Tillians and non-Van Tillians believe it is? Sometimes, what Van Til is saying about knowledge is simply very unclear, and that ambiguity makes interpretation difficult. This means that all of us, both Van Tillians and non-Van Tillians, need to be careful and charitable in our reading and in our writing.

The reason that this is a *philosophical* concern, however, is because the most ambiguous and unclear statements Van Til makes in all of his writings have to do with the topic of knowledge. In other words, the most ambiguous and unclear statements in his writings have to do with his epistemology. This is a serious concern because knowledge is the key theme running through every stage of Van Til's apologetic system of thought. To the extent that there is ambiguity and a lack of clarity in his theory of knowledge, there is ambiguity and a lack of clarity at the heart of his entire apologetic system. It would be one thing if it were 'very difficult to pin down precisely what Van Til believes' on some peripheral issue. It is another thing when his ambiguous language makes it very difficult to pin down what he believes on *the most central philosophical element of his apologetic thought.*

## The Idealism Controversy

There are a number of specific topics that could profitably be discussed in this chapter. I believe, however, that the most important philosophical issue to address is the perennial claim of idealist influence on the thought of Van Til.[9] This claim and the responses to it have resulted in an enormous amount of confusion and bitterness. The claim was made publicly as early as 1948 when J. Oliver Buswell claimed that Van Til was 'deeply

---

9. Van Til is not the only Reformed theologian to be associated with idealist philosophy. Joshua Farris and S. Mark Hamilton, for example, identify Jonathan Edwards as a proponent of philosophical idealism (specifically Berkeleyan idealism). See Farris and Hamilton, eds. *Idealism and Christianity*, vol. 1, *Idealism and Christian Theology* (New York: Bloomsbury, 2016), 2. Cf. also Oliver D. Crisp and Kyle C. Strobel, *Jonathan Edwards: An Introduction to His Thought* (Grand Rapids: William B. Eerdmans Publishing Company, 2018), 67-89, 106-116. Idealism has also been recognized as an influence on the nineteenth-century Mercersburg theologians. This includes men such as John Williamson Nevin and Emanuel Gerhart. On Nevin, for example, see William B. Evans, *A Companion to the Mercersburg Theology* (Eugene, OR: Cascade Books, 2019), 4. On Gerhart, see Annette G. Aubert, introduction to Emanuel Gerhart, *Christocentric Reformed Theology in Nineteenth-Century America* (Eugene, OR: Wipf & Stock, 2021), 9-10; cf. also Evans, *A Companion to the Mercersburg Theology*, 35.

mired in Hegelian idealistic pantheism.'[10] The claim was repeated in the early 1950s in a series of articles in *The Calvin Forum*. In the August–September 1953 issue, for example, Cecil De Boer argued that 'the new apologetic seems to have taken over uncritically the idealist theory of knowledge and truth, a theory leading logically to a kind of pantheism.'[11] In the same issue Jesse De Boer charged Van Til with appealing 'to idealist logic.'[12] In his book *A Theology of Grace*, James Daane claimed that Van Til's 'fundamental presuppositions lie embedded in the rational dialectical tradition of philosophic idealism.'[13] In 1984, in their book *Classical Apologetics*, R. C. Sproul, John Gerstner, and Arthur Lindsley pointed out the 'false idealistic supposition' behind Van Til's doctrine of analogical thinking.[14] In his 2019 book, *Reforming Apologetics*, J. V. Fesko notes 'clear connections between Van Til and idealism.'[15]

The claim that idealism influenced Van Til has not been made only by Van Til's critics, however. Van Til's proponents have made similar statements. John Frame, for example, observes that 'idealist philosophy is undoubtedly an influence upon Van Til.'[16] B. A. Bosserman goes so far as to say that Hegel is Van Til's most significant philosophical influence.[17] But how are such claims, made by both Van Tillians and non-Van Tillians, to be reconciled with Van Til's own repeated condemnations of idealism? Van Til repeatedly denied being an idealist and, in fact,

---

10. J. Oliver Buswell, 'The Fountainhead of Presuppositionalism,' *The Bible Today* 42, no. 2 (Nov. 1948). https://continuing.wordpress.com/2011/07/05/the-fountainhead-of-presuppositionalism/

11. Cecil De Boer, 'The New Apologetic,' *The Calvin Forum* 19, no. 1–2 (Aug–Sept 1953): 3.

12. Jesse De Boer, 'Professor Van Til's Apologetics, Part I: A Linguistic Bramble Patch,' *The Calvin Forum* 19, no. 1–2 (Aug–Sept 1953): 12. By 'idealist logic' he means 'idealist methodology.'

13. James Daane, *A Theology of Grace* (Grand Rapids: Wm. B. Eerdmans Publishing Company, 1954), 99.

14. R. C. Sproul, John Gerstner, and Arthur Lindsley, *Classical Apologetics: A Rational Defense of the Christian Faith and a Critique of Presuppositional Apologetics* (Grand Rapids: Zondervan, 1984), 313.

15. J. V. Fesko, *Reforming Apologetics: Retrieving the Classic Reformed Approach to Defending the Faith* (Grand Rapids: Baker Academic, 2019), 144.

16. Frame, *Cornelius Van Til: An Analysis of His Thought*, 245.

17. B. A. Bosserman, *The Trinity and the Vindication of Christian Paradox: An Interpretation and Refinement of the Theological Apologetic of Cornelius Van Til* (Eugene, OR: Pickwick, 2014), 1.

often criticized idealism.[18] Are those who make such claims about Van Til misrepresenting his views? This question cannot be answered in any satisfactory way until some important preliminary matters are settled.

## What is Idealism?

In the first place, if we are going to examine claims of idealist influence, it is necessary to have some understanding of what we mean by 'idealism.' When theologians suggest that Van Til is influenced by idealism, the reference is not to some kind of naïve optimism (e.g., an *idealistic* young anti-war activist) but to philosophical idealism. We need, therefore, a definition of such idealism. This is also a problem, however, because there are various versions of philosophical idealism, and they differ in some important ways. Berkeley's subjective idealism is not identical to Kant's transcendental idealism, for example, and neither of those is identical to Hegel's absolute idealism. British idealism differs in some ways from all three.[19] How then are we to understand idealism?

As Farris and Hamilton have observed, 'there is perhaps no other philosophical concept as elusive of definition as "idealism."'[20] They themselves offer as a basic definition of idealism the notion that only minds and ideas exist.[21] John Frame defines idealism as 'the view that the universe is fundamentally mental or spiritual.'[22] Along similar lines, A. C. Ewing says the one thing all versions of idealism have in common is 'the view that there can be no physical objects existing apart from some experience and this might perhaps be taken as the definition of idealism provided we regard *thinking* as a part of experience and do not

---

18. Some of these denials and criticisms will be noted below. Much of Van Til's book *The Defense of the Faith* is devoted to responding to such criticisms.

19. For a survey of the various types of philosophical idealism, see the relevant sections of volumes 4–8 of Frederick Copleston's *History of Philosophy* (New York: Doubleday, 1960–1966).

20. Farris and Hamilton, eds. *Idealism and Christianity*, vol. 1, *Idealism and Christian Theology*, 3.

21. Ibid. This definition aligns much more closely with the common interpretation of Berkeley's version of idealism than it does, for example, with Kant's version. Regardless of whether Berkeley actually believed this, Kant does not deny that a reality outside the human mind exists.

22. John Frame, *A History of Western Philosophy and Theology* (Phillipsburg: P&R Publishing Company, 2015), 756. This definition of idealism is similar to the definition of 'panpsychism,' a view held by a number of nineteenth-century idealists.

imply by experience passivity and provided we include under experience not only human experience but the so called Absolute Experience or the experience of a God such as Berkeley postulates.'[23]

These definitions all emphasize the point that, for idealists, reality is in one way or another mind-dependent, if not mind-exclusive. Jeremy Dunham, Iain Hamilton Grant, and Sean Watson, however, argue that idealism is not the view that *only* minds exist but is the view that minds *also* exist.[24] In other words, in their view, idealism is to be contrasted primarily with materialism, which affirms that *only* matter exists. What all of these definitions have in common, however, is an emphasis on a knowing mind as an indispensable element of reality.

It is important to recall that, in his own writings throughout his career, Van Til interacted extensively with the proponents of a specific version of idealism.[25] The specific version of idealism with which Van Til interacted most directly and most often was British idealism. British idealism shared common features with other forms of idealism, but if we are going to explore the possibility of British idealist 'influence' on Van Til, we will need some grasp of what was distinctive about this version of idealism. W. J. Mander has provided a helpful description of the emphases found among the proponents of British idealism. He explains:

> The Idealists had a distinctive conception of the world of knowledge, and of the place of philosophy within it. They insisted on its essential underlying unity, arguing that all ideas were systematically linked together into one whole with no fundamental divisions between the different departments of learning, the concepts and principles of one leading into those of another.[26]

Notice that the key emphasis of the British idealists is that knowledge is a unity in which all ideas are linked to one another. In other words, it is a kind of holism. While keeping the broader history and various

---

23. A. C. Ewing, *Idealism: A Critical Survey* (London: Methuen & Co, 1934), 3. Emphasis mine.

24. Jeremy Dunham, Iain Hamilton Grant, and Sean Watson, *Idealism: The History of a Philosophy* (London: Routledge, 2014), 4.

25. Timothy I. McConnel, 'The Influence of Idealism on the Apologetics of Cornelius Van Til,' *Journal of the Evangelical Theological Society* 48, no. 3 (Sept 2005): 563; cf. also Bosserman, *The Trinity and the Vindication of Christian Paradox*, 59.

26. W. J. Mander, *British Idealism: A History* (Oxford: Oxford University Press, 2011), 3.

types of idealism in mind, it is important, when discussing Van Til, to remain aware of this particular emphasis of British idealism.

## What is 'Influence'?

The second important observation we must make when discussing the influence of idealism is that the word 'influence' is incredibly vague. It can mean a number of different things, depending on the context. There are at least four possible ways in which philosophical 'influence' on a theologian could be understood:

1. Lexical Influence – In this case a theologian simply borrows philosophical terms and gives those terms Christian definitions.

2. Strategic influence – In this case, the major questions asked and the major problems raised by a particular philosophical school set the agenda in some way for a theologian's methodology.

3. Propositional influence – In this case, a theologian borrows what he believes to be individual true teachings from a philosophical system and incorporates them into his theological system.

4. Systemic influence – In this case, a philosophical system as a whole is adopted and then functions as a foundation for a theological system. This involves a complete synthesis of Christian theology with that philosophical system.

If any progress is to be made in the discussion about idealist 'influence' on Van Til's thought, we must recognize these different possible kinds of influence and specify which one we are talking about in any particular instance.

Van Til himself, as well as various Van Tillian scholars, regularly allude to these different kinds of philosophical 'influence' in their writings. With regard to 'Lexical Influence,' there does not appear to be much controversy. Van Til himself acknowledges taking philosophical words and putting Christian meaning into them.[27] John Frame observes that Van Til 'made liberal use of the idealist philosophical vocabulary ("concrete universal," "one and many," "absolute system," "eternal novelty," "limiting concept," "logic" [as a general term for "methodology"], the contrast between

---

27. Geehan, *Jerusalem and Athens*, 125-26.

"implication" and "linear inference," and even "presupposition").[28] Likewise, William D. Dennison notes, 'The fairest conclusion seems to be that Van Til's language was idealist, but the content and meaning of his terminology was not.'[29] In short, there is acknowledged idealist influence on Van Til's thought if, by 'influence' we mean that Van Til borrowed idealist terminology and gave it Christian meanings.

What about 'Strategic Influence'? Van Tillian scholars have also affirmed this type of idealist influence on Van Til. K. Scott Oliphint, for example, says that Van Til's 'extensive knowledge of idealism would shape his writing and his approach to apologetics and theology for the rest of his life.'[30] Similarly, Timothy I. McConnel argues that 'idealism provided Van Til a framework for problems to be dealt with.'[31] David Filson helpfully summarizes the nature of idealism's strategic influence on Van Til, saying, 'one must accept his programme as he intended, namely in an effort to interpret the philosophical currents of his day in light of Christian theism, employing particular philosophical nomenclature in an effort to push that current to its end, in the interest of the apologetic task.'[32] Filson's comments point to the connection between lexical and strategic influence in Van Til's work.

A potentially more significant question is whether idealism has had any 'Propositional Influence' on Van Til. Some prominent Van Tillian scholars have claimed that there is evidence of such influence. Oliphint, for example, says:

> Van Til took that which was formally true in idealism (due to common grace) and transplanted it into the Reformed Christian faith and there he nurtured and watered it to fruition because only in Christian 'soil' could these formally true ideas have their proper growing place. When he uses arguments, terms, and methods of idealism, therefore, we must

---

28. Frame, *Cornelius Van Til: An Analysis of His Thought*, 21.

29. Wiliam D. Dennison, *In Defense of the Eschaton: Essays in Reformed Apologetics*, ed. James Douglas Baird (Eugene, OR: Wipf & Stock, 2015), 15.

30. K. Scott Oliphint, 'Cornelius Van Til: Presuppositional Apologist,' in *The History of Apologetics: A Biographical and Methodological Introduction*, eds. Benjamin K. Forrest, Joshua D. Chatraw, and Alister E. McGrath, (Grand Rapids: Zondervan Academic, 2020), 480.

31. Timothy I. McConnel, 'The Influence of Idealism on the Apologetics of Cornelius Van Til,' *Journal of the Evangelical Theological Society* 48, no. 3 (Sept 2005): 558.

32. Filson, 'The Apologetics and Theology of Cornelius Van Til,' 57.

see them as surgically removed and then transplanted into the light of scriptural truth.[33]

Note that Oliphint is not claiming that Van Til adopted the entire system of philosophical idealism. Instead, Van Til took only that which was formally true in idealism. Echoing Oliphint, Gabe Fluhrer also argues that Van Til 'planted the grain of truth from [idealism] in the Reformed soil that nurtured him.'[34]

Van Til himself speaks of applying 'the method of idealist logicians in a way that these idealist logicians, because of their own anti-Christian theistic assumptions, cannot apply it.'[35] He says the true point the idealists make is that 'even the mere counting of particular things presupposes a system of truth of which these particulars form a part.'[36] Note in this statement the holism characteristic of British idealism. It is a point that he takes from idealism and replants in Reformed soil. In another place, Van Til writes,

> *The Idealists argued in the way that we have argued* above about the cow. They said that true knowledge cannot be obtained by a mere correspondence of an idea of the mind to an object existing apart from the mind. The *mind and the object of which it seeks knowledge are parts of one great system of reality and one must have knowledge of the whole of this reality before one has knowledge of any of its parts.* Accordingly, the Idealists said that the thing that really counted in knowledge was the coherence of any fact with all other facts. To know the place of a fact in the universe as a whole is to have true knowledge. *This position, as we shall see more fully later, approaches, in form, what we are after in our position.*[37]

Here, Van Til mentions several points within the idealist system that he believes are true points: 1) Knowledge of the whole system of reality, *including the knowing mind*, is necessary for knowledge of its parts;

---

33. K. Scott Oliphint, 'The Consistency of Van Til's Methodology,' *Westminster Theological Journal* 52, no. 1 (Spring 1990): 34.

34. Gabe Fluhrer, 'Reasoning by Presupposition: Clarifying and Applying the Center of Van Til's Apologetic,' PhD diss, (Westminster Theological Seminary, 2015), 33.

35. Van Til, *Christian Apologetics*, 150.

36. Ibid.

37. Van Til, *Survey of Christian Epistemology*, 2. Emphasis mine. It is also evident from this quote why idealism tended to be tied to a coherence theory of truth rather than a correspondence theory.

2) Knowledge requires understanding the relation of any fact with all other facts; and 3) Knowledge involves knowing a fact in relation to the universe as a whole. Note that all three points are saying essentially the same thing in different words. In all of them, Van Til is stating the holist theory of knowledge. Also note that in the first point, Van Til expresses his agreement with the idealist emphasis on a knowing mind as an indispensable element of reality.

Van Til immediately adds that the idealist position approaches the Christian position 'in form only' because idealists relate all knowledge to the Absolute rather than to the Christian God.[38] In other words, he agrees with the idealists' holistic definition of knowledge, but he believes the idealists have the wrong ultimate principle of interpretation. When Van Til replants the idealist theory of knowledge into Reformed soil, he replaces the idealist principle of interpretation (the Absolute) with the Christian principle of interpretation (the Triune God).

Finally, what about 'Systemic Influence'? Did Van Til adopt idealism as a systematic whole and then create a Christian-Idealist synthesis? I believe the answer is no.[39] At least as far back as 1930, Van Til stated that idealism 'is a foe of biblical Theism.'[40] Elsewhere, Van Til says that anyone who believes 'that idealist philosophy and Christianity can be harmonized' is mistaken.[41] In his book *Christianity and Idealism*, Van Til argues 'that the God of historic Christianity and the God of post-Kantian philosophy are basically at variance with one another.'[42] In the unabridged version of his book *The Defense of the Faith*, which includes extensive responses to his critics, Van Til provides numerous quotes from his earlier works and explains that anyone who reads these works will find

---

38. Ibid.

39. Some of the early critics who appear to assume systemic influence also add the charge of pantheism. That charge is puzzling because if there is anything that Van Til emphasizes throughout his writings, it is the Creator-creature distinction.

40. Cornelius Van Til, 'God and the Absolute,' *The Evangelical Quarterly* no. 2 (1930), in Cornelius Van Til and Eric H. Sigward, *The Articles of Cornelius Van Til*, Electronic ed. (Labels Army Company: New York, 1997).

41. Cornelius Van Til, 'The Christian Experience of Life,' *The Banner* no. 69 (1934), in Cornelius Van Til and Eric H. Sigward, *The Articles of Cornelius Van Til*, Electronic ed. (Labels Army Company: New York, 1997).

42. Cornelius Van Til, *Christianity and Idealism* (Philadelphia: The Presbyterian and Reformed Publishing Company, 1955), 107-08.

his thought 'to be informed by simple, generic Calvinism rather than by idealism, Hegelian rationalism, existentialism and/or phenomenalism.'[43]

By distinguishing the different possible kinds of philosophical 'influence,' we can gain some measure of clarity concerning the question of idealist 'influence' on Van Til. It seems clear, for example, that we can rule out systemic influence. While Van Til may have appropriated certain elements of idealism that he believed were true, he did not adopt any specific idealist system as a whole.[44] He did not create a comprehensive synthesis between Christian theology and Hegelianism, for example. There does appear to be clear evidence, on the other hand, of what I have called lexical influence, strategic influence, and propositional influence, and Van Tillian scholars themselves have acknowledged these three kinds of influence.

Distinguishing these different possible kinds of philosophical 'influence,' may also help us gain some additional measure of understanding concerning the history of the debate over idealism itself. Is it possible that the early critics of Van Til noticed the lexical, strategic, and/or propositional influence of idealism in Van Til and, because of his ambiguous language, mistook one or more of these three types of influence with systemic influence? Additionally, is it possible that Van Til and his early supporters, who knew that idealism was not a systemic influence on him, may have failed at times to understand how the other types of influence could easily be mistaken for systemic influence? This is, of course, speculation, but I am attempting to give both Van Til and his critics as much benefit of the doubt as possible. I believe Christian charity requires us to consider these possibilities.

How then should we consider these types of acknowledged influence in connection with the debate over Van Til's thought? The first kind of influence, lexical influence, should not be controversial. Christian theologians have borrowed words from philosophy since the early

---

43. Van Til, *The Defense of the Faith*, 23. While the word 'informed' here is extremely vague, I think the only way these statements and others made by Van Til could be made consistent with systemic idealist influence would be to charge Van Til with such a level of ignorance that he was unable to realize what he was doing or else to charge him with outright duplicity. I do not believe that Van Til was either ignorant or intentionally deceptive, so systemic influence is ruled out in my opinion.

44. In other words, Van Til did not do with idealist philosophy what process theologians did with the philosophy of Alfred North Whitehead.

centuries of the church. The Councils of Nicaea and Chalcedon, for example, made use of the terms *ousia* and *hypostasis* in their formulations of the doctrine of the Trinity and the doctrine of Christ. As long as borrowed terminology is carefully defined in such a way that remains consistent with the teaching of Scripture, this issue should not be a cause of major concern.

The existence of strategic philosophical influence should also not be a cause of concern since Christian apologists have always been strategically influenced by the currents of thought surrounding them. It is the thought world of an apologist's own time that must be engaged. Early Christian apologists were strategically influenced by various Greek and Roman philosophies. They addressed the problems raised by those forms of thought. Seventeenth- and eighteenth-century apologists were strategically influenced by the questions raised in the Enlightenment. They had to deal with rationalism, empiricism, deism, higher biblical criticism and more. This is a kind of 'influence' that is to be expected in every age.[45]

If idealism did not exercise a systemic influence on Van Til, and if there is nothing controversial or necessarily problematic about lexical or strategic influence, then we can focus on the issue of propositional influence. If Van Til has, in fact, taken certain things he believed were true from idealism and replanted them in Reformed soil, then there is some hope that the discussion about Van Til and idealism can be taken in a much more constructive direction. Rather than continue the fruitless and inherently confusing debate about a general and vague 'influence,' we can ask instead: 'What are the specific elements that Van Til took from idealism and replanted in Reformed soil?' If we can answer that question, we can then examine those specific elements in order to determine which, if any, are consistent with Scripture.

## Replanting Idealist Holism

Rather than attempt to cover every possible idealist element that Van Til might have replanted in Reformed soil, I will simply focus on one

---

45. For many months my own research has been driven by the questions Van Til raised. In that sense, Van Til has 'influenced' my thought. But such influence is not the equivalent of my having embraced Van Til's system of thought. Similarly, idealism raised many of the questions Van Til attempted to answer. Such influence cannot automatically be equated with the embrace of the idealist system of thought. It is merely strategic influence.

specific element that I believe has been generally overlooked in these discussions despite its importance in Van Til's system of thought. That specific element is epistemological holism.[46] In idealist philosophy, holism is often associated with the doctrine of internal relations.[47] David J. Crossley observes, 'If there is one central doctrine of absolute idealism it is the doctrine of internal relations. In the context of discussion of ethical and social issues this displays itself as the thesis of holism.'[48] Holism displayed itself not only in relation to ethical and social issues but also in relation to epistemology.

It is beyond the scope of this work to delve into the specific details of the historical debate over the doctrine of internal relations. In my reading of Van Til, I have not come across any substantive discussion of that specific issue or any discussion over the nature of such relations.[49] What is more significant for our purposes, in any case, is the consequence of the doctrine of internal relations on the idealist definition of knowledge. In his description of internal relations, the idealist philosopher Brand Blanshard notes this epistemological consequence:

> Put more formally, the theory is this: (1) that every term, i.e. every possible object of thought, is what it is in virtue of relations to what is other than itself; (2) that its nature is affected thus not by some of its relations only,

---

46. This topic hasn't been completely ignored. It was mentioned in passing by Cecil DeBoer in his 1953 article, 'The New Apologetic,' 4. It was also discussed briefly by Sproul, Gerstner, and Lindsley in their *Classical Apologetics*, 313-315. It has not, however, received the consideration it deserves. It is not possible, even here, to give it a thorough examination. My remarks in this section are preliminary. My hope is that they will encourage others to examine the issue more comprehensively.

47. James N. Anderson, 'Van Til and Analytic Philosophy' in *Thinking God's Thoughts After Him: Essays in the Van Til Tradition*, 2 vols. ed. Bradley Green (Eugene, OR: Wipf & Stock, forthcoming).

48. David J. Crossley, 'Holism, Individuation, and Internal Relations.' *Journal of the History of Philosophy* 15, no. 2 (Apr 1977): 183. Dennis Rohatyn provides a helpful explanation of internal relations explaining: 'It amounts to the following theses: (a) that every event, and every entity, in the world is somehow (causally or logically) tied to every other event, and every other object, in the universe, such that (b) to attain complete knowledge of any one thing or state of affairs, is to possess (automatically) knowledge of the whole, i.e. of all states of affairs and of all things.' See Rohatyn, 'Internal Relations.' *Philosophical Papers* 4, no. 2 (1975): 116.

49. One of the critics of this idealist view in the early twentieth century was Bertrand Russell. For an interesting critique of the holistic view (which he calls monism), see his *Philosophical Essays* (London: Longmans, Green, and Co., 1910), 150-69.

but in differing degrees by all of them, no matter how external they may seem; (3) that in consequence of (2) and of the further obvious fact that everything is related in *some* way to everything else, no knowledge will reveal completely the nature of any term until it has exhausted that term's relations to everything else.[50]

In other words, because every fact is related to every other fact, there is no full knowledge of any fact unless there is knowledge of that fact's relation to every other fact. Or, to put it in the words of another idealist philosopher, Bernard Bosanquet, 'each of two or more terms can only be understood if all are understood.'[51]

The British idealists were critical of a kind of empiricist methodology that dealt with facts in an atomistic manner. They sought to unify all facts. David Boucher and Andrew Vincent provide a helpful explanation:

> The British Idealists found in German philosophy two ideas that were to form the basis of their critiques of empiricist and sensationalist theories of knowledge. First, they contended that understanding is always contextual, and that which is to be understood has to be related to wider terms of reference, until ultimately the whole of experience or the Absolute is implicated. Put simply, there can be no isolated entities, facts or individuals. All have to be understood in their essential relatedness.[52]

What this ultimately means, according to Ewing, is that 'reality is a unity of a type something like that postulated by the coherence theory and we are near to Bradley's conclusion that we could know no one thing fully without knowing everything else also.'[53]

Having traced Van Til's theory of knowledge throughout his system of thought, it is abundantly evident that there is a 'propositional influence' of idealism here. Van Til has replanted this specific element of idealist epistemology into Reformed soil. As we have seen, he explicitly repeats this idealist understanding of knowledge dozens of times, and he assumes it throughout his writings. As just one example out of many,

---

50. Brand Blanshard, *The Nature of Thought*, 2 vols. (London: George Allen & Unwin Ltd, 1921), 2:452.

51. Bernard Bosanquet, *Logic, or the Morphology of Knowledge*, 2 vols. 2nd ed. (London: Humphrey Milford/Oxford University Press, 1911), 2:278.

52. David Boucher and Andrew Vincent, *British Idealism: A Guide for the Perplexed* (London: Continuum, 2012), 38-39.

53. Ewing, *Idealism: A Critical Survey*, 118.

he writes, 'we may say that we must know all about all things if we are to know anything about anything.'[54] This is true, he says, because 'All knowledge is inter-related.'[55] As Van Til explains, 'the mind of man is a unit. It cannot know one thing truly without knowing all things truly.'[56] These are merely a handful of the many instances where this idealist view of knowledge is expressed or implied by Van Til.

Of course, when Van Til replants this idealist understanding of true knowledge into Reformed soil, it is now the unified mind and plan of God within which all facts are said to be related. God's eternal plan now provides the ultimate unified context for all facts. Each fact can be truly known only in relation to the other facts in that plan and in relation to the God who decreed it. Van Til argues that according to the Christian view, 'nothing at all can be known truly of any fact unless it be known through and by way of man's knowledge of God.'[57] Van Til elaborates on this point, saying, 'it is this unity of the plan of God, founded as it is in the very being of God, that gives the unity that we look for between all the finite facts. If one should maintain that one fact can be fully understood without reference to all other facts, he is as much antitheistic as when he should maintain that one fact can be understood without reference to God.'[58] The idealist definition of knowledge remains the same, but the ultimate principle of interpretation changes when it is replanted in Reformed soil. The Triune God replaces the idealist Absolute as the final reference point in this holist theory of knowledge.[59]

This replanted idealist definition of true knowledge is crucial to every fundamental element in Van Til's apologetic system of thought. It is the reason God's omniscience is foundational to his system as the solution to the problem of knowledge. Because true knowledge ultimately requires a knowledge of all facts, only the omniscient God has a perfect system

---

54. Cornelius Van Til, 'A Christian Theistic Theory of Knowledge,' *The Banner* 66/1809 (6 Nov 1931), in Cornelius Van Til and Eric H. Sigward, *The Articles of Cornelius Van Til*, Electronic ed. (Labels Army Company: New York, 1997).

55. Van Til, *An Introduction to Systematic Theology*, 64.

56. Ibid.

57. Van Til, *Survey of Christian Epistemology*, 5.

58. Ibid., 6.

59. It may be worth noting that this is why Van Til will refer to God as the Christian's 'Absolute.' He seems to be saying, in effect, 'That which the idealists need and don't have exists only in the Christian system.'

of true knowledge. He eternally knows himself and every fact he has decreed as a unified plan. God is, therefore, the ultimate principle of interpretation, the final reference point for all true predication.

As creatures, human beings are finite, but Van Til says they can have true knowledge if their knowledge corresponds to God's exhaustive knowledge. They can achieve this correspondence by reasoning analogically. They do so by making God their final reference point and reinterpreting the facts that God has eternally preinterpreted. They correctly reinterpret the facts by looking at them in the light of God's revelation. If human beings do this, the result is that they have a finite reflection of God's exhaustive system of truth.

Because fallen man rejects God as the final reference point and replaces God with himself as the ultimate principle of interpretation, fallen man never knows any fact in its true relation to every other fact. Fallen man treats facts as brute facts and reasons univocally. Therefore, in principle, fallen man does not have and cannot have true knowledge of any fact. Note also that this idealist definition of true knowledge is the foundation for the distinction Van Til makes between the knowledge of believers and the knowledge of unbelievers when he discusses the antithesis. It is because unbelievers don't know any fact in its relation to God and to all other facts in God's plan that they do not have true knowledge of anything in principle.

Because fallen man does not have true knowledge of any fact, his knowledge of all particular facts is distorted. Because his knowledge of all particular facts is distorted, natural theology is impossible for fallen man. Because traditional apologetic methods assume that fallen man can have true knowledge of some facts without having knowledge of all facts, traditional apologetics must be rejected, and the method of presupposition must be used. As Van Til explains,

> This reasoning will accordingly have to be by way of presupposition. Since there is no fact and no law on which the two parties to the argument agree they will have to place themselves upon one another's positions for the sake of argument.[60]

Notice that the believer and unbeliever have to use the method of presupposition *because* they do not agree on any fact or any law. The

---

60. Van Til, introduction to *The Inspiration and Authority of the Bible*, 39.

reason they agree on nothing is ultimately explained by the idealist definition of knowledge. As even a cursory reading of Van Til will reveal, then, the replanted idealist understanding of true knowledge is a significant element in his apologetic system of thought. But should it be replanted in Reformed soil? That is the concern.

## Concerns with Idealist Holism

Non-Van Tillians are concerned with the replanting of the idealist theory of knowledge into Reformed soil for several reasons. In the first place, as we discovered in the previous chapter, the Bible does not teach an idealist view of knowledge. The Bible nowhere even suggests that only exhaustive knowledge is true knowledge or that in order for one to know anything one must know everything. Of course, the Bible teaches that God has exhaustive knowledge of all things, but the Bible does not teach that divine omniscience is the only kind of knowledge that counts as true knowledge. Finite and limited human knowledge is also treated as true knowledge in Scripture.

Second, the replanting of the idealist theory of knowledge into Reformed soil unwittingly introduces the potential for skepticism into Reformed theology. According to this theory of knowledge, every fact is related to every other fact and because of this, there is no true knowledge of any fact unless there is knowledge of that fact's relation to every other fact. Taken at face value, this means that in order for any knowledge to be true knowledge it must be infinitely exhaustive knowledge. The difficulty, on the surface, is self-evident. If we take this doctrine of true knowledge at face value, then only an omniscient being could have true knowledge. True knowledge would not even be theoretically possible for a finite human being. Taken at face value, then, this idealist theory of knowledge reduces any being without omniscience to total skepticism.

Van Til attempts to avoid this problem by asserting that true knowledge is possible for finite human beings. His explanation is that finite human beings can and do have true knowledge if they reason analogically and make God their final point of reference. If they look at all facts in the light of God's revelation, reinterpreting the facts God has eternally preinterpreted, they are able to have a finite reflection of God's exhaustive system of knowledge. That finite reflection is, by definition, not exhaustive, but Van Til says that it is true as far as it goes. If man reasons analogically, his knowledge will correspond with God's knowledge, and his finite reflection of God's knowledge will be true knowledge.

Van Til's assertion of true human knowledge alongside his assertion of the idealist theory of knowledge raises an obvious question. How can one consistently affirm the idealist premise that *only* exhaustive knowledge is true knowledge while also affirming that non-exhaustive human knowledge is true knowledge? If the phrase 'true knowledge' has the same meaning in each statement, then Van Til is contradicting himself. On the other hand, if the phrase 'true knowledge' has a different meaning in each statement, he is equivocating. Those appear to be the only options.

Has Van Til provided any other way to maintain both doctrines with any semblance of coherence and consistency? We have seen that when he asserts that the knowledge of God and the knowledge of man coincide at every point and at no point, this can be explained to some degree by distinguishing between an *act* of knowledge and a *fact* of knowledge. The knowledge of God and the knowledge of man coincide at every point if we are speaking of the *fact* of knowledge (the object of knowledge), but they coincide at no point if we are speaking of the *act* of knowledge (the mode or manner of knowledge). We have also seen that when Van Til asserts that unbelievers have no true knowledge and then asserts that they do have true knowledge, this can be explained to some degree by an appeal to common grace. Unbelievers know nothing truly, *in principle*, but because God restrains them from taking that interpretive principle to its logical end, they can and do know some truths despite their principle of interpretation.

Neither of those distinctions, however, resolves the problem we are addressing here. Common grace isn't a plausible explanation in this case because common grace is a means by which God restrains the sinner from taking his interpretive principle to its logical end. Common grace does not give a sinner exhaustive knowledge. Even if common grace removed all the effects of the fall and gave the unbeliever exactly the same knowledge as the believer it would not help here because no believer has exhaustive knowledge either. Common grace helps Van Til only in explaining the relation between two types of non-exhaustive human knowledge (the knowledge of believers and the knowledge of unbelievers). It does not help us explain how we can coherently affirm that only exhaustive knowledge is true knowledge while also affirming that non-exhaustive knowledge is true knowledge.

Does the distinction between an *act* of knowledge and a *fact* of knowledge help here? No, because in this case, we are not merely discussing individual facts but the whole unified system of facts and relations. That is the nature of the idealist definition: True knowledge of any fact requires knowledge of its relation to every other fact. Although Van Til allows that an individual fact as an individual object of knowledge can be the same for God and for man, he denies that man can have the same *system* of knowledge that God has. In other words, he denies that man can know any fact in relation to every other fact. In order for man to have the same system of knowledge that God has, man would have to exhaustively know every fact about God, every fact in the divine decree, and every relation of every fact to God and to every other fact. That is not possible because man is not God.

In short, Van Til denies that man's *act* of knowledge can ever be the same as God's *act* of knowledge, but more to the point here, he also denies that man can ever have an exact replica of God's perfect system of knowledge, which contains *all* the facts of God's knowledge. Man cannot have the same exhaustive knowledge of all facts that God has. All that man can have, according to Van Til, is a finite (i.e., non-exhaustive) reflection of God's exhaustive system of knowledge. In other words, all man can ever have is *non-exhaustive* knowledge, but if man cannot possibly have the same *exhaustive* system of knowledge as God, we are left with the original dilemma.

Van Til's doctrine of correspondence is his way of *allowing* for man's true non-exhaustive knowledge, but it does not *account* for that knowledge given his idealist definition of true knowledge. The doctrine of correspondence simply asserts that non-exhaustive knowledge *is* true knowledge. It does not explain *how* that affirmation is or even could be consistent with the affirmation that *only* exhaustive knowledge is true knowledge. It doesn't explain how one can affirm mutually exclusive statements. We are left with the original problem: the replanted idealist definition forces us to choose between the incoherence of equivocation and the incoherence of self-contradiction with respect to *the central element* in Van Til's system of thought, namely, his epistemology.

A third reason the replanting of the idealist theory of knowledge into Reformed soil is a concern is because the idealist theory of knowledge is a significant element of idealist philosophy and it represents a rather significant departure from the philosophical assumptions within which confessional Reformed theology was developed and defended. As noted above, when the generally realist philosophical assumptions of the early Reformed theologians were rejected and replaced with various Enlightenment philosophies, the theology itself changed and not for the better.

Van Til quite explicitly joins with post-Enlightenment era theologians in his disdain for classical realist philosophy. He argues that classical realism is hostile to Scripture and that it 'cannot allow for the Biblical doctrines of the Trinity, of creation or of providence.'[61] It appears that Van Til's rejection of classic realism is based on the idea that it necessarily involves adopting the complete systems of Plato or Aristotle, but whether this is the reason for his rejection of classic realism or not, the rejection of the philosophical assumptions of the early Reformed theologians creates significant theological problems. If the metaphysical and epistemological assumptions that provided the context for the Reformed church's development, formulation, and defense of Reformed theology is rejected, then Reformed theology itself becomes problematic.

It must be remembered that the theologians of the early Reformed church did not accept everything that philosophers such as Plato or Aristotle taught any more than Augustine, Anselm, or Aquinas did. Instead, they critically appropriated what they believed to be true and rejected what they believed to be false. They looked for the 'elements of truth' in thinkers such as Plato and Aristotle. To use the distinctions made above, philosophers such as Plato and Aristotle exercised a 'propositional influence' on them.

The philosophical framework of classical realism first began to come under fire by a small minority of thinkers in the Middle Ages. With the broader spread of nominalism beginning in the fourteenth century, the rise of skepticism during the Renaissance, the rise of rationalism and empiricism during the Enlightenment, and then Kantianism and

---

61. Van Til, *The Defense of the Faith*, 275.

idealism in the following centuries, the older philosophical framework was eventually discarded. The rejection of this realist philosophical framework has had a dramatic impact on Reformed theology as a whole and on the doctrine of God in particular.

When we examine the history of Enlightenment and post-Enlightenment theology, particularly regarding the doctrine of God, it becomes abundantly evident that when the older philosophical framework is abandoned, classical Trinitarian theism is not far behind. The rise of unitarianism, deism, pantheism, and panentheism during and after the Enlightenment is not a coincidence. Theologians who adopted the metaphysics and epistemology of the rationalists reformulated their doctrine of God to fit that new philosophical framework. Theologians who adopted the philosophy of the empiricists reformulated their doctrine of God to fit that framework. Theologians who adopted the philosophy of the idealists reformulated their doctrines of God to fit those philosophical frameworks.[62]

This brings us back to Van Til. As we have seen, Van Til, in agreement with most post-Enlightenment philosophers, rejected 'classical realism.' In short, he rejected the metaphysics and epistemology that provided the conceptual framework within which sixteenth and seventeenth century Reformed theology was developed, stated, and defended. Historically, what has happened when this philosophical context is rejected and replaced with a different philosophical context is that an internal tension is introduced, leading to different theologies and novel doctrines of God. Van Til's commitment to the Reformed confessions seems to have enabled him to live with the tension for the most part. The tension, however, remains for those who follow Van Til in the rejection of realist philosophy.

If history is any guide, Van Til's rejection of realist philosophy will eventually result in the revising of Reformed theology and the denial of classical theism by some who follow his lead. In fact, this seems to have already begun to occur. Some of his students have already begun to redefine and reject essential elements of classical biblical and Christian theism in order to bring their doctrine of God in line with newer philosophical views. In other words, it is arguable that Van Til's

---

62. See James Collins, *God in Modern Philosophy* (Chicago: Henry Regnery, 1959).

adoption of elements of post-Enlightenment idealism and his attempt to replant these in Reformed soil created an unstable mixture of ideas that has already begun to undermine the orthodox Reformed theology he wanted to defend.

## Conclusion

Van Til rightly affirms the biblical and Reformed doctrine of the omniscience of God. God does know all things. He knows all things eternally and perfectly. He has true knowledge. Van Til also rightly affirms that human beings can have and do have true knowledge. The knowledge that human beings have, however, is finite and limited. They do not know in the same manner that God knows, and they do not exhaustively know all facts. They do, however, have knowledge. Both of these doctrines are clearly taught in Scripture and in the theology of the Reformed churches. Both of these doctrines are also consistent with each other because Scripture does not define true knowledge in such a way that it is applicable to God and to God alone.

When Van Til replanted the idealist definition of knowledge into his apologetic system, he introduced something incompatible with the biblical doctrine of knowledge into the heart of his system, and it created internal incoherence. That incoherence creates a domino effect because of how prevalent the idealist definition of knowledge is throughout Van Til's entire system. This idealist definition also introduces incoherence into the larger body of Reformed doctrine where confessionally Reformed Van Tillians and non-Van Tillians stand in agreement because it adds an incongruous and unbiblical element into the Reformed theological system.

It introduces incoherence into Reformed theology because its definition of knowledge equates true knowledge exclusively with exhaustive knowledge (i.e., with infinite omniscience). If exhaustive knowledge *alone* is true knowledge, then whatever man has in his finite mind cannot possibly be true knowledge regardless of whether he is a believer or an unbeliever. Neither believers nor unbelievers have infinite omniscience because they are finite creatures. The idealist theory of knowledge, therefore, reduces such finite human beings to skepticism. If we assert that exhaustive knowledge *alone* is true knowledge *and* assert that man's non-exhaustive 'knowledge' is true knowledge, as Van

Til does, we are either asserting a blatant self-contradiction or else we are speaking equivocally about 'true knowledge.' In either case, we are speaking incoherently.

Non-Van Tillians believe such internal incoherence is completely unnecessary, however, because they believe that there is no compelling reason to replant this idealist definition of true knowledge into Reformed soil in the first place. They believe there is no compelling reason to assume that the idealist definition of knowledge is correct and many reasons to reject it as false. As we have seen, we find no positive scriptural support for it and abundant scriptural evidence against it. *Every* explicit and implicit indication in the Bible of the existence of true human knowledge (which cannot be anything but finite knowledge) directly contradicts the idealist definition of knowledge. In other words, if we evaluate the idealist theory of knowledge against the standard of Scripture, it fails.

It is one thing to plant a flower in your garden. A flower will grow and produce beautiful blooms. It is quite another to plant something that chokes out everything else in your garden. Such plants will soon overwhelm and kill every other plant in your garden. Replanting the idealist theory of knowledge into Reformed soil is much more akin to planting a fast-growing invasive vine than it is to planting a flower. If we find that a doctrine has been replanted into Reformed soil and we find that the new doctrine contradicts other doctrines that have abundant biblical and confessional support, that is a clear indication that the new doctrine is a false doctrine. The idealist theory of knowledge that Van Til replanted into Reformed soil is a false doctrine. It undermines clear biblical doctrines, and as such it must be uprooted by those concerned with faithfulness to Scripture.

# CHAPTER 8

# Theological Concerns

Although confessionally Reformed Van Tillians and non-Van Tillians agree on the vast majority of our theological doctrines (those contained in the confessional standards), Van Til did teach certain doctrines connected to his apologetic system of thought that have raised serious concerns. In this chapter, I will examine several of these doctrines and several of these theological concerns. As with the previous two chapters, I will not attempt an exhaustive discussion of every possible topic. Instead, I will look at those issues I believe to be most significant and most worthy of careful consideration by Van Tillians and non-Van Tillians alike. I will begin with one general theological concern before proceeding to a few specific theological concerns.

## Defining Reformed Theology

Van Til's lifelong goal was to develop an apologetic method that would be consistent with Reformed theology. With that in mind, the first important question that must be answered concerns how 'Reformed theology' is to be defined. We cannot determine whether an apologetic method is consistent with Reformed theology if we do not know what Reformed theology is. To a certain extent, the definition of Reformed theology can be determined easily by simply pointing to the Reformed confessions of the sixteenth and seventeenth centuries. It was during these centuries that the Reformed churches wrote doctrinal standards such as the Three Forms of Unity and the Westminster Confession and Catechisms. It was also during these centuries that the Reformed orthodox theologians wrote their extensive works of theology, defining and defending Reformed theology against its adversaries.

This introduces a complicating factor into our discussion because the Reformed orthodox theologians of the sixteenth and seventeenth centuries taught a form of natural theology and advocated traditional apologetic methods. Therein lies the problem. Van Til explicitly taught that after Calvin destroyed 'synthesis thinking,' the Reformed scholastic theologians returned the Reformed churches to such thinking.[1] Van Til believed that their traditional apologetic methods were rooted in such synthesis thinking and therefore those traditional apologetic methods were inconsistent with the pure Reformed theology taught by John Calvin.[2]

Van Til believed that the traditional apologetics taught by the Reformed scholastics is not only inconsistent with Reformed theology, it is in a state of 'compromise with unbelief at every point.'[3] According to Van Til, those who taught traditional apologetics compromised the doctrine of God, the doctrine of the divine decree, the clarity of God's revelation, the necessity and sufficiency of supernatural revelation, the authority of Scripture, the doctrine of man's creation in the image of God, the doctrine of the covenant, and the doctrine of sin.[4] In other words, Van Til had numerous theological concerns with what he believed was the compromised theology taught by the Reformed scholastics of the sixteenth and seventeenth centuries.

This raises an important question, however, since the Reformed theologians of the sixteenth and seventeenth centuries were the theologians who developed, defined, and defended historic Reformed theology in its original form. The basic parameters of Reformed theology were settled by the time of the Synod of Dordt (1618–1619) when it was determined that Remonstrant theology fell outside those boundaries.

---

1. Van Til, 'Herman Dooyeweerd and Reformed Apologetics,' in Cornelius Van Til and Eric H. Sigward, *The Pamphlets, Tracts, and Offprints of Cornelius Van Til*, Electronic ed. (Labels Army Company: New York, 1997).

2. I will address the alleged conflict between Calvin and the next generation of Reformed theologians in the following chapter.

3. Cornelius Van Til, 'Wanted – A Reformed Testimony,' *Presbyterian Guardian* 20/7 (16 July 1951), in Cornelius Van Til and Eric H. Sigward, *The Articles of Cornelius Van Til*, Electronic ed. (Labels Army Company: New York, 1997).

4. Van Til, *The Defense of the Faith*, 340-41.

Reformed theology reached its mature confessional formulation in the 1640s in the Westminster Standards. This is not to say, of course, that these early Reformed theologians were infallible or that there was no diversity to be found among them or that they replaced Scripture as the *principium cognoscendi* of theology, but it is to say that the basic parameters of the Reformed theological tradition did not remain in some kind of perpetual state of flux. There was a stable and definable Reformed theological tradition at this time.

The fact that there was a stable and definable Reformed theological tradition by this time is important because it means that the theologians of the sixteenth and seventeenth centuries played a unique foundational role in defining the Reformed tradition. Van Tillian scholars themselves have acknowledged this. Consider the words of K. Scott Oliphint, for example:

> In citing the Protestant scholastics, we are attempting to point out a large and substantial tradition in Protestant theological history, *disagreement with which places the burden of proof squarely on the one disagreeing*, and not on that tradition. Given the sheer intellectual weight of their work, no disagreement with them should be taken seriously that does not at the same time provide direct refutation of the exegesis and, following on that, the theology that is the sum and substance of that work.[5]

This is true because of the unique foundational role these theologians played. But what about Van Til's position? Van Til explicitly disagreed with the apologetic views of the Reformed scholastic theologians, but he also disagreed with what he believed were the numerous doctrinal compromises resulting from their synthesis thinking.

Where does this place Van Til in relation to the Reformed theological tradition? Van Til himself makes it abundantly clear that he disagrees with these early Reformed theologians because, according to him, they departed from the purity of Calvin's teaching and re-embraced synthesis thinking. But, as Oliphint has rightly pointed out, the burden of proof rests with the individual Reformed theologian who disagrees with the historic Reformed tradition exemplified in the writings of the Reformed scholastics. Has Van Til met that burden of proof?

---

5. K. Scott Oliphint, *Reasons for Faith: Philosophy in the Service of Theology* (Phillipsburg: P&R Publishing, 2006), xi. Emphasis mine.

As Oliphint explains, no disagreement with the Reformed scholastics should be taken seriously that does not directly refute their exegesis and refute the theology that rests on that exegesis. Van Til, however, cannot have possibly met this exegetical burden of proof since he did not do any substantive exegesis. Nor does he ever directly interact with any of the arguments of the Reformed scholastic theologians. In fact, it is difficult to determine whether he even read any of the Reformed scholastics at length.

A search in the electronic edition of the collected works of Van Til for some of the most prominent names among the Reformed scholastics reveals a half dozen mentions of Beza, three of which are references to Beza's biography of Calvin. The Leiden Synopsis is mentioned five times and Voetius is mentioned four times. Zanchius appears but only in a list of names. The names of Ursinus and Mastricht show up several times, but they are found in block quotes of other authors who are talking about the 1924 Synod of Kalamazoo. Similarly, Polanus' name appears a few times but when it does, it is only because Van Til is quoting Barth, and Barth mentions Polanus in those quotes. In a 1941 letter to a friend, Van Til does mention Francis Turretin only to say that 'Turretin does not impress me very favorably …'[6] Among these Reformed scholastics whose names Van Til does mention there is no interaction with any of their arguments, much less refutation.

There are others among the significant Reformed scholastics who do not even receive a mention. I found no references to Musculus, Vermigli, Ames, Wollebius, Witsius, Brakel, De Moor, Perkins, or Charnock. However, in contrast to the rather miniscule number of references to these giants of Reformed theology, the idealist philosopher Bernard Bosanquet is mentioned about 350 times in Van Til's collected works. According to the criteria Oliphint mentions, Van Til's disagreement with the Reformed scholastics simply cannot be taken seriously.

The concern here should be an obvious one. To the extent that Van Til dismisses or alters important doctrines taught by the theologians who originally defined the Reformed tradition, he is dismissing or

---

6. See Cornelius Van Til, 'Letter to an Unknown Friend dated 25 Dec 1941,' from Archives of Westminster Theological Seminary, as cited in Danny Olinger, 'Vos the Systematician: A Review Article,' *Ordained Servant* (Aug-Sep 2018): 12.

altering significant elements of the Reformed theological tradition. When we observe that the doctrines Van Til dismisses or alters are *precisely those that contradict his theory of knowledge and his apologetic views*, it gives every impression that Van Til was developing a novel Reformed theology that would be consistent with his apologetic system rather than developing a new apologetic system that would be consistent with Reformed theology.

By condemning the Reformed scholastic theologians and important elements of the original Reformed theological tradition, and by condemning all contemporary Reformed theologians who hold to that original theological tradition, Van Til is, in effect, saying that *his* definition of Reformed theology should be the standard by which all other Reformed theologians (including the theologians of the sixteenth and seventeenth centuries) should be judged. By doing this, Van Til is, in effect, insisting that his presuppositional apologetic methodology be the defining standard of the true Reformed tradition and that anything inconsistent with it must be rejected. It may not have been intentional, but it is what he is effectively saying, and it is the way his work has been treated by many of his students. When our centuries-old theological tradition is being changed in significant ways to conform to the views of one individual twentieth-century theologian, it should be a serious concern for all confessionally Reformed Christians. It is not a minor issue.

Van Til's statements about the early Reformed theologians forces the Reformed Christian to ask himself or herself why Van Til should be viewed as the standard by which all Reformed theology is defined. Van Til never even discussed the actual exegesis or arguments of the early Reformed theologians, much less refuted those arguments. The minimal number of references to the early Reformed scholastics in his writings and the non-existent interaction with their thought and their arguments makes it difficult to determine whether Van Til even read them before rejecting them as synthesizers and compromisers.[7] If he hasn't refuted them, however, we have to ask ourselves why his disagreement with them should be taken seriously?

---

7. It seems very likely that Van Til's knowledge of them was exclusively through secondary sources. As we will observe in the next chapter, Van Til's minimal interaction with primary sources and over-reliance on secondary sources created numerous problems in his system of thought.

## Natural Theology

At the heart of Van Til's rejection of traditional apologetics is his view that natural theology is impossible. Natural theology is 'the knowledge of God that is available to reason through the revelation of God in the natural order.'[8] In other words, natural theology is the knowledge of God based on general revelation. Such theology is impossible, according to Van Til, for several reasons. In the first place, the created order is under the curse of God. General revelation, therefore, is not as clear as it was before the fall. After the fall, 'darkness covers the "facts" or objects of knowledge.'[9] Second, the mind of fallen man is now corrupt.[10] As Van Til explains: 'After sin has entered the world, no one of himself knows nature aright, and no one knows the soul of man aright. How then could man reason from nature to nature's God and get anything but a distorted notion of God?'[11]

The third, and most important reason natural theology is impossible, according to Van Til, is related to his theory of knowledge. In order for man's knowledge to be true knowledge, man has to make God the ultimate principle of interpretation. Fallen man, however, makes himself the ultimate principle of interpretation, and because he does so, fallen man knows no fact as it truly is. If fallen man knows nothing in creation as it truly is, he cannot possibly reason from that non-knowledge to any true knowledge of God. Traditional natural theology, according to Van Til, wrongly assumes that man can have true knowledge of created facts and wrongly assumes that, by starting with such knowledge, man can reach some limited knowledge of God. For all of these reasons, natural theology must be rejected.

Van Til's rejection of natural theology is a concern for several reasons. It is a concern, in the first place, because while he rejects it, he also at the same time affirms it. Recall that Van Til teaches that fallen man now both knows God in one sense and does not know God in another sense.[12] He says, 'All men know not merely that *a* God exists, but they

---

8. Richard A. Muller, *Dictionary of Latin and Greek Theological Terms*, 2nd ed. (Grand Rapids: Baker Academic, 2017), 362.

9. Van Til, *Survey of Christian Epistemology*, 123.

10. Van Til, *An Introduction to Systematic Theology*, 164.

11. Ibid., 133.

12. Cornelius Van Til, *Common Grace and Witness-Bearing* (Phillipsburg, NJ: Lewis J. Grotenhuis, 1955), 9.

know that God, the *true* God, the *only* God, exists. They cannot be conscious of themselves, says Calvin, except they be at the same time conscious of God as their creator.'[13] Van Til explains:

> The picture of fallen man as given in Scripture is that he knows God but does not want to recognize him as God (Rom 1). That he knows God is due to the fact that all things in the universe about him and within him speak clearly of God. It is as 'knowing God' that man rebels against God.[14]

Note carefully what Van Til is saying here. He is saying that fallen man has knowledge of the true God and that fallen man's knowledge of the true God is rooted in the general revelation found in creation. That's a natural theology. In other words, in the same way that Van Til both affirms and denies that fallen man knows God, he both affirms and denies natural theology. This is a concern because this kind of equivocation inevitably leads to confusion.

Second, if Van Til is using 'natural theology' in the traditional sense of 'the knowledge of God that is available to reason through the revelation of God in the natural order,' his quasi-affirmation of it places him in some continuity with the very Reformed theologians he accuses of being compromisers for their affirmation of it. On the other hand, his simultaneous rejection of natural theology places him completely at odds with these same theologians. The fact that the Reformed theologians of the sixteenth and seventeenth centuries affirmed natural theology in the traditional sense is well beyond any reasonable dispute.[15] They differed from the Socinians who rejected natural theology, and they differed from rationalistic deists and others whose view of natural theology made human reason a theological *principium cognoscendi externum*. They had a doctrine of natural theology that was carefully

---

13. Ibid., 8.

14. Van Til, *A Christian Theory of Knowledge*, 34.

15. For surveys of the teaching of the Reformed orthodox on this subject, see, for example, Richard A. Muller, *Post-Reformation Reformed Dogmatics*, vol. 1, *Prolegomena to Theology*, 2nd ed. (Grand Rapids: Baker Academic, 2003), 270-310; Richard A. Muller, 'Was it Really Viral? Natural Theology in the Early Modern Reformed Tradition,' in *Crossing Traditions: Essays on the Reformation and Intellectual History*, ed. Maria-Cristine Pitassi and Daniela Solfaroli Camillocci, (Leiden: Brill, 2018), 507-531; J. V. Fesko, introduction to *Natural Theology*, Geerhardus Vos, trans. Albert Gootjes (Grand Rapids: Reformation Heritage Books, 2022), xvii-lxx; Michael Sudduth, *The Reformed Objection to Natural Theology* (London: Routledge, 2009), 9-40.

thought out, carefully qualified, and consistent with Scripture and the Reformed confessions.[16]

If Van Til is using 'natural theology' in the narrower sense as a virtual synonym for theistic proofs and is rejecting that specific idea because it is allegedly inconsistent with Reformed theology, then this is strong evidence that he is not attempting to develop an apologetic method that is consistent with Reformed theology but is instead developing a new version of Reformed theology that will be consistent with his apologetic system. This is true because the Reformed theologians who developed and defended confessional Reformed theology (the men who defined Reformed theology) had no qualms about using arguments for the existence of God. These arguments were not used as a rationalist foundation upon which supernatural theology was then constructed. When these early Reformed theologians bring up the arguments for the existence of God, it is typically for apologetic purposes – to refute atheists and Epicureans. A few examples from among these theologians will suffice.

Zacharius Ursinus (1534–1583), in his *Commentary on the Heidelberg Catechism*, presents eleven arguments for the existence of God, including a cosmological argument based on cause and effect.[17] In a collection of theses titled 'On God, or, That God Exists,' Franciscus Junius (1545–1602) presents a number of theistic arguments.[18] According to Junius, the natural man can be taught that God exists 'since there are certain demonstrations for God *a posteriori* (as they say), that is, from His works and effects' (Thesis 20). He then proceeds to outline an abridged version of Thomas Aquinas' 'Five Ways' of proving the existence of God.[19] Philippe Du-Plessis Mornay (1549–1623) wrote a massive work titled *De la verité de la religion chrestienne* (*On the Truth of the Christian Religion*). The entire lengthy first chapter is a collection of theistic proofs.[20] In his

---

16. See, for example, Francis Turretin, *Institutes of Elenctic Theology*, 3 vols., trans. George Musgrave Giger, ed. James T. Dennison, Jr. (Phillipsburg: P&R Publishing Company, 1992–1997), 1:6; cf. also Petrus van Mastricht, *Theoretical–Practical Theology*, vol. 1, *Prolegomena*, trans. Todd M. Rester, ed. Joel R. Beeke (Grand Rapids: Reformation Heritage Books, 2018), 83-84.

17. Zacharias Ursinus, *The Commentary on the Heidelberg Catechism*, 121-23.

18. Francis Junius, *Opera Theologica*, 2 vols. (Geneva: Caldoriani, 1607), 1:1777-78.

19. Ibid., 1778. See the Appendix for a full translation of 'On God, or, That God Exists.'

20. For an English translation, see Mornay, *A Woorke Concerning the Trewnesse of the Christian Religion*, trans. Philip Sidney and Arthur Golding (London: Thomas Cadman, 1587), 1-14.

*Institutions of Christian Religion*, Gulielmus Bucanus (d. 1603) shows 'the principal reasons to prove that there is a God' and includes the arguments from motion and from causality.[21] Edward Leigh (1602–1671) presents the same kinds of theistic proofs in his *Body of Divinity*.[22]

In Disputation 6 of the *Synopsis of a Purer Theology*, the kinds of proofs that can be used to demonstrate the existence of God are carefully set forth. For example:

> one can reason from the movement of the universe (and especially the constant and regulated motion of the heavens) to the prime mover and the author of motion (who exists in actuality) (Aristotle, *Metaphysics*, book 12, chapter 6). One can argue from the sequence of efficient causes to the first efficient cause where the sequence stops, and on which the other causes depend. Or one argues from the goals to the final goal and the force that determines the goal; from being, from the good, from perfection, up to the prime essence, the highest good and the most perfect nature.[23]

Francis Turretin (1623–1687) presents theistic proofs, including the argument from causality, in his *Institutes of Elenctic Theology*.[24] Stephen Charnock (1628–1680) presents a lengthy argument for a first cause in his *The Existence of God*.[25] Petrus Van Mastricht (1630–1706) provides an argument from created effects to the first cause in his *Theoretical-Practical Theology*.[26]

The point is that natural theology is an important element of classical Reformed theology. As Francis Turretin explains, 'The orthodox ... *uniformly* teach that there is a natural theology, partly innate (derived from the book of conscience by means of common notions

---

21. Gulielmus Bucanus, *Institutions of Christian Religion*, trans. Robert Hill (London: George Snowdon and Leonell Snowdon, 1606), 1-2.

22. Edward Leigh, *A Systeme or Body of Divinity* (London: A.M. for William Lee, 1662), 149.

23. Polyander, Johannes, Antonius Walaeus, Antonius Thysius, and Andreas Rivetus, *Synopsis Purioris Theologiae = Synopsis of a Purer Theology*, vol. 1, *Disputations 1-23*, ed. Dolf te Velde, trans Riemer A. Faber (Leiden: Brill, 2015), 153.

24. Turretin, *Institutes of Elenctic Theology*, 1:170.

25. Stephen Charnock, *The Complete Works of Stephen Charnock*, 5 vols. (Edinburgh: James Nichol/London: James Nisbet & Co., 1864), 1:150-51.

26. Petrus van Mastricht, *Theoretical–Practical Theology*, vol. 2, *Faith in the Triune God*, trans. Todd M. Rester, ed. Joel R. Beeke (Grand Rapids: Reformation Heritage Books, 2019), 116-17.

[*koinas ennoias*]) and partly acquired (drawn from the book of creatures discursively).[27] Classical Reformed theology teaches these doctrines because they are biblical doctrines. The mere fact that later theologians and heretics created a distorted rationalist version of natural theology does not justify the condemnation of those who taught a biblically faithful doctrine of natural theology.

## The Antithesis

A second theological concern is related to Van Til's doctrine of the antithesis. The most serious problem is that his doctrine of the antithesis is rooted in his idealist theory of knowledge, and this doctrine of the antithesis is the primary justification for Van Til's claim that the method of presupposition is the *only* biblically faithful method of apologetics. As Van Til explains,

> This reasoning will accordingly *have to* be by way of presupposition. *Since* there is no fact and no law on which the two parties to the argument agree they will *have to* place themselves upon one another's positions for the sake of argument.[28]

The method of presupposition is necessary for Van Til precisely because 'there is no fact and no law on which the two parties to the argument agree.' There is no fact on which they agree because one party (the believer) makes God the final reference point for predication while the other party (the unbeliever) makes man the final reference point. In other words, the antithesis between these mutually exclusive principles of interpretation makes the method of presupposition the only possible apologetic method. Van Til's doctrine of antithesis, however, raises some concerns.

If I might explain it this way, when Van Til is attempting to justify his claim that only the method of presupposition is proper, he appeals to an *absolute* antithesis with regard to the knowledge of individual facts and laws. As we saw, the method of presupposition is necessary for Van Til precisely because 'there is no fact and no law on which the two parties to the argument agree.'[29] However, if the antithesis is taken in an

---

27. Turretin, *Institutes of Elenctic Theology*, 1:6. Emphasis mine.
28. Van Til, introduction to *The Inspiration and Authority of the Bible*, 39. Emphasis mine.
29. Ibid.

absolute sense with regard to the unbeliever's knowledge of individual facts and laws, it would rule out the very possibility of communication between believers and unbelievers, thus ruling out the very possibility of apologetics.

As we have seen, however, Van Til himself does not assert an unqualified absolute antithesis in the present age with regard to knowledge. He does not deny the possibility of communication or apologetics. He knows that such a claim would fly directly in the face of Scripture and his own project. His assertion is that the absolute antithesis exists *in concrete practice* only after the eschatological separation of the sheep and the goats.[30] This is why Van Til so often qualifies the antithesis by saying that it is only *in principle* that the unbeliever knows no facts truly.[31] In practice, the unbeliever *does* have some true knowledge. The problem that a qualified antithesis creates in the argument for the method of presupposition is self-evident: the qualified antithesis allows the unbeliever to have true knowledge of facts. Since the claim that unbelievers have *no true knowledge* of facts is the very basis for the claim that the method of presupposition is necessary, this is a problem.

Some Van Tillian scholars, aware of this problem, de-emphasize Van Til's own qualified antithesis and move toward a more absolute antithesis. The problem here is that if the doctrine of the absolute antithesis exists in concrete practice only *after* the final eschatological separation of the sheep and the goats, then the only period of time during which Van Til's apologetic method of presupposition could be required would be during the eschaton when no apologetic method is necessary. On the other hand, if the antithesis is applied in an absolute sense in the present era before the final judgment, it results in an unbiblical over-realized eschatology. Consider, for example, what William Dennison has written about apologetics. He says:

> … the apologist stands not on earth pointing the unbeliever to heaven, where Christ is; rather, the apologist stands in heaven – in the *age to come* – pointing the unbeliever to heaven. In apologetics, the believer begins with his identity in Christ, as one who is part of Christ's bride located in

---

30. Cornelius Van Til, 'Common Grace: Third Article,' *Westminster Theological Journal* 9, no. 1 (Nov. 1946): 57, 74.

31. E.g., Van Til, *A Christian Theory of Knowledge*, 35, 229.

the heavenly places, and then he defends full-orbed Christian theism *from this glorified position.*[32]

Dennison, of course, does not deny that the believer lives in the already and the not yet, in the overlap of the ages between this world and the world to come.[33] However, by asserting that the believer addresses the unbeliever solely from his 'glorified position' in heaven, the not-yet is effectively ignored, and we slip into a dangerously over-realized eschatology. According to the confessionally Reformed understanding of Scripture, Christians are already justified, and we are already being sanctified, but we are not already glorified (WCF 32).[34] We still await the resurrection of our glorified bodies.

I mention this view merely to illustrate how easy it is for Van Til's equivocal language about the antithesis to lead to serious theological problems. It is Van Til's doctrine, however, with which we are primarily concerned. The significant point to observe when examining his doctrine of the antithesis is that he qualifies it by appealing to other doctrines such as common grace. As we have seen, he asserts repeatedly that fallen man does not apply his principle of interpretation consistently and does, in fact, know many facts.[35] Neither the unbeliever nor the believer is completely consistent as we have seen. Because an 'old man' exists in both the believer and the unbeliever, the antithesis in practice has fuzzy lines.[36]

To the extent that Van Til qualifies the antithesis, however, and to the extent that he allows for fallen man's knowledge of facts, he undermines the grounds for his claim that the method of presupposition is the only

---

32. William D. Dennison, *In Defense of the Eschaton: Essays in Reformed Apologetics*, ed. James Douglas Baird (Eugene, OR: Wipf & Stock, 2015), 107. Emphasis mine.

33. Ibid.

34. Dennison speaks of the redeemed man in terms of glorification repeatedly in his book. The believer sees 'all things through new glorified spectacles' (p. 108), and he responds to the attacks of unbelievers 'from this glorified status of union with Christ' (p. 111). Our present status, however, is one of sanctification, not glorification.

35. E.g., Van Til, Cornelius. *Christian Apologetics*, 132; *A Christian Theory of Knowledge*, 13-14, 36.

36. Van Til, introduction to *The Inspiration and Authority of the Bible*, 24-25. To use Van Til's own table saw illustration, if God's common grace often prevents the unbeliever from setting the saw blade at a wrong angle, the grounds for Van Til's apologetic claims are seriously weakened.

biblically faithful method of apologetics.[37] If there is agreement between believers and unbelievers with regard to any fact or law, the method of presupposition is not the only option. It is not absolutely necessary. Van Til acknowledged that the fact of the unbeliever's knowledge of the world is 'a difficult point.'[38] It is difficult for Van Til, however, only because it creates problems for his argument regarding the necessity of the method of presupposition. It is not a difficulty for those whose understanding of the antithesis is not shaped by an unbiblical idealist theory of knowledge with its all-or-nothing implications.

The difficulty for Van Til is that it does not matter whether the unbeliever's interpretive *principle* is completely antithetical to the believer's interpretive principle if God through common grace prevents the unbeliever from actually using his interpretive principle consistently and if that principle 'often' lies dormant.[39] If an unbeliever, for whatever reason, has true knowledge of any facts 'as far as it goes,' Van Til's case for the method of presupposition is undermined because in Van Til's system, *all* human knowledge is true only as far as it goes.

Van Til says that creaturely knowledge is true 'as far as it goes' if 'it corresponds to the knowledge that God has.'[40] Van Til also says, 'We are well aware of the fact that non-Christians have a great deal of knowledge about this world *which is true as far as it goes*.'[41] Regardless of the reason Van Til uses to explain an unbeliever's true knowledge of this world (i.e., facts), the very existence of *any* knowledge about this world destroys his own stated grounds for an exclusively presuppositional method of apologetics.

It is impossible to have it both ways. Either the antithesis between the believer's knowledge and the unbeliever's knowledge is absolute in practice

---

37. John M. Frame has recognized the problems with Van Til's doctrine of the antithesis. See, for example, his *Cornelius Van Til: An Analysis of His Thought*, 43, 192-210, so it is interesting that it is also Frame who has suggested a multi-perspectival approach to apologetics, which grants the legitimacy of non-presuppositional approaches if they are used in a complementary manner along with the presuppositional method. See Frame, *Selected Shorter Writings*, vol. 2 (Phillipsburg: P&R Publishing Company, 2015), 185-87.

38. Van Til, *An Introduction to Systematic Theology*, 63.

39. Cornelius Van Til, 'Reply to Professor J. Vanden Bosch,' *The Banner* 75/2246 (24 May 1940), in Cornelius Van Til and Eric H. Sigward, *The Articles of Cornelius Van Til*, Electronic ed. (Labels Army Company: New York, 1997).

40. Van Til, *Survey of Christian Epistemology*, 1-2.

41. Van Til, *An Introduction to Systematic Theology*, 63.

as well as in principle and we potentially have grounds for claiming that only the method of presupposition is viable (if we can figure out some way to communicate in such a situation), or the antithesis is not absolute in practice and we have no grounds for claiming that the method of presupposition is the only viable method in practice. The first option, a doctrine of absolute antithesis in practice as well as in principle, has to be rejected. It contradicts Scripture, destroys the very possibility of communication and apologetics, and was rightly denied by Van Til himself.

However, if we deny the doctrine of absolute antithesis in practice, as Van Til did, that denial leaves only the option Van Til himself chose, namely a qualified antithesis in practice. A qualified antithesis, however, does not have the same apologetic implications as an absolute antithesis because a qualified antithesis grants that unbelievers have 'a great deal of knowledge about this world.' A qualified antithesis does not imply the necessity of the method of presupposition, and it does not justify the blanket condemnation of all traditional methods of apologetics and the blanket condemnation of all non-Van Tillian Reformed theologians. The method of presupposition is only necessary if 'there is *no fact* and *no law* on which the two parties to the argument agree.'[42]

## One Person and Three Persons

The final theological concern we must discuss is related to Van Til's doctrine of God. I am referring specifically to Van Til's claim that God is both one person and three persons.[43] This doctrinal claim is a serious

---

42. Van Til, introduction to *The Inspiration and Authority of the Bible*, 39. Emphasis mine.

43. There is another theological issue indirectly related to Van Til and the doctrine of God that is a serious theological concern, but it has to do with the teaching of some of his proponents and not with Van Til himself. To be specific, it has to do with statements found in certain works that have been published by John M. Frame and K. Scott Oliphint.

For example, in his *The Doctrine of God* (Phillipsburg: P&R Publishing Company, 2002), 571, and in his *Systematic Theology: An Introduction to Christian Belief* (Phillipsburg: P&R Publishing Company, 2013), 377, Frame argues that 'God himself changes. ... changing as others change' (His *Systematic Theology* appears to have simply incorporated the text of his *Doctrine of God*). In both books, Frame expresses his view that there are 'two modes of existence in God,' a transcendent mode and an immanent mode (See *The Doctrine of God*, 572 and *Systematic Theology*, 378). Also, in both books, Frame thanks Vern Poythress 'for suggesting to me many of the ideas of this section' (See *The Doctrine of God*, 570, note 55 and *Systematic Theology*, 376, note 32).

In his book *God With Us: Divine Condescension and the Attributes of God* (Wheaton: Crossway, 2012), Oliphint taught something similar with his doctrine of God's 'essential attributes' and 'covenantal attributes' (p. 40). He argued that God takes on 'covenantal

issue because Van Til is a confessionally Reformed Christian and the Reformed confessions speak of the Triune God in terms of *one substance* and *three persons* (e.g., WCF, II.3) or *one essence* and *three persons* (Belgic Confession, Art. 8). In the Greek of the ancient Christian creeds, the formula is one *ousia* and three *hypostases*, and in Latin it is one *substantia* and three *personae* (or *subsistentiae*). Van Til, on the other hand, says,

---

attributes' in a way that is analogous to the Son's assuming of a human nature with its creaturely attributes (pp. 185-86). The analogy does not work, however, because in the unique case of the incarnation, the divine nature has/is the divine attributes, and the assumed human nature has the human attributes. Both natures belong to the one Person of the Son, but each nature retains its properties in the hypostatic union. The divine and human attributes are attributes of distinct natures belonging to the Son. The Triune God has essential attributes, and these essential attributes are attributes of the divine nature. But if the Triune God takes on covenantal creaturely attributes, what nature has those attributes? Oliphint speaks of these attributes being attributed to 'God as condescended,' which he parallels to the attribution of human attributes to 'God as incarnate' (p. 186), but the incarnation involves the assumption of a nature which has those human attributes. Presumably, condescension does not involve God's assumption of a second divine nature, but if it doesn't, it means that only the one divine nature could have these creaturely covenantal attributes. In short, each of these views ends up in its own way introducing a second level of being into God's divine nature in order to account for God's relation to his people, and each therefore ends up in its own way introducing the creaturely attribute of mutability into the divine nature of God. As we saw in chapter 1, for Van Til, the rejection of immutability is equivalent to the affirmation of correlativism, the idea that God and his creatures are mutually inter-dependent. As we saw, that idea is anathema to Van Til because it annihilates the very foundation of his entire apologetic system. While there is no indication that Frame's views on this matter have changed, it should be observed that Oliphint has made public statements saying that he has abandoned his proposal regarding the doctrine of God. His book, however, was in print for seven years before those statements were made, and he taught his proposal to many prospective pastors in the classroom for at least that many years. Those men are now ministering to God's people around the world. This means that this doctrine is still 'out there' and as such should be addressed regardless of whether Oliphint himself still believes or teaches it.

This correlativist doctrine of God should be of concern to Van Tillians given the fact that it destroys the foundation of Van Til's apologetic system and was anathema to Van Til himself. More importantly, it should be of concern to Van Tillians and non-Van Tillians alike because it destroys the foundation of orthodox Christian theology. A thorough study and refutation of this doctrine, while necessary, is beyond the scope of this book since this book is focused primarily on Van Til's thought. James Dolezal has made a good start with his book *All That is In God* (Grand Rapids: Reformation Heritage Books, 2017), but more work remains. I am not discussing it at length here because I am not discussing in detail any of the idiosyncratic views of Van Til's proponents unless those views can be definitively traced to Van Til himself. It is for this reason that I have not devoted any significant space to a discussion of reconstructionism or triperspectivalism either, even though I have concerns with both. Van Til himself can neither be credited with nor blamed for everything his students or published proponents teach.

'We speak of God as a person; yet we speak also of three persons in the Godhead.'[44] He asserts that God is 'one absolute person.'[45] After affirming that God is 'one in essence and three in person,' Van Til adds: 'Yet this is not the whole truth of the matter. We do assert that God, that is, the whole Godhead, is one person.'[46]

The reason why this is a serious theological concern should be self-evident. Van Til is making an assertion, which, on the face of it, appears to conflict with the doctrine of God taught in his own confessional standards, and the doctrine of God is not a peripheral matter. The doctrine of God impacts every other Christian doctrine because every other doctrine is related to God. The doctrine of Bibliology concerns Scripture, which is the Word *of God*. The doctrine of Anthropology concerns human beings who are created in the image *of God*. The doctrine of Christology concerns Jesus Christ, who is the Son *of God*. The doctrine of Soteriology concerns salvation, which is the redemptive work *of God*. The doctrine of Ecclesiology concerns the Church which is the people *of God*. The doctrine of Eschatology concerns the last things, which is the final goal *of God*. As Van Til himself acknowledges, 'Every doctrine is bound to be false if the first and basic doctrine of God is false.'[47] When, therefore, Van Til asserts that God is one person and three persons, it is a serious concern.

Given the fact that Van Til affirms the orthodox confessional teaching that God is 'three persons,' why does he then also affirm that God is 'one person'? According to Frame, Van Til is 'supplementing' the orthodox doctrine, not denying or replacing it.[48] Nathan Shannon says that Van Til makes this assertion in order 'to say that God is absolute personality, and that there is no sense in which God is impersonal.'[49]

---

44. Van Til, *An Introduction to Systematic Theology*, 348.

45. Ibid., 362.

46. Ibid., 363.

47. Van Til, *Christian Apologetics*, 31.

48. Frame, *Cornelius Van Til: An Analysis of His Thought*, 67.

49. Nathan D. Shannon, 'Christianity and Evidentialism: Van Til and Locke on Facts and Evidence.' *Westminster Theological Journal* 74, no. 2 (Fall 2012), 344. Note that if this is what Van Til is doing, it is another example of equivocation. When he affirms that God is 'three persons,' he uses the word person in one sense, and when he affirms that God is 'one person,' he uses the word 'person' in another completely different sense. If he wasn't equivocating, he would be uttering a self-contradictory statement. In other words,

If that was Van Til's motive, it is a strange one since the formulation found in the ancient creeds and in the Reformed confessions already denied that God is impersonal in its affirmation that God is tri-personal. A tri-personal God is not an impersonal God.[50] The orthodox Christian doctrine of the Trinity in its traditional formulation has never allowed room for any concept of God as some kind of impersonal force. In other words, Van Til's theological concern with the traditional formulation was completely unwarranted and unnecessary.

Regardless of his motive, however, the grounds for his assertion are worth examining. Van Til explains why he says that God is one person by drawing a parallel between the divine attributes and the three persons. Just as each of the attributes are 'coextensive with the being of God,' he argues, each of the persons is 'coterminous with the being of the Godhead.'[51] This much is true because neither the attributes nor the persons are accidental properties. God is non-composite (i.e., divine simplicity).

However, Van Til then adds that if each person is coterminous with the being of God, and if there is only one God, then each person must also be coinherent with the other persons.[52] An immediate problem arises when we see this parallel drawn, however, because in orthodox trinitarian theology, the three persons are not related to one another in exactly the same way that the attributes are related to one another. If they were, Christians could not be trinitarians.

As Francis Turretin explains, 'The attributes of God cannot really differ from his essence or from one another (as one thing from another) because God is most simple and perfect.'[53] Unlike each of the divine attributes,

---

he would be affirming nonsense. But as we have already observed in connection with his language about 'knowledge,' equivocal language introduces incoherence into these doctrines. A much wiser (and clearer) alternative is to use *different* words when referring to *different* things.

50. The church has also always affirmed the divine attributes of knowledge, volition, etc., all of which are attributes that do not describe an impersonal force.

51. Van Til, *An Introduction to Systematic Theology*, 363-64.

52. Ibid., 364.

53. Francis Turretin, *Institutes of Elenctic Theology*, 3 vols., trans. George Musgrave Giger, ed. James T. Dennison, Jr. (Phillipsburg: P&R Publishing Company, 1992–1997), 1:188; cf. also Petrus van Mastricht, *Theoretical–Practical Theology*, vol. 2, *Faith in the Triune God*, trans. Todd M. Rester, ed. Joel R. Beeke (Grand Rapids: Reformation Heritage Books, 2019), 116-117.

however, each of the three persons has 'an incommunicable property.'[54] Turretin is referring here to the personal properties of the three persons. In other words, he is reminding us that only the Father is eternally unbegotten and eternally begets. Only the Son is eternally begotten. Only the Holy Spirit eternally proceeds from the Father and the Son. These personal properties are distinguished from the essential properties of God. If the essential properties of the divine *ousia* are confused with the personal properties, we will not be able to affirm that the eternally begotten Son is *homoousios* with the eternally unbegotten Father.

Each of the three persons is the one divine *ousia*, but each of the three persons is the one divine *ousia* in a particular manner of subsistence. The Father eternally is the numerically one divine *ousia* in an eternally unbegotten and eternally begetting manner of subsistence. The Son eternally is the numerically one divine *ousia* in an eternally begotten manner of subsistence. The Holy Spirit eternally is the numerically one divine *ousia* in an eternally proceeding manner of subsistence. The divine attributes, on the other hand, are not the one divine *ousia* in different manners of subsistence defined in terms of unique personal properties. If we relate the three persons to one another in exactly the same way that the attributes are related to one another, we lose the distinction between the persons.[55]

In addition, the mutual indwelling (*perichoresis*) of the three persons does not destroy or blur the personal properties or the personal distinctions.[56] Turretin explains that if we confuse the persons and the essence, the result will either be monopersonalism or tritheism – one person or three essences.[57] He observes: 'If three persons in human

---

54. Ibid., 1:265.

55. For a helpful discussion of the technical terminology, see James Dolezal, 'Trinity, Simplicity and the Status of God's Personal Relations,' *International Journal of Systematic Theology* 16, no. 1 (Jan. 2014): 79-98.

56. I am not implying that Van Til says that the perichoresis destroys the personal properties. He affirms that God is three persons and affirms the personal properties. If he rejected the personal properties and any threeness in the Godhead, it would destroy his entire claim about the epistemological significance of God being one *and many*. What I am saying is that Van Til's language about the Trinity being 'one person' and 'three persons' is a case of theological equivocation, and since equivocation is incoherent, it always leads to doctrinal errors of one kind or another.

57. Turretin, *Institutes of Elenctic Theology*, 1:266.

things indicate three men, we ought [not] to infer that in divine things three persons are three Gods; or that the unity of the divine essence implies also a unity of person (as Socinus wishes).'[58]

If we assert that each of the persons is 'coterminous with the being of the Godhead' and if by that we mean that each of the persons shares in the same divine attributes or essential properties, then we are simply affirming that each person is God and that each person is *homoousios* with the other persons. That is part of classical Christian trinitarianism. However, if we say that each of the persons is 'coterminous with the being of the Godhead' and if by that we mean that they are also *exhaustively* coterminous with each other, there is a distinct danger of forgetting the personal properties or confusing the personal properties with the essential properties.

To say that the Son is *exhaustively* coterminous with the Father, for example, without distinguishing between essential properties and personal properties, would imply that the Son shares not only all of the essential properties of the Father (*homoousios*) but that he also shares the personal property of the Father, his 'eternal unbegottenness and eternal begetting.'[59] The danger is that we subtly shift from affirming the orthodox *homoousios* to affirming a heretical *homohypostasis*, effectively eliminating the distinction among the three persons and becoming unitarians in the process.

Formulating the precise boundaries of trinitarian orthodoxy took centuries, and one of the most important gains that was made in the fourth century was the realization that the church cannot use the same word to speak of what is one in God and what is three in God. The church discovered that such equivocation was a recipe for theological disaster.[60] A distinction had to be made between *ousia* and *hypostasis*. To assert that God is one person and that God is three persons, as Van Til does, is to reintroduce dangerously confusing language into the church. A wiser course would be to follow Zacharius Ursinus who wrote with

---

58. Ibid., 1:182.

59. It was the confusion of personal properties and essential properties that led Eunomius into heresy. He defined the divine *ousia* in terms of the personal property of unbegottenness. Given that definition, he concluded that the Son cannot be *homoousios* with the Father.

60. For a helpful overview of the fourth century trinitarian debates and the resulting trinitarian theology, see Lewis Ayres, *Nicaea and its Legacy: An Approach to Fourth–Century Trinitarian Theology* (Oxford: Oxford University Press 2004).

regard to the traditional trinitarian formulation: 'We, however, correctly retain the form of speech used by the church in her early and purer days, by holding fast to these terms.'[61]

It is highly ironic that Van Tillian scholars will defend Van Til for his departure from orthodox usage of Trinitarian terminology, while criticizing Gordon Clark for doing something very similar with his doctrine of Christ. The historically orthodox formulation established at the Councils of Ephesus and Chalcedon and taught in the Reformed confessions is that Christ is one person with two natures (Belgic Confession, Art. 19; WCF 8.2). Clark, however, asserts that Christ is 'two persons.' Van Tillian scholars are rightly very critical of Clark's formulation. Scott Oliphint, for example, says that by defining Christ as 'two persons,' Clark was critical of 'the entirety of historic, orthodox Christology, both Catholic and Protestant.'[62] But Van Tillian scholars will defend Van Til's 'one person and three persons' trinitarianism even though it too departs from the entirety of historic, orthodox Trinitarianism, both Catholic and Protestant. Similarly, the Clarkian, John W. Robbins, says that Van Til's 'one person and three persons' doctrine is a 'radically new heresy.'[63] But Robbins had no hesitation about defending Clark's 'two person' Christology. Those who are neither Clarkians nor Van Tillians are seriously concerned with both of these departures from the language and theology of the Reformed confessions and from historic Christian orthodoxy.

For decades, Van Tillians have defended Van Til's formulation and offered explanations of how it can be read in an orthodox sense, but even if we grant that Van Til intended it in an orthodox sense, no confessionally Reformed Christian should have ever defended it. Confessionally Reformed Van Tillians should have simply acknowledged that Van Til is a fallible human being. They could have explained that although he meant his language in an orthodox sense, the formula itself inevitably creates such confusion about Christianity's most foundational doctrine that it must be rejected. Good intentions are not an excuse for teaching dangerously false doctrines.

---

61. Zacharias Ursinus, *The Commentary on the Heidelberg Catechism*, trans. G. W. Willard (Phillipsburg, NJ: Presbyterian and Reformed Publishing Company, n.d.), 132.

62. K. Scott Oliphint, foreword to Van Til, *Common Grace and the Gospel*, xxvi, note 20.

63. John W. Robbins, *Cornelius Van Til: The Man and the Myth* (Jefferson, MD: The Trinity Foundation, 1986), 20.

Van Til's novel doctrine of the Trinity should certainly *never* under any circumstances be preached or taught to Christ's sheep in the pews. To go before Christian laymen and proclaim that God is 'one person' and 'three persons' is to speak in inherently ambiguous and confusing language. Such teaching will inevitably cause some of Christ's little ones to stumble into heresy. Christian ministers and theologians have a weighty responsibility to our Lord Jesus Christ for the care of his sheep. We do not show care for Christ's sheep by taking a doctrine that is already a difficult mystery and reformulating it in such a way that will lead his little ones to heretical conclusions about it.

Van Til's 'one person and three persons' doctrine adds nothing of any worth to trinitarian theology. It does not 'supplement' orthodox trinitarianism. It distorts it. It is just as serious a distortion of the Christian doctrine of God as the 'correlativist' view taught by some of his disciples. This theological novelty is unnecessary, equivocal, and positively harmful to the church and to the little ones in the church. Proclaiming this doctrine in the church *will* cause these little ones to stumble, and those who continue to proclaim it *will* be responsible. Attempts to justify this doctrine should stop. Our Reformed confessional formulation, found in chapter 2 of the Westminster Confession of Faith, is already both biblical and sufficient. It already denies that God is an impersonal force. It already provides boundaries against both tri-theism and Sabellianism. The orthodox doctrine of the Trinity simply does not need to be recast.

## Conclusion

The theological concerns addressed in this chapter cannot be said by any confessionally Reformed Christian to be insignificant. Van Til's condemnation of the early Reformed theologians as compromisers of Reformed doctrine has serious ramifications for our very definition of Reformed theology. Van Til's stated lifelong goal was to develop an apologetic methodology consistent with Reformed theology, but if the early Reformed theologians who helped codify Reformed theology in its ecclesiastical confessions of faith are condemned as doctrinal compromisers, then what exactly is the 'Reformed theology' with which our apologetic methodology must be consistent? Is Van Til really developing an apologetic method consistent with Reformed theology, or is he revising Reformed theology to make it fit with his apologetic methodology? The latter very much appears to be the case.

Van Til's doctrine of the antithesis also raises concerns because it lays bare an inconsistency at the very heart of his entire system of apologetic thought. Van Til's claim that the method of presupposition is the only biblically faithful method of apologetics has been the source of bitter disagreement among Reformed Christians for decades, but the case Van Til makes for the method of presupposition depends entirely on the doctrine of an absolute antithesis. Van Til's own qualifications of the absolute antithesis, however, undermine the foundation for the exclusive claims he makes for his apologetic method.

If the absolute antithesis is qualified, as it is by Van Til, to the extent that unbelievers can have knowledge of facts, the main reason for his condemnation of traditional apologetics and the main support for his own apologetic method is removed. Given the fact that Van Til's system of thought 1) replants an unbiblical idealist theory of knowledge into Reformed soil, 2) is contradicted by Scripture's own epistemology, 3) is not observed in any apologetic encounters described in Scripture, 4) implies that his novel apologetic methodology should be the standard by which true Reformed theology is defined, and 5) has an internally compromised foundation, there is no good reason for any biblically faithful and confessionally Reformed Christian to embrace it.

Van Til's doctrine of the Trinity should also raise serious concerns among confessionally Reformed Christians. Whatever may have been Van Til's motive, when he asserted that God is 'three persons,' and then also affirmed that God is 'one person,' he created a very serious theological problem in the Reformed churches because so many of his students are determined to defend him on this point. The doctrine of God is the most important doctrine in Christian theology. It impacts every other doctrine. A change in the doctrine of God changes every other Christian doctrine in one way or another. This is why revisionary doctrines of the attributes of God are so consequential. The same is true with revisionary doctrines of the Trinity.

Van Til's 'one person and three persons' doctrine of the Trinity is unbiblical, contrary to our ancient creeds, contrary to our Reformed confessions of faith, and it seriously endangers the souls of Christ's sheep whenever and wherever it is taught. It strikes at the vitals of the historic

Christian faith as much as a 'one nature and three natures' doctrine of the Trinity would. Of all the concerns there are with Van Til's system of thought, those related to his doctrine of the Trinity are by far the most serious. Regardless of how much Van Til was loved and admired by his students, he was neither a prophet nor an apostle. He was not infallible, and his writings are not inspired. Our love for Jesus Christ and his sheep must outweigh any love we have for any human teacher if and when that teacher makes such an egregious theological error. Biblical truth and faithfulness to the Lord Jesus is infinitely more important than party loyalty. We should not be recasting Reformed theology to conform to Van Til, and we should not be recasting Trinitarian orthodoxy to conform to Van Til. Van Til is not the Christian rule of faith.

# CHAPTER 9

# Historical Concerns

Cornelius Van Til was not a historian, but historical claims of various kinds are an important part of the case he makes for his apologetic system of thought. Van Til, for example, views the entire history of philosophy as the story of fallen man's attempts to create a system of knowledge based on autonomous human thought. As he explains, 'From the ancient Greeks to the present time, philosophy in general has worked upon the assumption that the mind of man can act independently of God.'[1] In a similar vein, Van Til sees the entire history of traditional Christian apologetics as a history of attempts to blend the Christian system of thought with autonomous Greek systems of thought. This created in Roman Catholicism 'a theism in which the God of Christianity and the God of Greek philosophy, particularly the Unmoved Mover of Aristotle, are ground together into a common mixture.'[2]

In Van Til's telling of the history of Christian theology, Thomas Aquinas is the primary example of Roman Catholic scholasticism (i.e., synthesis thinking). On the other hand, John Calvin was the first theologian to free himself from the synthesis thinking of scholasticism. He becomes the primary example of a pure biblical worldview. Calvin, 'alone of all the Reformers could rid himself of the last remnants of Platonic reasoning.'[3] The generation of theologians following Calvin,

---

1. Van Til, *Psychology of Religion*, 11.

2. Van Til, 'Defending the Faith,' in Cornelius Van Til and Eric H. Sigward, *The Articles of Cornelius Van Til*, Electronic ed. (Labels Army Company: New York, 1997).

3. Van Til, *Survey of Christian Epistemology*, 96.

however, returned the Reformed church to synthesis thinking.[4] According to Van Til, then, the Reformed scholastic theologians effectively betrayed Calvin's reformation by returning the Reformed churches to scholasticism. Post-reformation apologetics has followed in the footsteps of Thomas Aquinas and has adopted scholastic synthesis thinking. All of these historical claims set the stage for Van Til's appeal to adopt the apologetic method of presupposition.

Van Til's historical claims raise concerns primarily due to their many inaccuracies. There is no other way to put it. Van Til's representation of numerous historical facts and figures is simply false. To begin with, he engages in overly generalized surveys of the history of philosophy, apologetics, and theology. He, therefore, tends to lump a wide variety of thinkers into grossly oversimplistic categories. Second, in the case of several of the historical figures he discusses at length, there is little evidence that he has seriously engaged with any primary sources. His knowledge of Thomas Aquinas, for example, appears to be heavily dependent on secondary sources, and as we have already noted, he rarely even mentions any of the Reformed scholastic theologians, much less seriously engages with their exegetical and theological arguments.[5] All of this results in repeated misrepresentations and distortions of various historical figures.

This continual misrepresentation of historical figures is a concern for a number of reasons. In the first place, integrity requires that we make every attempt to represent accurately those with whom we are engaging. If we create strawmen deliberately, we are guilty of violating the ninth commandment. I do not believe Van Til was guilty of deliberate deception, but even if such misrepresentation is not deliberate, it reveals a dramatic lowering of the academic standards set by the theologians of Old Princeton. Regardless of what one thinks about B. B. Warfield or J. Gresham Machen, it is impossible to deny that they did their homework. They researched the primary sources. They did not create strawman arguments. Westminster Theological Seminary was founded

---

4. Van Til, 'Herman Dooyeweerd and Reformed Apologetics,' in Cornelius Van Til and Eric H. Sigward, *The Pamphlets, Tracts, and Offprints of Cornelius Van Til*, Electronic ed. (Labels Army Company: New York, 1997).

5. Van Til understands the importance of historical surveys. See, for example, his comments in his *Survey of Christian Epistemology*, xiii. The problem is that his own historical surveys distort history rather than surveying it.

to carry on the theological and academic legacy of Old Princeton. Van Til's historical claims repeatedly fail to measure up to the academic legacy of those Princetonian predecessors.

These continual misrepresentations are also significant because they are used by Van Til to support the case he makes for his specific apologetic system of thought. To the extent that his case rests upon false or distorted historical claims, that case is weakened. Recall how important Van Til's representation of medieval scholasticism and the theology of Thomas Aquinas is to his overall case. Recall how important his representation of John Calvin and the Reformed Scholastics is to his case. His representations of these figures play a major role in the way he defines 'Reformed' theology, and it is this definition of Reformed theology that he is using as a standard to measure the consistency of any apologetic methodology. To the extent that he misrepresents Thomas Aquinas, or John Calvin, or the Reformed Scholastics, he weakens important links in his case for presuppositional apologetics.

## Over Generalization

Van Til readily admitted that he was guilty in his writing of over generalizing. He says, 'One of my great faults has been to deal with very general and basic thrusts of a movement without giving adequate attention to details.'[6] Van Til understood that this was a fault, but what he perhaps did not clearly grasp is that his over generalizing often distorted the facts. Regarding the history of philosophy, for example, William Edgar explains that Van Til 'asserts that there is basically no difference in the types of unbelief since the earliest times. All philosophy suffers from the dilemma of Heraclitus against Parmenides.'[7] Similarly, Van Til lumps all forms of apologetic methodologies that differ from his own under the category of 'traditional apologetics.'[8] This allows Van Til to put everyone from Thomas Aquinas, to Bishop Butler, to B. B. Warfield into the same apologetic category.

The problem is that such over generalization distorts the truth. Consider the following statement as an illustration: 'There are only two

---

6. E. R. Geehan, ed., *Jerusalem and Athens*, 319-20.

7. William Edgar, 'Two Christian Warriors: Cornelius Van Til and Francis Schaeffer Compared,' *Westminster Theological Journal* 57, no. 1 (Spring 1995): 70.

8. E.g., Van Til, *The Defense of the Faith*, 340.

types of beings in existence: dogs and non-dogs.' In a very trivial sense this is a true statement, but the category of 'non-dogs' is such an over-generalized category that it serves almost no purpose. The category of beings in existence that are 'non-dogs' includes God, galaxies, humans, fish, elephants, trees, granite, and electrons. All of these, and many more, existing beings do have in common the fact that they are not dogs, but the assertion borders on the absurdly irrelevant.

The difference between God and everything else in the 'non-dogs' category alone is enough to show that it creates a distorted view of the facts. We cannot say, based on this distinction, that God and fish are 'basically' the same kind of existing beings. Similarly, when Van Til asserts that all forms of unbelief are basically the same and that all forms of non-Van Tillian apologetics are basically the same, he distorts the truth by glossing over the important differences.

Van Til credits Herman Dooyeweerd for his understanding of the history of philosophy as a history of synthesis thinking.[9] If this is so, then it is an example of the problems that occur when one depends too much on secondary sources. It is well beyond the scope of this book to provide a survey of the history of philosophy, but a reading of the works of the pre-Socratics, Plato, Aristotle, Sextus Empiricus, Plotinus, Proclus, Augustine, Boethius, Anselm, Aquinas, William of Ockham, Bacon, Descartes, Spinoza, Leibniz, Hobbes, Locke, Berkeley, Hume, Kant, Fichte, Schelling, Hegel, Kierkegaard, Nietzsche, etc., immediately reveals that Van Til's claim that there are basically only two philosophical standpoints borders on the absurd.[10]

There are significant and meaningful differences between realists and nominalists, between rationalists and empiricists, between idealists and materialists. There are as many differences among unbelieving philosophers as there are among non-dogs. It is certainly true that the most important difference among human beings is the difference between believers and unbelievers, but among both types of human

---

9. Van Til, *Christianity in Conflict*, in Cornelius Van Til and Eric H. Sigward, *The Pamphlets, Tracts, and Offprints of Cornelius Van Til*, Electronic ed. (Labels Army Company: New York, 1997); cf. also Van Til, *An Introduction to Systematic Theology*, 13.

10. For a helpful survey of the history of philosophy that does not ignore the important differences among the various individual philosophers, see Frederick Copleston, *History of Philosophy*, 9 vols. (New York: Doubleday, 1946–1975).

beings important differences remain. Even among believers, for example, Paul will say in one place that in Christ 'there is no male and female' (Gal. 3:28), but we do not conclude from this that there is 'basically no difference' between men and women (1 Cor. 11:2-16).

It is also important that we do not oversimplify the history of apologetics. It seriously distorts the truth to lump every non-Van Tillian into the 'Thomistic-Butler' category of apologetic method.[11] Van Til's 'Thomistic-Butler' category is a 'non-dogs' category. It is grossly over-simplified and profoundly unhelpful. Apologetics has developed over the centuries as the kinds of challenges and attacks against Christianity have changed. The earliest Christian apologists were dealing with Jewish and Roman persecution. Their apologetic works often address those in political power in an attempt to clear Christians of the slanderous charges that were being made (e.g., cannibalism). Medieval apologetic works often addressed pagans and Muslims and Jews. During the early Enlightenment era, apologists had to address new skeptical and rationalist claims. Apologists like Bishop Butler addressed the deists. It is misleading to categorize all apologetics as either Van Tillian or non-Van Tillian and then describe non-Van Tillian traditional apologetics as the 'Thomistic-Butler' method when even Thomas and Butler are very different from each other.[12]

## Misrepresenting Scholasticism

One of the most frequently encountered words in Van Til's writings is 'scholasticism.' For Van Til, 'scholasticism' is synonymous with what he calls 'synthesis thinking.' The principle of scholasticism is 'commingling Aristotelianism with Christian principles.'[13] Van Til explains, 'The scholastic idea is based on the conviction that the method of finding truth advocated by Aristotle and the method of finding truth advocated by Christianity can be brought into a synthesis.'[14] Throughout Van Til's writings, scholasticism is the term he uses to describe the flawed

---

11. E.g., Geehan, *Jerusalem and Athens*, 90.

12. For a helpful survey that looks closely at the differences among apologists over the centuries, see Benjamin K. Forrest, Joshua D. Chatraw, and Alister E. McGrath, eds., *The History of Apologetics: A Biographical and Methodological Introduction* (Grand Rapids: Zondervan Academic, 2020).

13. Van Til, *An Introduction to Systematic Theology*, 94.

14. Van Til, *The Defense of the Faith*, 286.

epistemology of the Roman Catholic Church. The word has become, in the minds of many Van Tillians, a catch-all term for everything we should avoid in theology and apologetics.[15]

The problem is that Van Til is using the wrong word to describe the phenomenon of 'synthesis thinking.' The word he is looking for is 'syncretism.' The word 'scholasticism,' on the other hand, refers to an academic *method* of doing theology.[16] It is a method adapted to the schools (*school*-asticism).[17] With sufficient evidence, it is certainly possible to build a case that a particular scholastic theologian was a syncretist who engaged in 'synthesis thinking,' but the word 'scholasticism' is not synonymous with syncretism.[18] Willem van Asselt rightly observes that scholasticism 'should not so much be associated with content but with method, an academic form of argumentation and disputation.'[19]

Not only was scholasticism not necessarily tied to any particular theological content, it was also not limited to one particular genre of writing. Dolf te Velde explains that 'various genres of writing existed in early modern scholasticism.'[20] He mentions the disputation, *Loci communes*, doctrinal digressions, manuals, and treatises.[21] All of these genres of scholastic writing shared certain features:

15. See, for example, John Frame, 'Scholasticism for Evangelicals: Thoughts on All That is in God by James Dolezal,' in *On Theology: Explorations and Controversies*, ed. John M. Frame (Bellingham, WA: Lexham Press, 2023), 101-117. For my response, see Mathison, 'Unlatched Theism: An Examination of John Frame's Response to *All That is in God*' at Tabletalk Online: https://tabletalkmagazine.com/posts/unlatched-theism-an-examination-of-john-frames-response-to-all-that-is-in-god/

16. See Richard A. Muller, *After Calvin: Studies in the Development of a Theological Tradition* (Oxford: Oxford University Press, 2003), 26; cf. also Ryan McGraw, *Reformed Scholasticism: Recovering the Tools of Reformed Theology* (London: T&T Clark, 2019), 3.

17. David C. Steinmetz, 'The Scholastic Calvin,' in *Protestant Scholasticism: Essays in Reassessment*, eds. Carl R. Trueman and R. Scott Clark (Eugene, OR: Wipf & Stock, 2005), 19.

18. The Reformed scholastic theologians in the transitional phase of high orthodoxy (*ca.* 1685–1725) and in the period of late orthodoxy (after 1725), for example, began to be more and more influenced by rationalist philosophy. See Richard A. Muller, *Post-Reformation Reformed Dogmatics*, vol. 1, *Prolegomena to Theology*, 2nd ed. (Grand Rapids: Baker Academic, 2003), 81-84.

19. Willem J. van Asselt, *Introduction to Reformed Scholasticism*, trans. Albert Gootjes (Grand Rapids: Reformation Heritage Books, 2011), 1.

20. Dolf te Velde, 'Introduction' to *Synopsis Purioris Theologiae = Synopsis of a Purer Theology*. Vol. 1, *Disputations 1–23* by Johannes Polyander, Johannes, Antonius Walaeus, Antonius Thysius, and Andreas Rivetus, trans. Riemer A. Faber (Leiden: Brill, 2015), 3.

21. Ibid., 3-4.

... a clear demarcation of the topic under discussion; a keen interest in definitions; a comprehensive treatment of relevant aspects by means of a topical structure; frequent usage of distinctions, partly to anticipate a treatment of the subject's various elements, partly to solve difficulties that are implied in the initial, undifferentiated statement; explicit statements of proofs and arguments supporting one's own position, and a corresponding refutation of counter-arguments.[22]

This is what scholasticism was. It was a method used to teach in the context of a school. Conflating the definitions of 'scholasticism' and 'syncretism,' as Van Til does, is historically inaccurate and unnecessarily confusing to students.

## Misrepresenting Thomas Aquinas

As mentioned above, in Van Til's retelling of the history of Christian theology and the history of philosophy, Thomas Aquinas becomes the primary example of Roman Catholic 'synthesis thinking.'[23] Van Til, for example, argues that Aquinas adopts the Aristotelian notion of the analogy of being.[24] His adoption of this Aristotelian principle, according to Van Til, then leads Aquinas to treat 'being' in such a way that the Creator-creature distinction is erased. As Van Til explains, 'Following Aristotle, Thomas Aquinas talks about *being* as such *before* making the distinction between the divine and created being. And this is fatal to Christian theology. It constitutes an attack on the basic distinction between God as self-contained and man as his creature.'[25] This synthesis of Aristotle and Christianity which destroys the Creator-creature distinction, is the fundamental problem Van Til discerns in medieval Roman Catholic philosophy. It is embodied, according to Van Til, most fully in the theology of Thomas Aquinas.

There is a problem, however, with Van Til's explanation of Aquinas' teaching on the Creator-creature distinction. The problem is that Van Til's explanation is demonstrably false.[26] There is nothing more

---

22. Ibid., 4.

23. E.g., Van Til, *Christian Apologetics*, 31.

24. Van Til, *Survey of Christian Epistemology*, 60.

25. Van Til, *Introduction to Systematic Theology*, 200.

26. Van Til also misunderstands Aquinas' doctrine of analogy, but that complex issue is beyond the scope of this work. For helpful discussions of what Aquinas

fundamental to Aquinas' theology than the metaphysical distinction between God and his creatures. This doctrine is emphasized by Aquinas throughout his career. It is taught in his early work *On Being and Essence*, for example, when Aquinas explains that God's being 'is being *distinct from* all other being.'[27] In his later work *On the Power of God*, Aquinas again emphasizes this basic point, saying, 'God's being which is his essence is not universal being, but being *distinct from* all other being: so that by his very being God is *distinct from* every other being.'[28] In the same work, he adds, 'God's relation to being is *different from* that of any creature's; for he is his own being, which cannot be said of any creature.'[29] In the *Summa Contra Gentiles*, Aquinas repeats the same idea, saying that God's 'being is *distinct from* all others.'[30]

---

teaches on the subject of analogy and the debates among Roman Catholics about his teaching, see Tommaso de Vio Cajetan, *The Analogy of Names, and the Concept of Being*, trans. Edward A. Bushinski (Eugene, OR: Wipf & Stock, 1953); Ralph McInerny, *Aquinas on Analogy* (Washington, D.C.: Catholic University of America Press, 1996); John F. Wippel, *The Metaphysical Thought of Thomas Aquinas* (Washington, D.C.: Catholic University of America Press, 2000), 501-75; John R. Mortensen, *Understanding St. Thomas on Analogy* (Rome: Aquinas Institute for the Study of Sacred Doctrine, 2006); Steven A. Long, *Analogia Entis* (Notre Dame: University of Notre Dame Press, 2011); Gyula Klima, 'Theory of Language,' in *The Oxford Handbook of Aquinas*, eds. Brian Davies and Eleonore Stump (Oxford: Oxford University Press, 2012), 379-85.

27. Thomas Aquinas, *On Being and Essence*, rev. ed., trans. Armand Maurer (Toronto: The Pontifical Institute of Mediaeval Studies, 1968), 61. Emphasis mine. Original Latin: Nec oportet, si dicimus quod Deus est esse tantum, ut in illorum errorem incidamus qui Deum dixerunt esse illud esse universale quo quaelibet res formaliter est. Hoc enim esse quod Deus est huius condicionis est ut nulla sibi additio fieri possit, unde per ipsam suam puritatem *est esse distinctum ab omni esse*.

28. Thomas Aquinas, *On the Power of God*, Third Book, trans. English Dominican Fathers (London: Burns Oates & Washbourne, 1932), Q. 7, art. 2, ad. 4. Emphasis mine. Original Latin: Ad quartum dicendum, quod esse divinum, quod est eius substantia, non est esse commune, sed est esse distinctum a quolibet alio esse. Unde per ipsum suum esse Deus differt a quolibet alio ente.

29. Thomas Aquinas, *On the Power of God*, Third Book, Q. 7, art. 7, *respondeo*. Emphasis mine. Original Latin: Deus autem alio modo se habet ad esse quam aliqua alia creatura; nam ipse est suum esse, quod nulli alii creaturae competit.

30. Thomas Aquinas, *Summa Contra Gentiles*, Latin/English Edition of the Works of St. Thomas Aquinas, vols. 11–12, trans. Fr. Laurence Shapcote, O.P., ed. John Mortensen and Enrique Alarcón (Green Bay, WI: Aquinas Institute, 2018), I, 26. Emphasis mine. Original Latin: Unde ex hoc ipso quod additionem, non recipit nec recipere potest, magis concludi potest quod Deus non sit esse commune, sed proprium: etiam ex hoc ipso *suum esse ab omnibus aliis distinguitur* quod nihil ei addi potest.

According to Thomas, God's being is distinct from creaturely being in many ways. God's being, for example, is pure act.[31] All creaturely being is a combination of potency and act. God's being is simple, but all creaturely being is composite. Aquinas says much more, but the basic point is clear. The distinction between God and his creation is foundational to Aquinas' entire discussion of the proofs for God's existence as well as to his entire discussion of God's attributes. It is an indispensable assumption of his entire theological system. And yet, despite his repeated affirmations of the distinction between the Creator and the creature, Van Til claims that Aquinas denies it.

It is important for us to understand why Van Til's misrepresentation of Aquinas is a problem. In the first place, again, simple academic integrity and honesty compel us to make every effort to accurately state the views of those with whom we disagree. Van Tillians have long complained about those early critics of Van Til who charged him with pantheism, but why did they complain? Because Van Til repeatedly teaches the metaphysical distinction between the Creator and his creatures. As difficult as he can be to interpret, the clear and repeated affirmations of the Creator-creature distinction rule out any pantheistic interpretation of Van Til's works. Should not the same principle of charitable interpretation be applied to Aquinas given his clear and repeated affirmations of the Creator-creature distinction and given the fundamental importance of that distinction to his entire theological system?[32] Of course it should, and it is deceitful to do otherwise.

---

31. Thomas Aquinas, *Summa Theologiae*, Latin/English Edition of the Works of St. Thomas Aquinas, vols. 13–20, trans. Fr. Laurence Shapcote, O.P., ed. John Mortensen and Enrique Alarcón (Lander, WY: Aquinas Institute, 2012), Ia, Q. 3, A. 2, *respondeo*.

32. Van Til's own misrepresentations of Aquinas appear to be due to a lack of familiarity with the primary sources. On a number of occasions, for example, Van Til cites the work of Arthur Lovejoy rather than Aquinas himself when describing Aquinas' teaching. See, Van Til, introduction to B. B. Warfield, *The Inspiration and Authority of the Bible*, 53-54; cf. also Van Til, 'Confessing Jesus Christ,' in *Scripture and Confession*, ed. John H. Skilton (Phillipsburg: Presbyterian and Reformed Publishing Co., 1973), 236. There was no excuse for this misrepresentation of Aquinas in Van Til's case, and there is no excuse for Van Tillians to continue the misrepresentation. It betrays a lack of academic integrity, and it is intellectually irresponsible. It is also the case that such misrepresentations no longer go unnoticed. See, for example, Richard A. Muller's review of K. Scott Oliphint's book on Aquinas, 'Reading Aquinas from a Reformed Perspective: A Review Essay,' *Calvin Theological Journal* 53, no. 2 (Nov 2018): 255-88. In his book, Oliphint repeated Van Til's demonstrably false claims about Aquinas' doctrine, and those false claims were publicly exposed in Muller's review.

Van Til's misrepresentation of Aquinas on the Creator-creature distinction is also important because it leads him to say that the Roman Catholic God and the Christian God are completely different Gods. If Aquinas and Rome eliminate the Creator-creature distinction, their God is inherently pantheistic. This creates problems for Reformed Christians, however, because the early Reformed theologians appropriated the existing late medieval doctrine of God from Rome. The Roman Catholic doctrine of God was not one of the points of doctrine that they rejected or reformed. If we are convinced that the Roman Catholic God is inherently pantheistic, then our own early Reformed theologians are condemned as well. Given that they are the men who wrote our Reformed confessions, we have a serious problem if we adopt Van Til's reading of history. Our problem is that we will have to reject the doctrine of God found in the Reformed Confessions written by these Reformed theologians.[33]

We have to remember that the Reformation was just that, a 'reformation.' It was an attempt to reform the faith and worship of the existing late medieval Roman Catholic Church. The early Reformed theologians were not a part of the so-called 'radical Reformation.' They were not restorationists. They did not throw out everything and attempt to start from scratch. They did not do with the doctrine of God what the Socinians did, becoming heretics in the process. They critically appropriated the theological works of theologians such as Thomas Aquinas.[34] They kept what was biblical (e.g., the doctrine of the Trinity, the doctrine of the hypostatic union), corrected that which had been severely distorted (e.g., the doctrine of justification, the doctrine of the sacraments), and threw out what was completely contrary to Scripture (e.g., the doctrine of the papacy, the doctrine of Mary).[35] They were able to be selective in their critical appropriation because they did not

---

33. As explained in chapter 8, rejecting the doctrine of God found in the Westminster Confession is precisely what John Frame is doing with the attributes of God and what Van Til did with his 'one person and three persons' trinitarian formulation.

34. See, for example, Matthew Levering and Marcus Plested, eds., *The Oxford Handbook of the Reception of Aquinas* (Oxford: Oxford University Press, 2021), especially chapters 9 and 14; cf. also Manfred Svensson and David VanDrunen, eds., *Aquinas Among the Protestants* (Chichester: Wiley Blackwell, 2018).

35. This is why treating Thomas Aquinas in an all-or-nothing manner is unhelpful. To go all in on Aquinas requires that one become Roman Catholic. To reject all that Aquinas taught (e.g., the Trinity, the deity of Christ, etc.) requires that one become a heretic.

subscribe to a replanted idealist theory of truth that forced them to treat every system in an all or nothing manner.

## Misrepresenting Calvin and the Calvinists

When we turn our attention away from Thomas Aquinas and toward Van Til's treatment of the Reformer John Calvin, we immediately notice a much greater sympathy. In Van Til's telling of the story, Calvin is the hero. In one place, for example, Van Til writes:

> … it is upon the development of these teachings of Calvin that we must depend for a consistent Christian epistemology. Calvin did not mix the categories of the temporal and eternal. He did not succumb to the temptation of giving man a false independence in the work of salvation. Hence he alone of all the Reformers could rid himself of the last remnants of Platonic reasoning.[36]

As Van Til puts it in his ThM thesis: 'Calvin is the never to be forgotten originator of the Reformed churches and in what a marvelous fashion was he true to that principle!'[37]

Despite his strong admiration for Calvin, Van Til misrepresents him on some points. In his *Institutes of the Christian Religion*, for example, Calvin makes an important distinction between the unbeliever's knowledge of earthly things and his knowledge of heavenly things. After discussing the effects of the fall on human beings, Calvin explains that fallen man has true, albeit clouded, knowledge of earthly things. Calvin then moves to a discussion of what fallen man can know about heavenly things. Here his answer is different.

> We must now explain what the power of human reason is, in regard to the kingdom of God, and spiritual discernments which consists chiefly of three things – the knowledge of God, the knowledge of his paternal favour towards us, which constitutes our salvation, and the method of regulating of our conduct in accordance with the Divine Law. With regard to the former two, but more properly the second, men otherwise the most ingenious are blinder than moles.[38]

---

36. Van Til, *Survey of Christian Epistemology*, 96.

37. Cornelius Van Til, 'Reformed Epistemology,' ThM thesis, Princeton Theological Seminary, 1925, in Cornelius Van Til and Eric H. Sigward, *Unpublished Manuscripts of Cornelius Van Til*, Electronic ed. (Labels Army Company: New York, 1997).

38. John Calvin, *Institutes of the Christian Religion*, trans. Henry Beveridge (Peabody, MA: Hendrickson Publishers, 2008), II.2.18.

According to Calvin, then, fallen man can have true knowledge of earthly things, but with regard to the knowledge of God's paternal favor toward us, fallen men are 'blinder than moles.'

Van Til surely has this passage in mind when he writes the following: 'Even Calvin, though by his doctrine of "common grace" he was in a much better position to do justice to the knowledge of non-Christian science without succumbing to it than others were, *did not bring out with sufficient clearness at all times that the natural man is as blind as a mole with respect to natural things as well as with respect to spiritual things.*'[39] Note what Van Til says here. He says that Calvin 'did not bring out' this point about the natural man. Of course, Calvin did not bring this point out, but that is because he denied it altogether. Calvin did not argue that fallen man is 'as blind as a mole with respect to natural things as well as with respect to spiritual things.' Calvin said that fallen man knows earthly things and is 'blind as a mole' with regard to certain heavenly things. Van Til's statement makes it appear as if Calvin asserted something he explicitly denied.

Only a few paragraphs later, Van Til attempts to bring himself and Calvin into closer doctrinal alignment by anachronistically interpreting Calvin as a proto-Van Tillian. He writes, 'The only distinction that will really help us is the one that Calvin developed, namely, that from an ultimate point of view the natural man knows nothing truly, but that from a relative point of view he knows something about all things. He knows all things *after a fashion*, and his fashion is best when he deals with earthly things such as electricity, etc.'[40] That, however, is not a distinction that Calvin developed. It is Van Til's distinction, and he is reading it back into Calvin. Van Til is again misrepresenting Calvin.

---

39. Van Til, *Introduction to Systematic Theology*, 148. Emphasis mine. It is worth observing that this comment about Calvin appears to be a paraphrase of a sentence from Bavinck's *Reformed Dogmatics*. Bavinck writes, 'Calvin too, although because of his theory of common grace he was in a much more favorable position than Luther, did not always succeed in transcending the ancient dualistic dichotomy between natural and supernatural revelation.' See Herman Bavinck, *Reformed Dogmatics*, vol. 1, *Prolegomena*, ed. John Bolt, trans. John Vriend (Grand Rapids: Baker Academic, 2003), 305-06. Both Bavinck and Van Til make their statements in the context of discussing Calvin's *Institutes* 2.2.12-13. The similarity of thought, then, appears to be more than coincidence, but Van Til does not credit Bavinck.

40. Ibid., 150.

Turning to the Reformed Scholastics and their relation to Calvin, we have observed in a previous chapter that Van Til tends to assume that Calvin defined Reformed theology in its purest form and that the next generation of Reformed theologians departed from his pure theology. This is very much a type of the 'Calvin vs. the Calvinists' thesis, and it seriously distorts the truth about both Calvin and the next generation of Reformed theologians. The 'Calvin vs. the Calvinists' thesis has been subjected to intense historical research over the last several decades and has been found to be completely unwarranted. This is acknowledged by contemporary Van Tillians as well as by non-Van Tillians, so it should not remain a source of controversy.[41]

## Misrepresenting Joseph Butler (and Aquinas Again)

One of the historical figures frequently mentioned by Van Til in his writings is the Anglican Bishop and apologist Joseph Butler (1692–1752). Butler is famous for his book, *The Analogy of Religion Natural and Revealed to the Constitution and Course of Nature*. It was originally published in 1736. This book was enormously influential, becoming a standard textbook in prestigious universities. Butler's *Analogy* was written specifically as a response to the deism that had arisen out of the rationalism of the Enlightenment. Deists, such as Lord Herbert of Cherbury (1583–1648) and Matthew Tindal (1657–1733), believed that there is a God who created the universe, but they did not believe in special revelation or miracles. They denied the doctrine of the Trinity and the atonement. For the deists, human reason is sufficient to discover all there is to know about God.

As David McNaughton explains, Butler's strategy is to start with what the deists grant, namely, the existence of a God who designed and created all things, and to use their own methods of reasoning to

---

41. See, for example, Richard A. Muller, 'Calvin and the "Calvinists": Assessing Continuities and Discontinuities Between the Reformation and Orthodoxy: Part One,' *Calvin Theological Journal* 30, no. 2 (Nov 1995): 345-75, and also 'Calvin and the "Calvinists": Assessing Continuities and Discontinuities Between the Reformation and Orthodoxy: Part Two,' *Calvin Theological Journal* 31, no. 1 (Apr 1996): 125-60. Among the Van Tillian scholars who have acknowledged the refutation of this thesis are Richard Gaffin, Moises Silva, and Jeffrey Jue. See K. Scott Oliphint and Lane G. Tipton, eds., *Revelation and Reason: New Essays in Reformed Apologetics* (Phillipsburg: P&R Publishing, 2007), 39, note 55; 75; 174-75.

examine the truth claims of Christianity. His argument is that by using our reason we can discover far more truth than the deists grant.[42] The title of Butler's book is based on the fact that he attempts to argue his case using analogical reasoning. McNaughton explains, 'Arguments by analogy start from a known pattern of events and argue that in a similar but not identical situation, we will find a similar pattern.'[43] Butler, for example, draws analogies between what we know of this present life and what that might mean for a knowledge of a future life. The use of such analogies results in probabilistic arguments. Part I of the *Analogy* is devoted to Natural Religion, namely, to what we can discover through the use of our reason. Part II is devoted to Revealed Religion and attempts to show that there is no good reason for the deists to reject it.[44]

Butler explains, 'Probable evidence is essentially distinguished from demonstrative by this, that it admits of degrees; and of all variety of them, from the highest moral certainty, to the very lowest presumption.'[45] He argues that while God has absolute certainty, for finite creatures, 'probability is the very guide of life.'[46] We all assume, he says, that based on the fact that the sun has risen every morning of our life, it will probably rise again tomorrow morning, and we all act on that likelihood. Butler explains that he plans to apply the principle of analogous argumentation to the subject of religion:

> … my design is to apply it to that subject in general, both natural and revealed: taking for proved, that there is an intelligent Author of Nature, and natural Governor of the World. For as there is no presumption against this prior to the proof of it: so it has been often proved with accumulated evidence; from this argument of analogy and final causes; from abstract reasonings; from the most ancient tradition and testimony; and from the general consent of mankind. Nor does it appear, so far as I can find, to

---

42. David McNaughton, introduction to Joseph Butler, *The Analogy of Religion*, ed. David McNaughton (Oxford: Oxford University Press, 2021), xiv.

43. David McNaughton, 'Joseph Butler' in *The History of Apologetics*, eds. Benjamin K. Forrest, Joshua D. Chatraw, and Alister E. McGrath (Grand Rapids: Zondervan Academic, 2020), 362.

44. Ibid., xv.

45. Joseph Butler, *The Analogy of Religion*, ed. David McNaughton (Oxford: Oxford University Press, 2021), 3.

46. Ibid., 4.

be denied by the generality of those who profess themselves dissatisfied with the evidence of religion.[47]

Notice that Butler is not setting out in the *Analogy* to prove the existence of an intelligent Designer. There is no argument for the existence of God in his work. He is assuming it because it is not denied by the deists to whom his work is directed.

Butler then sets the stage for his argument. He says, 'Let us then … turn our thoughts to what we experience to be the conduct of nature with respect to intelligent creatures; which may be resolved into general laws or rules of administration, in the same way as many of the laws of nature respecting inanimate matter may be collected from experiments.'[48] He then describes the next step: 'let us compare the known constitution and course of things, with what is said to be the moral system of nature; the acknowledged dispensations of providence, or that government which we find ourselves under, with what religion teaches us to believe and expect; and see whether they are not analogous and of a piece.'[49] Butler argues that if we do this we will see that they are analogous and of a piece and therefore 'both may be traced up to the same general laws, and resolved into the same principles of divine conduct.'[50]

There is much more to Butler's work, but I mention all of this because when we look at the way in which Van Til describes Butler's work, we notice a common pattern. In one place, for example, Van Til says, 'Butler followed Thomas …'[51] In another place, Van Til says that the argument of Butler's *Analogy* 'is closely similar to that which is found, for instance, in the *Summa Contra Gentiles* of Thomas Aquinas.'[52] Elsewhere, he writes, 'Bishop Butler's approach to the question of interpretation is to all intents and purposes the same as that of Aquinas.'[53] The problem is

---

47. Ibid., 6.

48. Ibid., 7.

49. Ibid.

50. Ibid.

51. Cornelius Van Til, 'Scripture and Reformed Apologetics,' in *The New Testament Student and Theology,* ed. John H. Skilton (Nutley, NJ: Presbyterian and Reformed, 1976), in Cornelius Van Til and Eric H. Sigward, *The Articles of Cornelius Van Til,* Electronic ed. (Labels Army Company: New York, 1997).

52. Van Til, *Christian Apologetics*, 100.

53. Van Til, *The Protestant Doctrine of Scripture*, 20.

that regardless of one's opinion of Butler's methodology, it is not the same as that of Thomas Aquinas, nor is it 'closely similar.'

Butler's *Analogy* is written specifically as an apologetic text addressing deism, and his methodology is focused on the use of analogies, such as that between the present life and the future life. Butler is attempting to persuade deists to see that given their own starting assumptions about reason they should affirm much more than they have been willing to do. Butler is attempting to show that by the use of reason we can reach a likely conclusion regarding numerous truths that rationalistic deists deny. He is also attempting to show that, contrary to what the deists are saying, there is nothing unjust about the idea of God giving special revelation to some and not to all. His entire argument is shaped by the nature of his intended audience's stated beliefs, and he did not adopt his apologetic strategy from Aquinas.

Thomas Aquinas was a Dominican whose primary task was the teaching of Scripture and theology to other Christians. He taught aspiring theologians in a university setting for approximately seven years, and he taught fellow Dominicans in Dominican priories for approximately twenty-five years.[54] He wrote commentaries on Scripture as well as commentaries on theological works such as Peter Lombard's *Sentences* and on philosophical works such as those of Aristotle. He also wrote scholastic disputations on a wide variety of questions in theology and philosophy. His two most well-known works, however, are the *Summa Theologiae* and the *Summa Contra Gentiles*.

The *Summa Theologiae* represents Aquinas' mature theological views, but this work is misunderstood if it is treated as an apologetics text. The *Summa Theologiae* was written by Aquinas for the theological training of fellow Christians in the Dominican order. The entire work assumes that both the author and the reader are Christians who believe in the articles of faith set forth in the Nicene Creed.[55] As Brian Davies explains, 'Aquinas offers the *Summa* as an extended treatment of the truths of Christianity based on the Bible.'[56] The first part of the *Summa*, which provides the context for all that follows, is titled *De sacra doctrina*. For

---

54. Brian Davies, *Thomas Aquinas's Summa Theologiae: A Guide & Commentary* (Oxford: Oxford University Press, 2014), 9.

55. Ibid., 13.

56. Ibid., 18.

Aquinas, this term is 'equivalent to divine revelation as provided in the Bible.'[57] Aquinas even treats the terms *sacra doctrina* and *sacra Scriptura* interchangeably at times.[58]

This definition of *sacra doctrina* must be kept in mind if Aquinas' *Summa* is to be properly understood for what it is. Aquinas states in the Prologue to the *Summa* that his purpose in the book is 'to treat of whatever belongs to the Christian religion in such a way as may befit the instruction of beginners.'[59] The 'beginners' are other Dominicans, less knowledgeable about Scripture and theology than Thomas. He says he will try to set forth what belongs to *sacra doctrina*.[60] If the following articles under Question 1 are read in this light, it is abundantly evident that Aquinas is not doing in this work what Butler was doing many years later in his *Analogy*.[61] Aquinas is writing a work to assist in teaching

---

57. Ibid.

58. E.g., Thomas Aquinas, *Summa Theologiae*, Ia, Q. 1, A. 2, *ad secundum*.

59. Thomas Aquinas, *Summa Theologiae*, Ia, prologue.

60. Ibid.

61. In Article 1, for example, Aquinas asks whether any science ('knowledge') is needed in addition to philosophy, which deals with what can be known by reason alone. He answers yes. There is other knowledge, namely, the inspired Scripture. In his divine revelation, God has given men truths that exceed human reason. This was necessary, he says, for salvation. In Article 2, Aquinas asks whether *sacra doctrina* (the teaching found in special revelation) is a science. He argues that it is. In Article 3, Aquinas argues that *sacra doctrina* is one science because it considers things as divinely revealed. In Article 4, he argues that *sacra doctrina* is concerned with God. In Article 5, Aquinas argues that *sacra doctrina* is nobler than all other sciences because it derives its certainty from divine knowledge and because of its subject matter. He points out that *sacra doctrina* does not derive its principles from any philosophical sciences but simply makes use of them as handmaidens. In Article 6, Aquinas argues that *sacra doctrina* derives its knowledge from divine revelation and *not through natural reason*. Anything found in the philosophical sciences contrary to the science of *sacra doctrina* is to be rejected as false. In Article 7, Aquinas explains that God is the object of *sacra doctrina*. In Article 8, Aquinas asks whether *sacra doctrina* is a matter of argument. He answers that *sacra doctrina* does not attempt to prove its principles, the articles of faith. Instead, it starts with those principles and uses them to prove other truths. Since Scripture is the highest science, Aquinas argues that it can dispute with a person who denies its principles (articles of faith) only if that person admits some truths derived from divine revelation. We can argue for the articles of faith from Scripture against heretics. We can argue with a person who rejects one article from another article that he accepts. But if a person rejects all divine revelation, we cannot prove any articles of faith to him. All we can do is answer his objections. Aquinas adds that *sacra doctrina* does not use human reason to prove faith but to make clear the things that faith believes. It uses the authority of philosophers only as probable arguments. The authority of Scripture is the only incontrovertible truth. All

other Dominicans the doctrines of Scripture as he understands them. He is not writing a work of apologetics.

Unlike the *Summa Theologiae*, the *Summa Contra Gentiles* is an apologetic work, but even here, it is evident that Butler is not following Aquinas. Aquinas is, to be sure, interested in what truths reason can discover without appealing to revelation. He believes some truths about God can be discovered by reason, while other truths about God are beyond the reach of reason. But Aquinas doesn't adopt rationalist principles, even for the sake of argument. In his commentary on Boethius' *De Trinitate*, for example, Aquinas explains that 'error arises if, in matters of faith, reason has precedence of faith and not faith of reason, to the point that one would be willing to believe only what he could know by reason, when the converse ought to be the case.'[62]

The *Summa Contra Gentiles* was originally titled *A Book on the Truth of the Catholic Faith against the Errors of Unbelievers*. The contrast between truth and error in the original title describes the content of the book. The purpose of the *Summa Contra Gentiles*, for example, is explained in chapter 1 in a discussion of the wise man. Aquinas explains that the wise man has a twofold office: 'to meditate and publish the divine *truth*' and 'to refute the *error* contrary to truth.'[63] In the following chapter, Aquinas again explains the purpose of his work. It is 'to declare the *truth* which the Catholic faith professes, while weeding out contrary *errors*.'[64] He then explains why it is difficult to refute errors. He gives two reasons: 'First, because we do not know the sacrilegious assertions of each erring individual well enough to refute their errors with arguments from what they say.'[65] The second reason has to do with the kinds of people who are in error:

> … some of them, like the Mohammedans and pagans, do not agree with us as to the authority of any Scripture by which they may be convinced in the same way as we are able to dispute with the Jews by means of the Old Testament, and with heretics by means of the New. But the former accept

---

of this provides the context for the discussion of the existence of God in Question 2 and everything else in the remainder of the *Summa*.

62. Thomas Aquinas, *Commentary on the De Trinitate of Boethius*, Q. 2, A.1.

63. Thomas Aquinas, *Summa contra Gentiles*, I, 1. Emphasis mine.

64. Thomas Aquinas, *Summa contra Gentiles*, I, 2. Emphasis mine.

65. Thomas Aquinas, *Summa contra Gentiles*, I, 2.

neither. Thus we need to have recourse to natural reason, to which all are compelled to assent. And yet this is deficient in the things of God. But while we are occupied in the inquiry about a particular *truth*, we shall show what *errors* are excluded thereby, and how demonstrable truth is in agreement with the faith of the Christian religion.[66]

The first three books of the *Summa Contra Gentiles* address those who do not accept the authority of Scripture and who must be approached with natural reason. In the fourth book, Aquinas argues that although the Articles of Faith cannot be demonstrated to be true, it is not unreasonable to believe them.[67] Butler's content and method differs significantly from Aquinas's content and method.

## Conclusion

Van Til's over generalization of the history of philosophy, apologetics, and theology and his misrepresentations of various individual figures within those histories is a serious concern primarily because it distorts the truth. It is also a failure to measure up to the academic standards the founders of Westminster Seminary set for themselves when they declared their intention to carry on the legacy of Old Princeton. The legacy of Old Princeton is one of rigorous and competent academic research. It is a legacy of academic integrity. The Old Princetonians worked hard to understand the views of those they wrote and spoke about. They read and digested the primary sources. To the extent that scholars follow Van Til's approach to history, they abandon the rigorous academic legacy of Old Princeton.

Van Til's over generalizations also effectively turn all of church history into a kind of legend with mythological archetypes of good and evil. In this tale, Thomas Aquinas, with his scholasticism, becomes the mythological archetype of evil, while John Calvin becomes the

---

66. Thomas Aquinas, *Summa contra Gentiles*, I, 2. Emphasis mine.

67. In another place, Thomas speaks of another category of error, namely, those who deny principles. He says, 'We must note, however, that, as the Philosopher says in *Metaphysics*, IV, against those who deny principles there can be no unqualified demonstration which proceeds from what is more known simply. But we may use a demonstration to contradiction which proceeds from those things which are supposed by our adversary, which things are, for the time being, less known simply.' See Thomas Aquinas, *Commentary on Aristotle's Physics*, trans. Richard J. Blackwell, Richard J. Spath, and W. Edmund Thirlkel (London: Routledge & Kegan Paul, 1963), Book I, lect. 3, 24.

mythological archetype of good. The Reformed Scholastics betray Calvin and align themselves with the forces of evil. Van Til then steps into the story as the new hero, calling all of us to return to the pure Reformed theology of Calvin. We can do this only if we accept Van Til's idealist theory of knowledge and the apologetic methodology that rests upon it.

In all of his retelling of history, it seems to matter little what any particular theologian, philosopher, or apologist actually taught. What matters is what Van Til assumes they *must have* taught given his own philosophical presuppositions even when what he says they *must have* taught differs from what they actually did teach. What matters is preserving the mythological narrative. This kind of revisionary history, however, is academically irresponsible and completely unhelpful to anyone seeking an accurate understanding of history, theology, philosophy, or apologetics.

The misrepresentations of scholasticism, of Thomas Aquinas, of John Calvin, of the Reformed Scholastic theologians, and of Joseph Butler are all used by Van Til to support his case for his apologetic system of thought. Regardless of Van Til's intention, to the extent that his representation of them is inaccurate, it weakens various elements of his overall case for the method of presupposition. Van Til rested a lot of his case on the Calvin vs. the Calvinist thesis, for example. It shaped his view of the Reformed theology with which he said our apologetic methodology should be consistent. When we discover that the Calvin vs. the Calvinists thesis is demonstrably false, we discover that the Reformed Scholastics are among those who defined the Reformed theology with which our apologetic methodology should be consistent. We can no longer claim that our apologetic methodology is Reformed if it rejects their theology and their apologetics.

# CHAPTER 10

# Practical Concerns

In this chapter, I will explain some practical concerns with Van Til's system of thought. This will necessarily involve a discussion not only of Van Til himself but also some of his students. As I have explained elsewhere, the focus of this book is the thought of Van Til. I have deliberately refrained from any substantive evaluation of the views of his students unless a particular view could be directly traced to Van Til. My choice to remain focused on Van Til is the reason that I have not devoted any significant space to topics such as reconstructionism, triperspectivalism, or the so-called covenantal attributes of God. I have not addressed them at length because Van Til himself did not teach any of those views. A lengthy discussion of those topics, while certainly worthwhile, would distract from the specific focus of this book.

It is impossible, however, to avoid all mention of Van Til's students when discussing the practical concerns non-Van Tillians have with his system of thought when those practical concerns include the potential implications of his thought. Van Til's apologetic proposal was a novel one in the early twentieth century, and it often takes many years before the implications of a new theological proposal are worked out. There is, obviously, more room for error in a discussion such as this, because these kinds of implications are more difficult to verify than direct statements. Some of the concerns I raise in this chapter, therefore, should be understood as precisely that: concerns that I believe need to be carefully considered rather than summarily dismissed.

## Recasting Reformed Theology

Van Til, as we have seen, characterized the entire medieval period as one of 'synthesis thinking,' an attempt to combine the tenets of Christianity with Aristotelian philosophy. According to Van Til, John Calvin is the theologian who first escaped fully from synthesis thinking. Unfortunately, the Reformed scholastic theologians of the next generation returned the Reformed churches to such compromised thinking.[1] According to Van Til, these theologians betrayed the pure Reformed theology taught by John Calvin. Their traditional apologetic methods were inconsistent with Calvin's Reformed doctrine and must be abandoned. Furthermore, as Van Til explains, the traditional apologetics taught by the Reformed scholastics compromised with unbelief.[2] According to Van Til, those who taught traditional apologetics compromised every major doctrine of Reformed theology.[3]

I have already discussed the problem Van Til's condemnation of the Reformed scholastic theologians creates with regard to defining what Reformed theology is. By condemning the Reformed scholastic theologians, Van Til is effectively redefining the Reformed theological tradition. Whether he realized it or not, it seems evident that Van Til was developing a Reformed theology that would be consistent with his method of apologetics rather than developing a method of apologetics that would be consistent with Reformed theology. The practical result is that Van Til is *effectively* saying that his presuppositional apologetic methodology should be the defining standard of the true Reformed tradition. Non-Van Tillians do not believe that a twentieth century apologetic methodology that is completely dependent upon a modernist theory of knowledge is or should be the standard of what counts as true Reformed theology.

The redefinition of Reformed theology is itself a serious problem, but it is very possible that Van Til's condemnation of the Reformed

---

1. Van Til, 'Herman Dooyeweerd and Reformed Apologetics,' in Cornelius Van Til and Eric H. Sigward, *The Pamphlets, Tracts, and Offprints of Cornelius Van Til*, Electronic ed. (Labels Army Company: New York, 1997).

2. Cornelius Van Til, 'Wanted – A Reformed Testimony,' *Presbyterian Guardian* 20/7 (16 July 1951), in Cornelius Van Til and Eric H. Sigward, *The Articles of Cornelius Van Til*, Electronic ed. (Labels Army Company: New York, 1997).

3. Van Til, *The Defense of the Faith*, 340-41.

scholastic theologians had other unintended consequences as well. I began studying Van Til's writings again because I had noticed that two of his most well-known students (John M. Frame and K. Scott Oliphint) were publishing works on the doctrine of God that appeared to be contrary to the Reformed confessions of faith (e.g., in the denial of divine immutability and the suggestion of two modes of existence in the Divine Being). I began reading Van Til again in an attempt to discern whether there was something in his writings that might account for this. I did not find anything in Van Til that would directly link him to such doctrines. In fact, he himself would have considered any denial of immutability to be an example of what he called 'correlativism,' and there is no question that he would have harshly condemned any proponent of such teachings. This is because he directly connects divine immutability to divine independence or aseity.[4]

Although Van Til himself did not teach these specific doctrines, it is possible that his repeated strong condemnations of the Reformed scholastics might have had an indirect connection to their development. Again, I am not blaming Van Til for anything any of his students taught. I am merely attempting to understand how one element of his thought might have unintentionally created an environment in which the prevalence of such strange theological moves make sense. Consider, for example, the history of the institution most comprehensively shaped by Van Til's system of thought, Westminster Theological Seminary. One of the things that is most striking to any observer of the history of Westminster Seminary is the continual attempts at 'recasting' doctrines that are at the very heart of confessional Reformed theology.[5] It is also striking to observers that several of these attempts at recasting have led to serious controversies and upheavals at the seminary.

Obviously, Van Til himself recast Reformed apologetics, but he also recast the doctrine of the Trinity. His colleague, John Murray, recast covenant theology.[6] These attempts at recasting were accepted with little or no resistance at the seminary. A later WTS professor of theology,

---

4. Van Til, *Christian Apologetics*, 24.

5. I am borrowing the word 'recasting' from John Murray. See his *The Covenant of Grace: A Biblico-Theological Study* (London: The Tyndale Press, 1953), 5.

6. Murray, *The Covenant of Grace*. Murray taught at Westminster Seminary in Philadelphia from 1930 to 1966.

Norman Shepherd, attempted to recast the doctrine of justification.[7] WTS Professor of Old Testament, Peter Enns attempted to recast the doctrine of inspiration.[8] Theology professors John Frame and K. Scott Oliphint have, in their own individual ways, attempted to recast the doctrine of God's attributes.[9]

All of those attempts at recasting created controversies. For our purposes, the important thing to observe is that none of these are peripheral doctrines. The doctrine of the Trinity, God's attributes, covenant theology, justification, and biblical inspiration, are among the most fundamental doctrines of Reformed theology. Changes in those doctrines strike at the vitals of our faith. So why are such serious attempts at doctrinal recasting occurring again and again at the institution most influenced by Van Til's system of thought?

Could this recurring phenomenon have any connection to Van Til's teaching? Given his profound influence on the seminary after Machen's death, it is a question that we are forced to ask. Based on what we find in Van Til's books and class syllabi, it is clear that those who were his students had the idea drilled into their heads year after year that the traditional apologetics and the natural theology of the sixteenth and seventeenth century Reformed theologians led those theologians to compromise every major doctrine of Reformed theology. For decades, Van Til's students were trained to think of the theologians who defined the Reformed tradition and who wrote the Reformed confessions as 'scholastics,' as men who had betrayed John Calvin's theological legacy and returned the Reformed churches to a Roman Catholic type of 'synthesis thinking.'

---

7. See O. Palmer Robertson, *The Current Justification Controversy* (Unicoi, TN: The Trinity Foundation, 2003). Shepherd taught at Westminster Seminary in Philadelphia for almost twenty years, from 1963 to 1981. According to both John Frame and John Muether, Van Til defended Shepherd's teaching against charges of unorthodoxy. See Frame, *Cornelius Van Til: An Analysis of His Thought*, 393, and John Muether, *Cornelius Van Til: Reformed Apologist and Churchman*, 221.

8. Peter Enns, *Inspiration and Incarnation: Evangelicals and the Problem of the Old Testament* (Grand Rapids: Baker Academic, 2005). Enns taught at Westminster Seminary in Philadelphia from 1994 to 2008.

9. See Frame, *The Doctrine of God*, and his *Systematic Theology*. See also Oliphint, *God With Us: Divine Condescension and the Attributes of God* (Wheaton: Crossway, 2012). Frame taught at Westminster Seminary in Philadelphia from 1968 to 1980 and then at Westminster Seminary in California from 1980 to 2000. Oliphint has been a professor at Westminster Seminary in Philadelphia since 1991.

What questions might such teaching lead Van Til's students to ask? That is not difficult to answer. They might ask: 'If the early Reformed theologians were so wrong about these important doctrines, what else might they have been wrong about? If they corrupted every major doctrine of the Reformed faith, shouldn't we try to purify those doctrines? If they corrupted every major doctrine of the Reformed faith, how badly distorted are the Reformed confessions?' When we see Van Til year after year giving his students such a deeply negative assessment of the generations of men who developed confessional Reformed theology and who wrote the works defending that theology, we have to ask whether his teaching could have played a role in leading so many to stray repeatedly from the teaching of the Reformed confessions by recasting fundamental doctrines of the Reformed faith.[10]

In a 1997 journal article, John Frame shares some information about his time as one of Van Til's students at Westminster Seminary during the first half of the 1960s. What he shares is telling and worth our consideration:

> During my student years, I was never asked to read any of the Reformed confessions, or Calvin's *Institutes,* except in small bits. I never read any official standards of church government or discipline, not to mention Robert's Rules of Order. We used Hodge and Berkhof in our systematics classes, but for the most part we were graded not on our reading but on our knowledge of Murray's lectures.[11]

What is most concerning about Frame's statement is his claim about the lack of required study of the Reformed confessions while a student at WTS. This is concerning because WTS exists to train men for the ministry in *confessionally* Reformed churches such as the OPC. These men are required to subscribe to Reformed confessional standards. In order to intelligently subscribe to the Reformed confessions, however, one must know the Reformed confessions and the system of theology

---

10. The importance of seriously considering this question is made even more evident when we note that in the last several decades, the students of Van Til's students have continued to recast vital Reformed doctrines and in doing so have moved even farther from historic confessional Reformed theology. One prominent example of this can be seen in the work of those who created the so-called 'Federal Vision' theology.

11. John M. Frame, 'In Defense of Something Close to Biblicism: Reflections on Sola Scriptura and History in Theological Method,' *Westminster Theological Journal* 59, no. 2 (Fall 1997): 279.

contained within them. One must know how each element in that system of theology relates to the other elements. Without such knowledge, one may not understand how changes to one element in the system of theology ('recasting') will impact other elements in the system.

Why, then, would the teaching of the Reformed confessions have been so minimized in the seminary curriculum during Frame's student days? Why were students effectively cut off from so much of their Reformed heritage? We have to ask whether this was another consequence of Van Til's repeated condemnations of the Reformed theologians of the sixteenth and seventeenth centuries. These were the theologians who wrote the Reformed confessions, and if those theologians were corrupted and compromised by 'synthesis thinking,' as Van Til teaches, it would not be a huge leap to conclude that the confessions they wrote were also corrupted and compromised by 'synthesis thinking.'

Is it possible that Van Til's condemnation of the Reformed scholastic theologians was a contributing factor in the doctrinal controversies that we have witnessed throughout the history of the seminary he helped build? We cannot answer that question with absolute certainty, but it is difficult to see how such repeated condemnations of the theologians who wrote and defended the Reformed confessions would not lead at least some men to treat the confessional doctrines of God, of justification, of inspiration, as doctrines that needed to be cleansed of foreign elements in the same way that apologetics had been cleansed of foreign elements by Van Til.

J. Gresham Machen founded Westminster Seminary to carry on the legacy of old Princeton. One aspect of that legacy is reflected in the words of the great Princetonian Charles Hodge. In 1872, Hodge said, 'I am not afraid to say that a new idea never originated in this Seminary.'[12] Part of old Princeton's legacy was an aversion to theological novelty. Had Machen lived, perhaps that aspect of the old Princeton legacy would have continued, but after Machen's death, Van Til was the effective leader of the new school, and his repeated condemnations of the early Reformed theologians may have been part of the reason why so much theological recasting and novelty has taken place at the institution he decisively shaped.

---

12. A. A. Hodge, *The Life of Charles Hodge D.D. LL.D.* (New York: Charles Scribner's Sons, 1880),521.

## The Antithesis Revisited

In a previous chapter, I observed that Van Til's system of thought contains an internal tension between his doctrine of the antithesis and his doctrine of common grace. I have already looked at the problems he creates for his system when he qualifies the absolute epistemological antithesis. Because it is the absolute epistemological antithesis that necessitates the method of presupposition, the moment that this antithesis is qualified, for whatever reason, the method of presupposition is no longer necessitated. There are, however, other problems that have resulted from Van Til's doctrine of the antithesis.

Because of the internal tension in Van Til's system between the absolute antithesis *in principle* and the qualified antithesis *in practice*, some Van Tillians have tended to emphasize the absolute antithesis to the virtual exclusion of the common grace qualifications.[13] As a result of an over-emphasis or exclusive emphasis on the antithesis, these Van Tillians treat the unbeliever as if he has no knowledge of any fact in practice as well as in principle. They reject Calvin's argument that unbelievers have knowledge of earthly things but are blind as a mole with respect to heavenly things. They reject his claim that we can learn about earthly things from such unbelievers. Ironically, they are also rejecting a significant element of Van Til's own teaching in their zeal to defend Van Til's teaching.

Because they conclude that the unbeliever has no knowledge of anything, they also conclude that we cannot learn anything from any source other than the Bible. This over-emphasis on the antithesis, therefore, leads to a kind of distorted biblicism. It leads some Van Tillians to approach every field of human knowledge and practice as if the only source of knowledge for that field of knowledge is the Bible as read through Van Tillian lenses. It attempts to ignore what we can learn from the study of creation itself and from unbelievers who have a knowledge of earthly things.[14]

---

13. This kind of unqualified antithesis is commonly found among social media Van Tillians who have not read much of Van Til himself or who have simply missed the scattered references to the common grace qualifications in his writings.

14. I say 'attempts' because this is never workable in actual practice. Even those who consider themselves to be the strongest adherents to this type of biblicism have learned things from sources other than the Bible. All of them have learned to speak at least

One example of this is reconstructionism, which originated as R. J. Rushdoony's application of Van Til's system of thought to the study of the civil magistrate and the civil law.[15] Another example is nouthetic counseling, which arose when Jay Adams applied Van Til's system to the practice of counseling.[16] Other examples are found in the chapters of Gary North's edited *Festschrift* for Van Til. These chapters seek to approach fields including mathematics, sociology, economics, and psychology through the lenses of a biblicism informed by Van Til's system of thought.[17] To the extent that such approaches ignore what can be learned from unbelievers and from a study of God's creation, they depart from Van Til's own qualifications of the antithesis and, more importantly, they depart from the teaching of Scripture.

## Movement Van Tillianism

Another practical concern is what John Frame has described as 'Movement' Van Tillianism.[18] Van Til was seen by many of his students as the leader of a movement, and when you have movement leaders, one's faithfulness is determined by one's unquestioned loyalty to the leader. The practical concern non-Van Tillians have about movement Van Tillians is the same concern they have about those who treat any Christian leader in this way. There is always the danger in such cases that

---

one human language, for example. They have learned what the words of that language signify. If they know the meaning of any words not found in the Bible, they didn't learn those meanings from the Bible. Any of them who know how the circulatory system of a human body works learned it from a source other than the Bible. Any of them who know how igneous rocks are formed learned it from a source other than the Bible. I could go on. The point is that the Bible is sufficient for the purposes for which it was intended by God. It wasn't intended to provide knowledge of the circulatory system or the inner workings of a cell or the process of photosynthesis or Maxwell's equations. Those things have to be learned by using our God-created sensory and rational faculties to study the things God has made.

15. See Michael J. McVicar, *Christian Reconstruction: R. J. Rushdoony and American Religious Conservatism* (Chapel Hill: The University of North Carolina Press, 2015), 13-14, 34-35.

16. See Brian Keith Baker, 'Integrating Principles and Practices of Apologetics with Biblical Counseling,' DMin thesis, Southern Baptist Theological Seminary, 2018.

17. Gary North, ed., *Foundations of Christian Scholarship: Essays in the Van Til Perspective* (Vallecito, CA: Ross House Books, 1979).

18. Frame, *Cornelius Van Til: An Analysis of His Thought*, 11.

the movement leader will be treated as virtually infallible and beyond criticism. That is the way in which cults develop. It is not consistent with the teaching of Scripture.[19]

For those who treat Van Til in this way, any criticism of Van Til is automatically dismissed without serious consideration, and any critic is automatically dismissed as either stupid or evil. For a 'Movement' Van Tillian, to consider the criticisms and concerns of non-Van Tillians in a fair and serious manner and to read such critics with any charity would be an act of disloyalty to the movement. The job of the 'Movement' Van Tillian, when he encounters a criticism of Van Til, is not to treat the critic as a brother and to prayerfully examine the criticism to determine whether it has any merit. The job is to assume from the outset that there cannot possibly be any merit in such a criticism and then to immediately dismiss it in order to reassure others in the movement.

The irony of this is that Van Til did not think of himself in this way, and he did not treat all criticisms in this way. As we saw in the Introduction, Van Til treated those in the church with whom he disagreed as brothers in Christ. As the book *Jerusalem and Athens* illustrates repeatedly, he carefully considered criticisms of his views and typically responded with a Christian attitude.[20] He certainly expressed his disagreements without reservation, and he pointed out what he saw as errors in the thinking of his critics. He does not, however, engage in the kind of insulting and patronizing language that 'Movement' Van Tillians have been prone to use. In other words, in their zeal to follow Van Til, 'Movement' Van Tillians are actually being unfaithful to Van Til's own method of engagement with his Reformed critics.

## Practical Apologetics and Evangelism

Turning to the actual practice of evangelism and apologetics, another concern non-Van Tillians have with Van Til's system of thought is that,

---

19. Peter was an apostle of Christ, but even he was not beyond the possibility of criticism. Paul had to oppose him with regard to his attitude toward Gentiles (Gal. 2:11-14).

20. E. R. Geehan, ed. *Jerusalem and Athens: Critical Discussions on the Philosophy and Apologetics of Cornelius Van Til* (Phillipsburg: P&R Publishing Company, 1971). Frame has indicated that Van Til could have done a better job in his interactions with Clark during the ordination controversy. See Frame, *Cornelius Van Til: An Analysis of His Thought*, 109-13. Even if that is granted, by the end of their lives Clark and Van Til spoke charitably of one another. See Douma, *The Presbyterian Philosopher*, 240-42.

in spite of its aims, it discourages the average Christian from engaging with unbelievers. Remember that the method of presupposition involves two stages. In the first stage, the Christian steps into the shoes of his opponent for the sake of argument and offers an internal critique of the unbeliever's worldview. In his critique of the non-Christian view, the Christian seeks to demonstrate that the non-Christian system is internally self-contradictory. The goal is 'to reduce our opponent's position to absurdity.'[21] In the second stage, the Christian asks the unbeliever to step into the Christian's shoes and then shows the unbeliever that only the Christian worldview can account for human knowledge and human predication.

The first stage of the method of presupposition is where the average Christian immediately faces the most discouraging difficulties. In order to step into the unbeliever's worldview and offer an intelligent internal critique of it, the Christian must have a thorough grasp of the unbeliever's worldview. He must know its elements well enough to be able to show its internal self-contradictions. The difficulty the Christian encounters at this point is the fact that there are multitudes of vastly different unbelieving worldviews. How is he to deal with this?

Van Til attempts to overcome this difficulty by treating all unbelieving systems as if they were basically the same. This, however, is an unhelpful over-generalization that seriously distorts the truth. Claiming that all unbelieving worldviews are basically the same because they are all non-Christian is no more helpful than saying that God, galaxies, and geese are all basically the same because they are all non-dogs.[22] In practice, this approach to apologetics tends to force the Christian into offering pat answers that do not deal with the actual questions a specific unbeliever is asking. The Christian who uses such formulaic answers on the assumption that all unbelievers are basically the same quickly discovers that such an assumption is unhelpful and quickly realizes that the unbelievers he must deal with are complicated individual human beings.

An apologetic methodology that lumps all unbelieving worldviews into one over-simplified category is not helpful in the real world where

---

21. Van Til, *Survey of Christian Epistemology*, 205.

22. By treating them all the same, it also fails to take into account that some unbelieving worldviews have more elements of truth than others.

Christians deal with real people. Real people are varied in their views. Van Til's particular argument might be useful if one encounters a specific individual who is deeply mired in nineteenth-century idealist philosophy and who also has an obsessive concern about the problem of human predication, but that describes very few if any people the average Christian might encounter in the real world. Today a Christian is more likely to encounter a teenager dabbling in witchcraft, or a college student who says logic is a tool of oppression, or a co-worker who is into all kinds of conspiracy theories, or a neighbor who is a Hindu, or a cousin who has bought into transgender ideology.

One simply cannot step into the shoes of the materialist worldview and demonstrate its absurdity in exactly the same way one steps into the shoes of the subjective idealist worldview and demonstrates its absurdity. One cannot step into the shoes of the Buddhist worldview and demonstrate its internal problems in exactly the same way one steps into the shoes of the Muslim worldview and demonstrates its internal problems. One has to actually take the time to study a non-Christian worldview in order to understand its specific internal problems well enough to critique them intelligently. But who among us has mastered all of the hundreds or thousands of unbelieving worldviews well enough to show how each reduces to absurdity?

Real unbelievers are not as simplistic as textbook unbelievers. If a Christian desires to use the Van Tillian method of presupposition and then discovers that real unbelievers are very different from one another, he will quickly become overwhelmed because he will realize that the internal critique of unbelieving worldviews required as the first stage of that method cannot be used effectively without a mastery of the various unbelieving worldviews he encounters. A method of apologetics that requires a Christian to have a mastery of every worldly philosophy and religion is not a method that will be of much practical use in the church. The Christian needs instead to study Scripture to observe the way in which the Gospel was proclaimed to real unbelievers and the way it was defended by faithful men and women.

## A Final Practical Concern

The final practical concern I have is related to the discussion of 'Movement' Van Tillianism above. One of the things I have noticed as I have observed this debate over the last thirty years is that many of my fellow students and friends who were the most zealous 'Movement' Van Tillians were far more interested in talking about apologetics than they were in doing apologetics. For many of them, apologetics became more a matter of defending Cornelius Van Til than defending the Christian faith. Many of my friends were more than happy to argue with fellow Christians about this or that nuance of Van Til's thought until all hours of the night, but they showed little interest in actually talking about Jesus Christ to real flesh and blood unbelievers.

In short, my concern is that the debate over Van Til has been more of a distraction than a help in the actual task of evangelism and apologetics.[23] I am concerned that it has distracted Van Tillians and non-Van Tillians alike. I am not suggesting that Van Til should not have raised the concerns he raised or that non-Van Tillians should not have responded to Van Til. I am not advocating an anti-intellectualist approach to these issues. What I am saying is that in my experience it has become apparent that the legitimate discussion among Reformed Christians about the proper *method* of apologetics has sometimes distracted from the actual *practice* of apologetics. What is the point, however, of arguing endlessly about the proper method of addressing an unbeliever if the Reformed Christians who zealously fight over apologetic methods never actually address an unbeliever?

We as Christians are called to proclaim the Gospel of Jesus Christ to a lost and dying world, to actual human beings enslaved to sin and death and darkness. We are called to be always prepared to make a defense to anyone who asks us for a reason for the hope that is in us, and we are called to do so with gentleness and respect (1 Peter 3:15). The legitimate discussions we have as Christians about the proper apologetic method should also be done with gentleness and respect. More importantly, however these discussions should contribute to the actual proclamation of the Gospel and to the actual defense of the faith. If discussions of apologetic methodology remain ends in themselves, we are being unfaithful to our Lord.

---

23. This debate was largely the result of Van Til's condemnation of all non-Van Tillian theologians as compromisers. That is why I include this concern in this chapter even though the concern itself now extends to non-Van Tillians as well as Van Tillians.

# Conclusion

Many of the practical concerns non-Van Tillians have with Van Til's apologetic system are implications of elements of his thought discussed elsewhere in this book. The idealist theory of knowledge, for example, creates internal inconsistencies with Van Til's doctrine of the antithesis, a doctrine that is crucial to his system. The idealist theory of knowledge results in an all-or-nothing approach to knowledge that causes Van Til to distort the history of philosophy, theology, and practical apologetics. It is an unbiblical theory that should be uprooted from Reformed soil.

One aspect of historical theology that is seriously distorted by Van Til is the teaching of the Reformed Scholastic theologians of the sixteenth and seventeenth centuries. His repeated condemnations of them results in a redefinition of the very meaning of 'Reformed' theology. This redefinition undermines Van Til's claim that he is seeking to develop an apologetic method that is consistent with Reformed theology. It is also possible that Van Til's repeated condemnations of the Reformed theologians of the sixteenth and seventeenth centuries helped create an atmosphere in which the radical recasting of fundamental doctrines of the Reformed faith has become an all too common occurrence.

It is also concerning to see Van Til regularly treated as if he were infallible and as if his works were beyond any possibility of criticism. Van Til was a Reformed minister of the Gospel. He was neither a prophet nor an apostle, and it should go without saying among Reformed Christians that he should not be venerated in the same way that cult leaders and Roman Catholic saints are venerated. Respect and admiration for a man are one thing. Fanatical adulation is quite another. The movement mentality surrounding Van Til exacerbated an already complicated debate by elevating Van Til's works to a sort of quasi-canonical status and by treating as an apostate anyone who raised questions or concerns about Van Til. Thankfully, there are those among the current generation of Van Tillian scholars who have abandoned the movement mentality and are reading Van Til with a more critical eye, but 'Movement' Van Tillianism is alive and well in many circles.

Finally, all of us, Van Tillian and non-Van Tillian alike must endeavor to keep the debate over apologetic methodology in perspective. These debates should be in service of a clearer presentation of the Gospel and a clearer defense of the hope that is within us. Debates over apologetic methodology cannot be allowed to replace the actual proclamation of the Gospel to unbelievers. Debates over the best way to defend the faith cannot be allowed to replace the actual defense of the faith.

These debates among Van Tillian and non-Van Tillian brothers in Christ are glorifying to God and edifying to the church only if they are used as a way of helping 'one another as together we present the name of Jesus as the only name given under heaven by which men must be saved.'[24] That is the spirit in which I have attempted to present these concerns. That is the spirit in which I pray that they are received. My hope is that this will drive us back to Scripture in order to help us more faithfully obey our Lord Jesus Christ.

24. Cornelius Van Til, 'My Credo,' in *Jerusalem and Athens: Critical Discussions on the Philosophy and Apologetics of Cornelius Van Til*, ed. E. R. Geehan (Phillipsburg: P&R Publishing Company, 1971), 3.

# Conclusion

I strongly believe that the debate over Van Til's apologetic system of thought is an important debate that is well worth the effort to carefully consider. I believe that the concerns Van Til raised about traditional apologetics are worth careful consideration, and I believe that the concerns raised by non-Van Tillians about his apologetic system are worth careful consideration. Unfortunately, in this debate, careful consideration has often been the casualty of confused remarks coming from both sides. For decades, this debate has been made more difficult than necessary because of various misunderstandings on both sides. I have attempted in this book to clear away some of those distracting misunderstandings first, by presenting in a concise and comprehensible way Van Til's own system of thought, and then, by explaining a number of the concerns non-Van Tillians have with that system of thought. I have attempted to do these things without adding to the confusion and misunderstanding. Where I have failed, I ask the reader's forgiveness.

## An Appeal to Non-Van Tillians

To those readers who, like myself, are not Van Tillians, please remember that Van Til was an ordained elder in a confessional Reformed church and that he subscribed to the Westminster Standards. That means that he should be treated as a brother in Christ. That also means that we have a lot of agreement with him on many confessional doctrines. Since non-Van Tillians typically do not accept an all-or-nothing idealist theory of knowledge, it should be easy for us to understand that a man can be wrong on some points and right on others. A mistake in one place does not necessarily invalidate everything a man teaches. Even numerous mistakes do not invalidate everything a man teaches.

Those among the non-Van Tillians who appreciate Thomas Aquinas surely recognize this with regard to Thomas' teaching. Reformed theologians who appreciate Thomas do not reject everything he said even though he was wrong on many points of doctrine. They critically evaluate his teaching, appropriate what was right, and discard what was wrong. If Reformed non-Van Tillians can do that with Thomas Aquinas, Reformed non-Van Tillians can do that with Cornelius Van Til.

Confessionally Reformed non-Van Tillians should not be mirror images of 'Movement' Van Tillians. Confessionally Reformed non-Van Tillians do not have to reject something just because Van Til said it or accept something just because a critic of Van Til said it. Confessionally Reformed non-Van Tillians should critically evaluate the things Van Til says and critically evaluate the things his critics say. Van Til is not infallible, but neither is any critic of Van Til. That includes me, and it includes this book. I have attempted to represent accurately Van Til's teaching. I have attempted to explain accurately some of the problems that exist in his system of thought. But I am not infallible. I can be mistaken.

## An Appeal to Van Tillians

To those readers who are Van Tillians, please remember that many of Van Til's critics were and are men who subscribe to the Westminster Standards. There is much on which we agree. Also remember the way in which Van Til himself spoke to his critics at the beginning of *Jerusalem and Athens*. Remember that he said: 'I hope that by doing this we may be of help to one another as together we present the name of Jesus as the only name given under heaven by which men must be saved.'[1] In other words, he didn't treat his critics as apostates. If Van Tillians and non-Van Tillians could begin to treat each other with mutual respect as brothers in Christ, it would go a long way toward moving this discussion in a more edifying direction.

---

1.   Cornelius Van Til, 'My Credo,' in *Jerusalem and Athens: Critical Discussions on the Philosophy and Apologetics of Cornelius Van Til*, ed. E. R. Geehan (Phillipsburg: P&R Publishing Company, 1971), 3.

This does not mean that we cannot or should not be direct and forthright about our views and about what we believe to be serious problems in the thinking of those brothers with whom we disagree. If we can treat each other as brothers in Christ, however, perhaps we can stop treating one's view regarding Van Til's apologetic methodology as if it were on the same level of importance as one's view of the resurrection of Jesus. We could treat it as what it actually is, a family discussion over the apologetic implications of a shared Reformed theology.

This would mean actually listening to the concerns of non-Van Tillians and prayerfully considering them, instead of attempting to be the first person online to find a way to hastily dismiss them. Is it really completely absurd, for example, for a confessionally Reformed Christian to be concerned when Van Til affirms that God is three persons and then adds that God is also one person? Are radical changes to the doctrine of the Trinity merely trifles? Is the concern about the replanting of a modernist theory of knowledge into Reformed soil really unworthy of any thoughtful consideration? The point is that respectful consideration is not a one-way street.

One of my hopes is that this book will encourage Van Tillians and non-Van Tillians alike to explore more deeply Reformed theologians of the sixteenth and seventeenth centuries other than Calvin. Of course, we should continue to read and study Calvin, but we should also read Zacharias Ursinus' *Commentary on the Heidelberg Catechism*, for example. Or William Ames' *The Marrow of Sacred Divinity*. Those who haven't already should read Francis Turretin's *Institutes of Elenctic Theology* or Petrus van Mastricht's *Theoretical-Practical Theology*. We should read Stephen Charnock and John Owen. We should read the writings of the Westminster Divines, men such as Anthony Burgess, Thomas Goodwin, and William Twisse. As I noted in a previous chapter, Van Tillian scholars themselves have begun acknowledging that the old Calvin vs. the Calvinists thesis is false. We should, therefore, read and study both Calvin and the Calvinists.

## Toward a Reformed Apologetics

Cornelius Van Til's goal of developing an apologetic methodology consistent with Reformed theology was an admirable goal. For the reasons I have explained throughout this book, however, I do not believe he succeeded in achieving that goal. I do not embrace Van Til's apologetic system of thought because the evidence indicates that it is contrary to the teaching of Scripture, that it conflicts with the historic Reformed theological tradition, and that it is fundamentally rooted in an unbiblical modernist theory of knowledge. In short, I do not embrace Van Til's apologetic system because it is neither biblical nor Reformed.

If it is true that Van Til failed in achieving his goal, how should confessionally Reformed Christians go about developing an apologetic that is actually consistent with Reformed theology? How should we go about attempting to achieve the goal Van Til set for himself? Although a full exegetical and theological case for such a Reformed apologetic would require a separate full-length book, I would like to share a few preliminary thoughts on what is necessary to achieve such a goal.

In the first place, if we are going to develop an apologetic that is consistent with Reformed theology, we have to know what Reformed theology is. We cannot determine whether an apologetic system is consistent with Reformed theology without a clear and objective definition of Reformed theology. Furthermore, we cannot start with an apologetic methodology and then adapt a theology to it and then call that theology 'Reformed theology.' We must start with a solid understanding of real historical Reformed theology if we are to have any hope of achieving our goal.

So, where do we go if we want to know what real historical Reformed theology is? We must go first to the confessions and catechisms of the Reformed churches. These corporate statements of faith are concise public confessions that distinguish Reformed theology from Roman Catholic theology, Lutheran theology, Arminian theology, Socinian theology, and more. The Reformed confessional standards that are in widest use today are the Three Forms of Unity and the Westminster Standards. Confessionally Reformed Christians believe these standards contain the system of theology taught in Scripture. These Reformed Confessions will have to be the base line standard in the development of a Reformed apologetic. Of course, these Reformed confessions will have to be interpreted within their own historical, ecclesiastical, theological, and philosophical context.

We will also have to look to the Reformed theologians of the sixteenth and seventeenth centuries. These were the men who developed the doctrines that were included in the Reformed confessions. This development of Reformed theology was the result of intensive and extensive exegetical labors. These men also wrote the massive theological works proclaiming and defending the teaching of the Reformed confessions. Because many of these works were written for use in *schools*, many of these works adopt a *scholastic* methodology, but that methodology helped them in the proclamation and defense of Reformed theology. In short, Reformed theology is defined primarily by the Reformed confessions and secondarily by the Reformed theologians of the sixteenth and seventeenth centuries. Departures from that theology, such as are found in seventeenth century Arminian theology or twenty-first century Federal Vision theology, are not Reformed theology.

If we are to develop an apologetic consistent with Reformed theology, it must be consistent with the historical Reformed theology that was developed and defended in the sixteenth and seventeenth centuries. We will have to be aware that this historic Reformed theology did not toss out everything that previous theologians such as Thomas Aquinas said. We will have to be aware that this historic Reformed theology did not reject natural theology. We will have to be aware that this historic Reformed theology had not yet fallen into the trap of various Enlightenment and post-Enlightenment philosophical views. It had not yet adopted the various forms of rationalism or empiricism or idealism. We will also have to understand that appeals to return to the teaching of historic traditional Reformed theology are not appeals to return to 'the vomit of Rome.'[2]

Second, if we are going to develop an apologetic that is consistent with Reformed theology, we must develop an apologetic that conforms to what we find in Scripture. We cannot presuppose our apologetic and then read Scripture through that lens. We must start with what we actually find in Scripture and evaluate our apologetic in light of that. This means that we will have to look at what Scripture teaches and assumes about things like knowledge and then compare various human theories of knowledge to the biblical standard. We will also have to look at the way in which believers deal with unbelievers in Scripture. Our apologetic will not be a biblical or Reformed apologetic

---

2. See Fesko, *Reforming Apologetics*, xv.

if it contradicts what the Bible teaches or else twists Scripture to conform to an apologetic theory.

Third, if we are going to develop an apologetic that is consistent with Reformed theology, we must uproot any unbiblical philosophical elements that have been planted in Reformed soil. The early Reformed theologians uprooted unbiblical Greek philosophical elements from late medieval Roman Catholicism, but pagan Greek ideas are not the only concern. Neither the biblical authors nor the authors of the Reformed confessions, for example, taught or assumed the idealist theory of knowledge that is foundational to the Van Tillian method of presupposition. The biblical teaching related to knowledge flatly contradicts the idealist theory of knowledge. To the extent that this idealist theory of knowledge is a part of our apologetic system, that apologetic system is contrary to Scripture and contrary to Reformed theology.

Finally, an apologetic that is consistent with Reformed theology will be an apologetic that can be understood by any intelligent Christian, and it will be one that can be put into practice. Those who adopt it will actually be able to use it rather than merely talk about it. A consistently Reformed apologetic will be an apologetic like that of Paul's, one that accompanies the proclamation of the Gospel of Jesus Christ whether that proclamation is to Jews or Greeks. It will be an apologetic that follows Paul in starting on whatever shared ground one has with his audience, such as the Old Testament with Jews and natural reason with the Athenians (Acts 17). It will be an apologetic that is always ready to answer the real questions real unbelievers ask rather than giving pat answers on the assumption that all unbelievers are obsessively concerned with the problem of human predication. A consistently Reformed apologetic will, Lord willing, serve the purpose of glorifying God.

# Appendix

## 'On God, or, That God Exists'

### By Franciscus Junius

*Franciscus Junius (1545–1602) is best known in the English-speaking world for his work* A Treatise on True Theology *(1594) since it is among the few works of Junius to be translated into English.[1] The following work is a collection of theological theses that were among those disputed during Junius' time teaching in Heidelberg. These* Heildelberg Theses *along with those developed during his time in Leiden cover a number of theological topics and are collected in the first volume of Junius' Opera Theologica.[2] The relevance of this collection of theses, titled 'De Deo Seu Deum Esse' ('On God, or, That God Exists'),[3] is its clear statement of Reformed natural theology including the possibility of demonstrating to unbelievers the existence of God. It is also relevant to the topic of this book because in these theses, Junius presents an 'abridged' version of the 'Five Ways' of Thomas Aquinas.[4]*

1. The proper subject and material of sacred Scripture is God.

2. 'God' in Greek and Latin means the same as the Hebrew term *Dai* (דּי), which refers to sufficiency and self-existence (αὐτοαρχῇ) in and through itself.

---

1. Franciscus Junius, *A Treatise on True Theology*, trans. David C. Noe (Grand Rapids: Reformation Heritage Books, 2014).

2. Ibid., xx.

3. Franciscus Junius, *Opera Theologica*, 2 vols. (Geneva: Caldoriani, 1607), 1:1777-78.

4. The following translation was produced by my colleague Levi Berntson who has graciously allowed me to include it in this volume.

3. Both nature itself and Scripture testify that God exists.

4. Therefore, those who either have faith in natural light or in the supernatural light exposited in holy Scripture never doubt that God exists.

5. But whoever restrains the truth of God and of nature in a lie will deny this by blinding their minds and by forcing their wills to particular desires (Ps. 14), however much they have been overwhelmed by supernatural light and by the natural light of the conscience.

6. The supernatural light is the testimony of the Spirit of God in our minds (1 Cor. 2:10).

7. The supernatural eye of our mind is faith (Heb. 11:1).

8. This light effects the mind, and from this light the mind understands so that we believe that God exists.

9. But neither of these can be grasped by the natural man, since it is supernatural and spiritual (1 Cor. 2:14).

10. This is the case because both the supernatural and the spiritual can be grasped by man only in a supernatural and spiritual manner, and this is not present in the natural man.

11. The medium or instrument for both lights is the Word of God, preached and written.

12. And even this cannot be grasped usefully except in a supernatural and spiritual way.

13. Now, briefly let us teach that this is the case: those who receive God believe that God exists, and that He is the rewarder (μισθαποδότης) for those who seek Him (Heb. 11:6).

14. Those who are illuminated by natural light alone have some common notions (Rom. 1), often called 'principles,' which are complementary to supernatural light.

15. Indeed, these notions are remnants and corrupted seeds of that first nature which was destroyed by man which God has preserved in man by His own blessing.

16. From these notions, man understands that he is considered by God spoiled and damnable, and he is rendered inexcusable by the conscience (Rom. 1:19).

17. Now the conscience is that internal light of nature which is a constant and inescapable testimony to this (Rom. 2:15).

18. According to this conscience, the natural man knows and can be taught that God exists.

19. He knows, since it is of his nature by itself to know that God exists (Acts 14; 17).

20. He can be taught, since there are certain demonstrations for God *a posteriori* (as they say), that is, from His works and effects.

21. There are five ways of these demonstrations from the creation of the world which have been explained by various men: the nature of things, governance, motion, the nature of the efficient cause, and its mode.

22. *The nature of things*: Since things are so distinguished among themselves by grades, such that however much all things are in a nature, yet some of them are said to be more good, true, etc., and others less so.

23. Now that which is most in any kind is the efficient cause of all things of that same kind, and what is most true is also supremely existent.

24. Therefore, whatever is the one supreme being, transcends all kinds. That same thing is the principle of all things and the cause for all things which exist so that they are (Acts 17), and this is God.

25. *Governance and its order*: For whatever exists in the nature of things is directed toward its own end by a certain intention, either an alien intention or its own intention.

26. Even those things which are directed by their own intention are directed not only by their own mutable and deficient nature, but they are directed by the intention of an unchangeable, incorruptible, and necessary-of-itself intention.

27. And not only are individual things individually directed toward their own immediate end, but also they are directed collectively to one highest and common end of all things.

28. But this intention of direction cannot be deployed toward a just order except by the highest intelligence by which all things in nature are ordered to this end in a most wise way (Acts 14), and this intelligence is God.

29. *Motion*: For whatever is moved, insofar as it is moved, is moved by another thing which moves it; either this is a secondary mover which moves by a power which moves it to action, or a primary and highest mover which alone is act.

30. But this primary mover which moves all things cannot be anything except one (Acts 17), and so this is God.

31. Some might suppose causes of motion *ad infinitum*, but this is most absurd.

32. *The nature of the efficient cause*: For just as in all things as motion, so is the order of all efficient causes from the first to the last and highest.

33. But there is no other cause of the first efficient cause (John 5), for if there were, it would not be first; and this first cause is God.

34. *The mode of the efficient cause*: For every mode is either possible or necessary.

35. Inferior to a necessary mode is a possible mode, which can exist and not exist, just as potency is inferior to act.

36. That which is in act is necessary, and cannot be otherwise, even if it has its necessity from elsewhere or does not have a cause of its own necessity,

37. But what is necessary of itself, having no cause of necessity from elsewhere but is a cause of necessity on other things and imposes a mode on those things, is that first cause of all things and of the second mode. And this cause is God.

38. And so, from the testimonies of the divine light and our nature, we conclude that God exists, and that those men who deny it are self-condemned (αὐτοκατακρίτοις, [Tit. 3:11]), since they do not hesitate to bark at the divine and natural testimonies with certain wickedness.

# Bibliography

Ahvio, Juha. *Theological Epistemology of Contemporary American Confessional Reformed Apologetics*. Helsinki: Luther-Agricola Society, 2005.

Allen, Michael, and Scott R. Swain, eds. *The Oxford Handbook of Reformed Theology*. Oxford: Oxford University Press, 2020.

Ameriks, Karl, ed. *The Cambridge Companion to German Idealism*. Cambridge: Cambridge University Press, 2000.

Ames, William. *The Marrow of Theology*. Translated by John Dykstra Eusden. Grand Rapids: Baker Books, 1997.

————. *A Sketch of the Christian's Catechism*. Translated by Todd M. Rester. Classic Reformed Theology, edited by R. Scott Clark. Grand Rapids: Reformation Heritage Books, 2008.

————. *The Substance of Christian Religion*. London: Thomas Davies, 1659.

Anderson, James N. 'If Knowledge Then God: The Epistemological Theistic Arguments of Alvin Plantinga and Cornelius Van Til.' *Calvin Theological Journal* 40, no. 1 (Apr 2005): 49-75.

————. 'Presuppositionalism in the Dock: A Review Article.' *Reformed Faith & Practice* 7, no. 1 (May 2022): 74-85.

Anderson, Owen. *Reason and Worldview: Warfield, Kuyper, Van Til and Plantinga on the Clarity of General Revelation and Function of Apologetics*. Lanham: University Press of America, 2008.

Asselt, Willem J. van. *Introduction to Reformed Scholasticism.* Translated by Albert Gootjes. Reformed Historical–Theological Studies, edited by Joel R. Beeke and Jay T. Collier. Grand Rapids: Reformation Heritage Books, 2011.

———. 'Protestant Scholasticism: Some Methodological Considerations in the Study of its Development.' *Nederlands archief voor kerkgeschiedenis* 81, no. 3 (2001): 265-274.

Asselt, Willem J. van, Michael D. Bell, Gert van den Brink, Rein Ferwerda. *Scholastic Discourse: Johannes Maccovius (1588–1644) on Theological and Philosophical Distinctions and Rule.* Publications of the Institute for Reformation Research, edited by William den Boer. Apeldoorn: Instituut voor Reformatieonderzoek, 2009.

Asselt, Willem J. van, and Eef Dekker, eds. *Reformation and Scholasticism: An Ecumenical Enterprise.* Texts & Studies in Reformation & Post-Reformation Thought, edited by Richard A. Muller. Grand Rapids: Baker Academic, 2001.

Aubert, Annette G. *The German Roots of Nineteenth-Century American Theology.* Oxford: Oxford University Press, 2013.

Ayres, Lewis. *Nicaea and its Legacy: An Approach to Fourth-Century Trinitarian Theology.* Oxford: Oxford University Press, 2004.

Bagchi, David, and David C. Steinmetz, eds. *The Cambridge Companion to Reformation Theology.* Cambridge: Cambridge University Press, 2004.

Bahnsen, Greg L. *Always Ready: Directions for Defending the Faith.* Edited by Robert R. Booth. Atlanta: American Vision, 1996.

———. *An Answer to Frame's Critique of Van Til: Profound Differences Between the Traditional and Presuppositional Methods.* Glenside: Westminster Seminary Bookstore, n.d.

———. 'A Conditional Resolution of the Apparent Paradox of Self-Deception.' PhD diss, University of Southern California, 1978.

———. 'The Crucial Concept of Self-Deception in Presuppositional Apologetics.' *Westminster Theological Journal* 57, no. 1 (Spring 1995): 1-31.

———. 'Inductivism, Inerrancy, and Presuppositionalism.' *Journal of the Evangelical Theological Society* 20, no. 4 (Dec 1977): 289-305.

———. 'Machen, Van Til, and the Apologetical Tradition of the OPC.' In *Pressing Toward the Mark: Essays Commemorating Fifty Years of the Orthodox Presbyterian Church*, edited by Charles G. Dennison and Richard C. Gamble, 259-294. Philadelphia: The Committee for the Historian of the Orthodox Presbyterian Church, 1986.

———. *No Other Standard: Theonomy and its Critics*. Tyler, TX: Institute for Christian Economics, 1991.

———. 'Pragmatism, Prejudice, and Presuppositionalism.' In *Foundations of Christian Scholarship*, edited by Gary North, 241-292. Vallecito, CA: Ross House Books, 1979.

———. *Presuppositional Apologetics: Stated and Defended*. Edited by Joel McDurmon. Powder Springs: American Vision Press, 2008.

———. 'Socrates or Christ: The Reformation of Christian Apologetics.' In *Foundations of Christian Scholarship*, edited by Gary North, 191-239. Vallecito, CA: Ross House Books, 1979.

———. *Van Til's Apologetic: Readings and Analysis*. Phillipsburg: P&R Publishing, 1998.

Baird, James Douglas. 'Analogical Knowledge: A Systematic Interpretation of Cornelius Van Til's Theological Epistemology.' *Mid-America Journal of Theology* 26 (2015): 77-103.

Baker, Brian Keith. 'Integrating Principles and Practices of Apologetics with Biblical Counseling.' DMin thesis, Southern Baptist Theological Seminary, 2018.

Ballor, Jordan J. 'Natural Law and Protestantism—A Review Essay.' *Christian Scholar's Review* 41, no. 2 (Winter 2012): 193-209.

Barnes, Jonathan, ed. *The Complete Works of Aristotle*. 2 vols. Princeton: Princeton University Press, 1984.

Barrett, Jordan P. *Divine Simplicity: A Biblical and Trinitarian Account*. Minneapolis: Fortress Press, 2017.

Barrett, Matthew. *None Greater: The Undomesticated Attributes of God*. Grand Rapids: Baker Books, 2019.

———. *Simply Trinity: The Unmanipulated Father Son, and Holy Spirit*. Grand Rapids: Baker Books, 2021.

Bartholomew, Craig G. *Contours of the Kuyperian Tradition: A Systematic Introduction.* Downers Grove: IVP Academic, 2017.

Bauerschmidt, Frederick Christian. *Thomas Aquinas: Faith, Reason, and Following Christ.* Christian Theology in Context, edited by Timothy Gorringe, Serene Jones, and Graham Ward. Oxford: Oxford University Press, 2013.

Bavinck, Herman. *Philosophy of Revelation: A New Annotated Edition.* Edited by Cory Brock and Nathaniel Gray Sutanto. Peabody, MA: Hendrickson Publishers, 2018.

———. *Reformed Dogmatics.* 4 vols. Edited by John Bolt. Translated by John Vriend. Grand Rapids: Baker Academic, 2003–2008.

Beach, J. Mark. 'Abraham Kuyper, Herman Bavinck, and "The Conclusions of Utrecht 1905".' *Mid-America Journal of Theology* 19 (2008): 11-68.

Beeke, Joel R. 'Van Til and Apologetics.' *New Horizons* 16, no. 5 (May 1995): 5-6.

Beiser, Frederick C., ed. *The Cambridge Companion to Hegel.* Cambridge: Cambridge University Press, 1993.

———. *German Idealism: The Struggle Against Subjectivism, 1781–1801.* Cambridge: Harvard University Press, 2002.

———. *Hegel.* Routledge Philosophers, edited by Brian Leiter. New York: Routledge, 2005.

———. *Late German Idealism: Trendelenburg and Lotze.* Oxford: Oxford University Press, 2013.

Békefi, Bálint. 'Van Til versus Stroud: Is the Transcendental Argument for Christian Theism Viable?' *TheoLogica* 2, no. 1 (2018): 136-60.

Belt, Hendrik van den. 'Autopistia: The Self-Convincing Authority of Scripture in Reformed Theology' PhD diss, University of Leiden, 2006.

Berkeley, George. *Principles of Human Knowledge and Three Dialogues.* Edited by Howard Robinson. Oxford: Oxford University Press, 1996.

Berkhof, Louis. *Systematic Theology.* New Combined Edition. Grand Rapids: William B. Eerdmans Publishing Company, 1996.

Beza, Theodore. *A Briefe and Pithie Summe of the Christian Faith.* Translated by Robert Fills. London: Richard Serll, 1565.

Blanshard, Brand. *The Nature of Thought.* 2 vols. London: George Allen & Unwin Ltd, 1921.

Bolt, John, ed. *Five Studies in the Thought of Herman Bavinck.* Lewiston, NY: Edwin Mellon, 2011.

————. *A Free Church, A Holy Nation: Abraham Kuyper's American Public Theology.* Grand Rapids: William B. Eerdmans Publishing Company, 2001.

Bosanquet, Bernard. *Implication and Linear Inference.* London: Macmillan and Co., Ltd., 1920.

————. *Logic, or the Morphology of Knowledge.* 2 vols. Second edition. London: Humphrey Milford/Oxford University Press, 1911.

————. *The Principle of Individuality and Value.* London: Macmillan and Co., Ltd., 1912.

Bosse, Brian. 'Van Tillian Presuppositional Apologetics: A Critique Concerning Certainty.' http://www.fallacydetective.com/images/uploads/Critique-VanTil.pdf

Bosserman, B. A. *The Trinity and the Vindication of Christian Paradox: An Interpretation and Refinement of the Theological Apologetic of Cornelius Van Til.* Eugene, OR: Pickwick, 2014.

Boucher, David, and Andrew Vincent. *British Idealism: A Guide for the Perplexed.* London: Continuum, 2012.

Bradley, F. H. *Appearance and Reality: A Metaphysical Essay.* London: Swan Sonnenschein & Co., 1893.

————. *Essays on Truth and Reality.* Oxford: Clarendon Press, 1914.

Brakel, Wilhelmus à. *The Christian's Reasonable Service.* 4 vols. Translated by Bartel Elshout. Edited by Joel R. Beeke. Grand Rapids: Reformation Heritage Books, 1992.

Bratt, James D. *Abraham Kuyper: Modern Calvinist, Christian Democrat.* Library of Religious Biography, edited by Mark A. Noll, Nathan O. Hatch, and Allen C. Guelzo. Grand Rapids: William B. Eerdmans Publishing Company, 2013.

———. *Dutch Calvinism in Modern America: A History of a Conservative Subculture*. Grand Rapids: Wm. B. Eerdmans Publishing Company, 1984.

Brock, Cory C., and N. Gray Sutanto. *Neo-Calvinism: A Theological Introduction*. Bellingham, WA: Lexham Academic, 2022.

Bucanus, William. *Institutions of Christian Religion*. Translated by Robert Hill. London: George Snowdon and Leonell Snowdon, 1606.

Bullinger, Henry. *The Decades*. Edited by Thomas Harding. 2 vols. Grand Rapids: Reformation Heritage Books, 2004.

Butler, Joseph. *The Analogy of Religion*. Edited by David McNaughton. Oxford: Oxford University Press, 2021.

Butner, D. Glenn, Jr. *Trinitarian Dogmatics: Exploring the Grammar of the Christian Doctrine of God*. Grand Rapids: Baker Academic, 2022.

Calvin, John. *Institutes of the Christian Religion*. 2 vols. Edited by John T. McNeill. Translated by Ford Lewis Battles. Library of Christian Classics. Philadelphia: The Westminster Press, 1960.

Cajetan, Tommaso de Vio. *The Analogy of Names, and the Concept of Being*. Translated by Edward A. Bushinski. Eugene, OR: Wipf and Stock, 2009.

Cessario, Romanus. *A Short History of Thomism*. Washington, D.C.: The Catholic University of America Press, 2003.

Clark, R. Scott. *Recovering the Reformed Confession: Our Theology, Piety, and Practice*. Phillipsburg: P&R Publishing, 2008.

Clowney, Edmund P. 'Preaching the Word of the Lord: Cornelius Van Til, V.D.M.' *Westminster Theological Journal* 46, no. 2 (Fall 1984): 233-53.

Cobb, John B., Jr., and David Ray Griffin. *Process Theology: An Introductory Exposition*. Louisville: Westminster John Knox Press, 1976.

Collett, Don. 'Apologetics: Van Til and Transcendental Argument.' *Westminster Theological Journal* 65, no. 2 (Fall 2003): 289-306.

Collingwood, R. G. *An Essay on Philosophical Method*. Oxford: The Clarendon Press, 1933.

_____. *Speculum Mentis or The Map of Knowledge*. Oxford: The Clarendon Press, 1924.

Collins, James. *God in Modern Philosophy*. Chicago: Henry Regnery, 1959.

Copleston, F. C. *Aquinas*. London: Penguin Books, 1955.

Cowan, Steven B. *Five Views on Apologetics*. Counterpoints, edited by Stanley N. Gundry. Grand Rapids: Zondervan, 2000.

Cowan, Steven B., and James S. Spiegel, eds. *Idealism and Christianity*. Vol. 2, *Idealism and Christian Philosophy*. New York: Bloomsbury, 2016.

Crampton, W. Gary. 'Why I Am Not a Van Tilian.' *The Trinity Review* (Sep 1993): 1-5.

Crisp, Oliver D. and Fred Sanders, eds. *Advancing Trinitarian Theology: Explorations in Constructive Dogmatics*. Grand Rapids: Zondervan, 2014.

Crossley, David J. 'Holism, Individuation, and Internal Relations.' *Journal of the History of Philosophy* 15, no. 2 (Apr 1977): 183-194.

Cumming, Nicholas A. *Francis Turretin (1623–87) and the Reformed Tradition*. St. Andrews Studies in Reformation History, edited by Bridget Heal. Leiden: Brill, 2020.

Daane, James. *A Theology of Grace*. Grand Rapids: Wm. B. Eerdmans Publishing Company, 1954.

Davies, Brain. *The Thought of Thomas Aquinas*. Oxford Clarendon Press, 1992.

Davies, Brian and Eleonore Stump, eds. *The Oxford Handbook of Aquinas*. Oxford: Oxford University Press, 2012.

David, Stephen T., Daniel Kendall, and Gerald O'Collins, eds. *The Trinity*. Oxford: Oxford University Press, 1999.

de Bary, Philip. *Thomas Reid and Scepticism: His Reliabilist Response*. London: Routledge, 2002.

De Boer, Cecil. 'The New Apologetic.' *The Calvin Forum* 19, no. 1–2 (Aug–Sept 1953): 3-7.

De Boer, Jesse. 'Professor Van Til's Apologetics, Part I: A Linguistic Bramble Patch.' *The Calvin Forum* 19, no. 1–2 (Aug–Sept 1953): 7-12.

————. 'Professor Van Til's Apologetics, Part II: God and Human Knowledge.' *The Calvin Forum* 19, no. 3 (Oct 1953): 27-34.

————. 'Professor Van Til's Apologetics, Part III: God and Human Knowledge.' *The Calvin Forum* 19, no. 4 (Nov 1953): 51-57.

DeMar, Gary, ed. *Pushing the Antithesis: The Apologetic Methodology of Greg L. Bahnsen.* Powder Springs, GA: American Vision, 2007.

Dennison, Charles G. 'Tragedy, Hope, and Ambivalence: The History of the Orthodox Presbyterian Church 1936–1962. Part One: Tragedy.' *Mid-America Journal of Theology* 8, no. 2 (Fall 1992): 147-159.

————. 'Tragedy, Hope, and Ambivalence: The History of the Orthodox Presbyterian Church 1936–1962. Part Two: Hope.' *Mid-America Journal of Theology* 9, no. 1 (Spring 1993): 26-44.

————. 'Tragedy, Hope, and Ambivalence: The History of the Orthodox Presbyterian Church 1936–1962. Part Three: Ambivalence.' *Mid-America Journal of Theology* 9, no. 2 (Fall 1993): 248-278.

Dennison, Charles G. and Richard C. Gamble, eds. *Pressing Toward the Mark: Essays Commemorating Fifty Years of the Orthodox Presbyterian Church.* Philadelphia: The Committee for the Historian of the Orthodox Presbyterian Church, 1986.

Dennison, James T., Jr., ed. *Reformed Confessions of the 16th and 17th Centuries in English Translation.* 4 vols. Grand Rapids: Reformation Heritage Books, 2008–2014.

Dennison, William D. 'Analytic Philosophy and Van Til's Epistemology.' *Westminster Theological Journal* 57, no. 1 (Spring 1995): 33-56.

————. *In Defense of the Eschaton: Essays in Reformed Apologetics.* Edited by James Douglas Baird. Eugene, OR: Wipf & Stock, 2015.

————. *Paul's Two-Age Construction and Apologetics.* Eugene, OR: Wipf & Stock, 2000.

————. 'Van Til and Common Grace.' *Mid-America Journal of Theology* 9, no. 2 (Fall 1993): 225-47.

Descartes, René. *The Philosophical Writings of Descartes.* Vol. 1. Translated by John Cottingham, Robert Stoothoff, and Dugald Murdoch. Cambridge: Cambridge University Press, 1985.

———. *The Philosophical Writings of Descartes*. Vol. 2. Translated by John Cottingham, Robert Stoothoff, and Dugald Murdoch. Cambridge: Cambridge University Press, 1984.

———. *The Philosophical Writings of Descartes*. Vol. 3, *The Correspondence*. Translated by John Cottingham, Robert Stoothoff, Dugald Murdoch, and Anthony Kenny. Cambridge: Cambridge University Press, 1991.

———. *Principles of Philosophy*. Translated by Valentine Rodger Miller and Reese P. Miller. Dordrecht: D. Reidel Publishing Company, 1982.

DeYoung, Kevin. 'Franciscus Junius, Old Princeton, and the Question of Natural Theology: A Response to Shannon's "Junius and Van Til on Natural Knowledge of God"' *Westminster Theological Journal* 83, no. 2 (Fall 2021): 251-66.

Dodds, Michael. J. *The One Creator God in Thomas Aquinas & Contemporary Theology*. Washington, D.C.: The Catholic University of America Press, 2020.

———. *The Unchanging God of Love: Thomas Aquinas and Contemporary Theology on Divine Immutability*. Second edition. Washington, D.C.: The Catholic University of America Press, 2008.

Dolezal, James E. *All That is in God: Evangelical Theology and the Challenge of Classical Christian Theism*. Grand Rapids: Reformation Heritage Books, 2017.

———. *God Without Parts: Divine Simplicity and the Metaphysics of God's Absoluteness*. Eugene, OR: Pickwick Publications, 2011.

———. 'Trinity, Simplicity and the Status of God's Personal Relations' *International Journal of Systematic Theology* 16, no. 1 (Jan. 2014): 79-98.

Doolan, Gregory T. *Aquinas on the Divine Ideas as Exemplar Causes*. Washington, D.C.: Catholic University of America Press, 2008.

Dooyeweerd, Herman. *A New Critique of Theoretical Thought*. Vol. 1, *The Necessary Presuppositions of Philosophy*. Translated by David H. Freeman and William S. Young. Grand Rapids: Paideia Press, 1984.

————. *A New Critique of Theoretical Thought*. Vol. 2, *The General Theory of the Modal Spheres*. Translated by David H. Freeman and H. De Jongste. Grand Rapids: Paideia Press, 1984.

————. *A New Critique of Theoretical Thought*. Vol. 3, *The Structures of Individuality of Temporal Reality*. Translated by David H. Freeman and H. De Jongste. Grand Rapids: Paideia Press, 1984.

————. *A New Critique of Theoretical Thought*. Vol. 4, *Index of Subjects and Authors*. Translated by H. De Jongste. Grand Rapids: Paideia Press, 1984.

————. *Reformation and Scholasticism in Philosophy*. Vol. 1, *The Greek Prelude*. Edited by Robert D. Knudsen. Translated by Ray Togtmann. The Collected Works of Herman Dooyeweerd, edited by D. F. M. Strauss, Series A, vol. 5. Grand Rapids: Paideia Press, 2012.

————. *Reformation and Scholasticism in Philosophy*. Vol. 2, *The Philosophy of the Cosmonomic Idea and the Scholastic Tradition in Christian Thought*. Edited by Lyn Boliek, Ralph Vunderink, and Harry Van Dyke. Translated by Magnus Verbrugge. The Collected Works of Herman Dooyeweerd, edited by D. F. M. Strauss, Series A, vol. 5/2. Grand Rapids: Paideia Press, 2013.

Dorrien, Gary. *Kantian Reason and Hegelian Spirit: The Idealistic Logic of Modern Theology*. Chichester: Wiley Blackwell, 2012.

Douma, Douglas J. *The Presbyterian Philosopher: The Authorized Biography of Gordon H. Clark*. Eugene, OR: Wipf & Stock, 2016.

Dowey, Edward A., Jr. *The Knowledge of God in Calvin's Theology*. Grand Rapids: William B. Eerdmans Publishing Company, 1994.

Duby, Steven J. *Jesus and the God of Classical Theism: Biblical Christology in Light of the Doctrine of God*. Grand Rapids: Baker Academic, 2022.

Dulles, Avery. *A History of Apologetics*. San Francisco: Ignatius Press, 1999.

Dunham, Jeremy, Iain Hamilton Grant, and Sean Watson. *Idealism: The History of a Philosophy*. London: Routledge, 2014.

Edgar, William. *The Face of Truth: Lifting the Veil*. Phillipsburg: P&R Publishing, 2001.

_____. *Reasons of the Heart: Recovering Christian Persuasion*. Grand Rapids: Baker Book House, 1996.

_____. 'Two Christian Warriors: Cornelius Van Til and Francis Schaeffer Compared.' *Westminster Theological Journal* 57, no. 1 (Spring 1995): 57-80.

_____. 'Why I Am a Presuppositionalist.' *New Horizons* 16, no. 5 (May 1995): 7-8.

Eglinton, James. *Bavinck: A Critical Biography*. Grand Rapids: Baker Academic, 2020.

Eliot, T. S. *Knowledge and Experience in the Philosophy of F. H. Bradley*. London: Faber and Faber, 1964.

Ellis, Brannon. *Calvin, Classical Trinitarianism, & the Aseity of the Son*. Oxford: Oxford University Press, 2012.

Emery, Gilles. *The Trinity: An Introduction to Catholic Doctrine on the Triune God*. Translated by Matthew Levering. Thomistic Ressourcement Series, edited by Matthew Levering and Thomas Joseph White. Washington, D.C.: The Catholic University of America Press, 2011.

Emery, Gilles, and Matthew Levering, eds. *Aristotle in Aquinas's Theology*. Oxford: Oxford University Press, 2015.

_____. *The Oxford Handbook of the Trinity*. Oxford: Oxford University Press, 2011.

Ewing, A. C. *Idealism: A Critical Survey*. London: Methuen & Co, 1934.

Fahim, Sherif. 'Kantian Epistemology vs. Reformed Epistemology.' *Puritan Reformed Journal* 12, no. 1 (Jan 2020): 125-52.

Fairbairn, Donald, and Ryan M. Reeves. *The Story of Creeds and Confessions: Tracing the Development of the Christian Faith*. Grand Rapids: Baker Academic, 2019.

Farris, Joshua R., and S. Mark Hamilton, eds. *Idealism and Christianity*. Vol. 1, *Idealism and Christian Theology*. New York: Bloomsbury, 2016.

Ferrier, James F. *Institutes of Metaphysic: The Theory of Knowing and Being*. Edinburgh and London: William Blackwood and Sons, 1854.

Feser, Edward. *Aquinas: A Beginner's Guide*. London: Oneworld Publications, 2009.

———. *Scholastic Metaphysics: A Contemporary Introduction*. Heusenstamm: Editiones Scholasticae, 2014.

Fesko, J. V. *The Covenant of Redemption: Origins, Development, and Reception*. Reformed Historical Theology, edited by Herman J. Selderhuis. Göttingen: Vandenhoek & Ruprecht, 2016.

———. 'Introduction.' In *Natural Theology*, Geerhardus Vos, translated by Albert Gootjes, xvii-lxx. Grand Rapids: Reformation Heritage Books, 2022.

———. *Reforming Apologetics: Retrieving the Classic Reformed Approach to Defending the Faith*. Grand Rapids: Baker Academic, 2019.

Fesko, J. V., and Guy M. Richard. 'Natural Theology and the Westminster Confession of Faith.' In *The Westminster Confession into the 21st Century*, Vol. 3, edited by Ligon Duncan, 223-66. Fearn: Mentor, 2009.

Filson, David Owen. 'The Apologetics and Theology of Cornelius Van Til.' *Foundations* 79 (Nov 2020): 32-59.

Flint, Thomas P., and Michael C. Rea, eds. *The Oxford Handbook of Philosophical Theology*. Oxford: Oxford University Press, 2009.

Fluhrer, Gabe. 'Reasoning by Presupposition: Clarifying and Applying the Center of Van Til's Apologetic' PhD diss, Westminster Theological Seminary, 2015.

Forrest, Benjamin K., Joshua D. Chatraw, and Alister E. McGrath, eds. *The History of Apologetics: A Biographical and Methodological Introduction*. Grand Rapids: Zondervan Academic, 2020.

Frame, John M. *Apologetics: A Justification of Christian Belief*. Phillipsburg: P&R Publishing Company, 2015.

———. 'Cornelius Van Til.' In *Handbook of Evangelical Theologians*, edited by Walter A. Elwell, 156-167. Grand Rapids: Baker Books, 1993.

———. *Cornelius Van Til: An Analysis of His Thought*. Phillipsburg: P&R Publishing Company, 1995.

————. *The Doctrine of God*. A Theology of Lordship. Phillipsburg: P&R Publishing Company, 2002.

————. *The Doctrine of the Knowledge of God*. A Theology of Lordship. Phillipsburg: P&R Publishing Company, 1987.

————. *A History of Western Philosophy and Theology*. Phillipsburg: P&R Publishing Company, 2015.

————. 'In Defense of Something Close to Biblicism: Reflections on Sola Scriptura and History in Theological Method.' *Westminster Theological Journal* 59, no. 2 (Fall 1997): 269-291.

————. *Nature's Case for God: A Brief Biblical Argument*. Bellingham, WA: Lexham Press, 2018.

————. *No Other God: A Response to Open Theism*. Phillipsburg: P&R Publishing Company, 2001.

————. *On Theology: Explorations and Controversies*. Bellingham, WA: Lexham Press, 2023.

————. 'Reply to Mark W. Karlberg.' *Mid-America Journal of Theology* 9, no. 2 (Fall 1993): 297-308.

————. 'Reply to Richard Muller and David Wells.' *Westminster Theological Journal* 59, no. 2 (Fall 1997): 311-318.

————. *Salvation Belongs to the Lord: An Introduction to Systematic Theology*. Phillipsburg: P&R Publishing Company, 2006.

————. *Selected Shorter Writings*, Vol. 1. Phillipsburg: P&R Publishing Company, 2014.

————. *Selected Shorter Writings*, Vol. 2. Phillipsburg: P&R Publishing Company, 2015.

————. *Selected Shorter Writings*, Vol. 3. Phillipsburg: P&R Publishing Company, 2016.

————. *Systematic Theology: An Introduction to Christian Belief*. Phillipsburg: P&R Publishing Company, 2013.

————. 'Systematic Theology and Apologetics at the Westminster Seminaries.' In *The Pattern of Sound Doctrine*, edited by David VanDrunen, 73-98. Phillipsburg: P&R Publishing Company, 2004.

————. *Theology in Three Dimensions: A Guide to Triperspectivalism and its Significance*. Phillipsburg: P&R Publishing Company, 2017.

————. 'Van Til on Antithesis.' *Westminster Theological Journal* 57, no. 1 (Spring 1995): 81-102.

————. 'Van Til and the Ligonier Apologetic.' *Westminster Theological Journal* 47, no. 2 (Fall 1985): 279-99.

————. *Van Til: The Theologian*. Phillipsburg: Pilgrim Publishing Company, 1976.

Frame, John M. and Steve Hays. 'Johnson on Van Til: A Rejoinder.' *The Evangelical Quarterly* 76, no. 3 (Jul 2004): 227-39.

Francks, Richard. *Modern Philosophy: The Seventeenth and Eighteenth Centuries*. Fundamentals of Philosophy, edited by John Shand. London: Routledge, 2003.

Gaffin, Richard B., Jr. 'Some Epistemological Reflections on 1 Cor. 2:6-16.' *Westminster Theological Journal* 57, no. 1 (Spring 1995): 103-24.

Gallagher, Kenneth T. *The Philosophy of Knowledge*. New York: Fordham University Press, 1982.

Gamble, Richard C. *The Whole Counsel of God*. Vol. 3, *God's People in the Western World*. Phillipsburg: P&R Publishing Company, 2021.

Garber, Daniel and Michael Ayers, eds. *The Cambridge History of Seventeenth-Century Philosophy*. 2 vols. Cambridge: Cambridge University Press, 1998.

Garcia, Mark A. 'Preface.' In *In Defense of the Eschaton: Essays in Reformed Apologetics*, William D. Dennison, edited by James Douglas Baird, xiii-xviii. Eugene, OR: Wipf & Stock, 2015.

Gaukroger, Stephen. *Francis Bacon and the Transformation of Early-Modern Philosophy*. Cambridge: Cambridge University Press, 2004.

Geehan, E. R., ed. *Jerusalem and Athens: Critical Discussions on the Philosophy and Apologetics of Cornelius Van Til*. Phillipsburg: P&R Publishing Company, 1971.

Geisler, Norman. *Thomas Aquinas: An Evangelical Appraisal*. Grand Rapids: Baker Book House, 1991.

Gerson, Lloyd P. *Ancient Epistemology*. Key Themes in Ancient Philosophy, edited by Catherine Osborne and G. R. F. Ferrari. Cambridge: Cambridge University Press, 2009.

Gilson, Étienne. *The Christian Philosophy of St. Thomas Aquinas*. Translated by L. K. Shook. Notre Dame, IL: University of Notre Dame Press, 1994.

————. *Methodical Realism: A Handbook for Beginning Realists*. Translated by Philip Trower. San Francisco: Ignatius Press, 1990.

Gleason, Ron. *Herman Bavinck: Pastor, Churchman, Statesman, and Theologian*. Phillipsburg: P&R Publishing Company, 2010.

Godfrey, W. Robert. 'The Westminster School' In *Reformed Theology in America: A History of its Modern Development*, edited by David F. Wells, 89-101. Grand Rapids: William B. Eerdmans Publishing Company, 1985.

Gomes, Alan W. 'Some Observations on the Theological Method of Faustus Socinus (1539–1604).' *Westminster Theological Journal* 70, no. 1 (Spring 2008): 49-71.

Gordon, Bruce. *Calvin*. New Haven: Yale University Press, 2009.

Goudriaan, Aza. *Reformed Orthodoxy and Philosophy, 1625–1750: Gisbertus Voetius, Petrus van Mastricht, and Anthonius Driessen*. Brill's Series in Church History, edited by Wim Janse. Leiden: Brill, 2006.

Goyette, John, Mark S. Latkovic, and Richard S. Myers, eds. *St. Thomas Aquinas and the Natural Law Tradition: Contemporary Perspectives*. Washington D.C.: The Catholic University of America Press, 2004.

Grabill, Stephen John. 'Theological Foundation for a Reformed Doctrine of Natural Law.' PhD diss., Calvin Theological Seminary, 2004.

Green, Bradley G., ed. *Thinking God's Thoughts After Him: Essays in the Van Til Tradition*. 2 vols. Eugene, OR: Wipf & Stock, forthcoming.

Greene, William Brenton. 'The Metaphysics of Christian Apologetics: I. Reality.' *The Presbyterian and Reformed Review* 9, no. 33 (Jan. 1898): 60-82.

————. 'The Metaphysics of Christian Apologetics: II. Duality.' *The Presbyterian and Reformed Review* 9, no. 34 (Apr. 1898): 261-288.

————. 'The Metaphysics of Christian Apologetics: III. Personality.' *The Presbyterian and Reformed Review* 9, no. 35 (Jul. 1898): 472-499.

————. 'The Metaphysics of Christian Apologetics: IV. Morality.' *The Presbyterian and Reformed Review* 9, no. 36 (Oct. 1898): 659-694.

Gregory, Thomas M. 'Apologetics Before and After Butler: A Tribute to Van Til.' In *Pressing Toward the Mark: Essays Commemorating Fifty Years of the Orthodox Presbyterian Church*, edited by Charles G. Dennison and Richard C. Gamble, 351-367. Philadelphia: The Committee for the Historian of the Orthodox Presbyterian Church, 1986.

Grote, John. *Exploratio Philosophica: Rough Notes on Modern Intellectual Science*, Vol. 1. Cambridge: Deighton, Bell, and Co., 1865.

————. *Exploratio Philosophica*, Vol. 2. Edited by Joseph Bickersteth Mayor. Cambridge: The University Press, 1900.

Haig, Albert. 'Modernity, "Radical Orthodoxy," and Cornelius Van Til: A Journey of Rediscovery of Participatory Theism.' *Colloquium* 47, no. 2 (Nov 2015): 257-73.

Haines, David, ed. *Without Excuse: Scripture, Reason, and Presuppositional Apologetics*. Leesburg, VA: The Davenant Press, 2020.

Hakkenberg, Michael A. 'The Battle over the Ordination of Gordon H. Clark, 1943–1948.' In *Pressing Toward the Mark: Essays Commemorating Fifty Years of the Orthodox Presbyterian Church*, edited by Charles G. Dennison and Richard C. Gamble, 329-50. Philadelphia: The Committee for the Historian of the Orthodox Presbyterian Church, 1986.

Hall, Alexander W. *Thomas Aquinas and John Duns Scotus: Natural Theology in the High Middle Ages*. London: Continuum, 2007.

Halsey, Jim S. *For a Time Such as This: An Introduction to the Reformed Apologetics of Cornelius Van Til*. Phillipsburg: Presbyterian and Reformed Publishing Company, 1976.

————. 'A Preliminary Critique of *Van Til: The Theologian*.' *Westminster Theological Journal* 39, no. 1 (Fall 1976): 120-36.

Hamilton, Floyd E. *The Basis of the Christian Faith: A Modern Defense of the Christian Religion*. Revised edition. New York: Harper & Row Publishers, 1964.

Hankins, James. *The Cambridge Companion to Renaissance Philosophy*. Cambridge: Cambridge University Press, 2007.

Harinck, George, Marinus De Jong, and Richard Mouw, eds. *The Klaas Schilder Reader: The Essential Theological Writings*. Bellingham, WA: Lexham Academic, 2022.

Harris, Henry S. *Hegel's Ladder*. Vol. 1, *The Pilgrimage of Reason*. Indianapolis: Hackett Publishing Company, 1997.

———. *Hegel's Ladder*. Vol. 2, *The Odyssey of Spirit*. Indianapolis: Hackett Publishing Company, 1997.

Hart, Darryl G. 'The Princeton Mind in the Modern World and the Common Sense of J. Gresham Machen.' *Westminster Theological Journal* 46, no. 1 (Spring 1984): 1-25.

Hart, D. G., and John Muether. 'Why Machen Hired Van Til.' *Ordained Servant* 6, no. 3 (July 1997). https://www.opc.org/OS/MachenVanTil.html

Hatch, Nathan O. *The Democratization of American Christianity*. New Haven: Yale University Press, 1989.

Haykin, Michael A. G., and Mark Jones, eds. *Drawn Into Controversie: Reformed Theological Diversity and Debates Within Seventeenth-Century British Puritanism*. Gottingen: Vandenhoek & Ruprecht, 2011.

Hazony, Yoram. *The Philosophy of Hebrew Scripture*. Cambridge: Cambridge University Press, 2012.

Hegel, Georg Wilhelm Friedrich. *Encyclopaedia of the Philosophical Sciences, Part One: Science of Logic*. Translated and edited by Klaus Brinkmann and Daniel O. Dahlstrom. Cambridge: Cambridge University Press, 2010.

———. *Encyclopaedia of the Philosophical Sciences, Part Two: Philosophy of Nature*. Translated by A. V. Miller. Oxford: The Clarendon Press, 1970.

———. *Encyclopaedia of the Philosophical Sciences, Part Three: Philosophy of Mind*. Translated by W. Wallace and A. V. Miller. Revised by Michael Inwood. Oxford: Clarendon Press, 2007.

———. *The Phenomenology of Spirit*. Translated and edited by Terry Pinkard. Cambridge: Cambridge University Press, 2018.

————. *The Science of Logic.* Translated and edited by George Di Giovanni. Cambridge: Cambridge University Press, 2010.

Heidegger, Johann Heinrich. *The Concise Marrow of Theology.* Translated by Casey Carmichael. Classic Reformed Theology, edited by R. Scott Clark and Casey Carmichael. Grand Rapids: Reformation Heritage Books, 2019.

Helm, Paul. *Calvin at the Centre.* Oxford: Oxford University Press, 2010.

————. *Faith & Understanding.* Grand Rapids: Wm. B. Eerdmans Publishing Company, 1997.

————. *John Calvin's Ideas.* Oxford: Oxford University Press, 2004.

Helseth, Paul Kjoss. 'The Apologetical Tradition of the OPC: A Reconsideration.' *Westminster Theological Journal* 60, no. 1 (Spring 1998): 109-129.

————. *Right Reason and the Princeton Mind: An Unorthodox Proposal.* Phillipsburg: P&R Publishing Company, 2010.

Heslam, Peter S. *Creating a Christian Worldview: Abraham Kuyper's Lectures on Calvinism.* Grand Rapids: William B. Eerdmans Publishing Company, 1998.

Hochschild, Joshua P., et al., eds. *Metaphysics Through Semantics: The Philosophical Recovery of the Medieval Mind.* International Archives of the History of Ideas, edited by Guido Giglioni. Cham: Springer, 2023.

Hodge, Charles. *Systematic Theology.* 3 vols. Grand Rapids: Wm. B. Eerdmans Publishing Company, 1965.

Hoover, David P. *The Defeasible Pumpkin: An Epiphany in a Pumpkin Patch.* Hatfield, PA: Interdisciplinary Biblical Research Institute, 1997. https://ibri.org/Books/DefeasiblePumpkin/htm/doc.html

————. 'For the Sake of Argument: A Critique of the Logical Structure of Van Til's Presuppositionalism.' *IBRI Research Report* 11 (1982). https://ibri.org/RRs/RR011/11vanTil.htm

Hughes, John J., ed. *Speaking the Truth in Love: The Theology of John M. Frame.* Phillipsburg: P&R Publishing Company, 2009.

Hume, David. *An Enquiry Concerning Human Understanding.* Edited by Peter Millican. Oxford: Oxford University Press, 2007.

———. *A Treatise of Human Nature*. Edited by L. A. Selby-Bigge. Oxford: The Clarendon Press, 1888.

Hunt, Jason Bennett. 'Cornelius Van Til's Doctrine of God and Its Relevance for Contemporary Hermeneutics.' PhD diss, University of Chester, 2017.

Israel, Jonathan I. *Radical Enlightenment: Philosophy and the Making of Modernity 1650–1750*. Oxford: Oxford University Press, 2001.

Ive, Jeremy G. A. 'The Contribution and Philosophical Development of the Reformational Philosopher, Dirk H. Th. Vollenhoven.' *Philosophia Reformata* 80, no. 2 (Nov 2015): 159-77.

Jensen, Steven J. *The Human Person: A Beginner's Thomistic Psychology*. Washington, D.C.: The Catholic University of America Press, 2018.

Joachim, Harold H. *The Nature of Truth*. Oxford: Clarendon Press, 1906.

Johnson, Jeffrey D. *The Failure of Natural Theology: A Critical Appraisal of the Philosophical Theology of Thomas Aquinas*. Conway, AR: Free Grace Press, 2021.

Johnson, John J. 'Is Cornelius Van Til's Apologetic Method Christian, or Merely Theistic?' *The Evangelical Quarterly* 75, no. 3 (Jul 2003): 257-68.

Jones, Henry. *A Faith That Enquires*. London: Macmillan and Co., Ltd., 1922.

Kant, Immanuel. *Critique of Pure Reason*. Translated and edited by Paul Guyer and Allen W. Wood. Cambridge: Cambridge University Press, 1998.

———. *Prolegomena to Any Future Metaphysics*. Translated and edited by Gary Hatfield. Cambridge: Cambridge University Press, 2004.

Karlberg, Mark W. 'John Frame and the Recasting of Van Tilian Apologetics: A Review Article.' *Mid-America Journal of Theology* 9, no. 2 (Fall 1993): 279-96.

Kenny, Anthony. *Aquinas on Mind*. Topics in Medieval Philosophy, edited by John Marenbon. London: Routledge, 1993.

Kerr, Fergus. *After Aquinas: Versions of Thomism*. Malden, MA: Blackwell Publishing, 2002.

————. *Twentieth-Century Catholic Theologians*. Malden, MA: Blackwell Publishing, 2007.

Kirkham, Richard L. *Theories of Truth: A Critical Introduction*. Cambridge, MA: The MIT Press, 1995.

Kleutgen, Josef. *Pre-Modern Philosophy Defended*. Translated by William H. Marshner. South Bend: St. Augustine's Press, 2019.

Klubertanz, George P. *St. Thomas Aquinas on Analogy*. Chicago: Loyola University Press, 1960.

Knudsen, Robert D. 'The Legacy of Cornelius Van Til.' *New Horizons* 16, no. 5 (May 1995): 3-4.

————. 'The Transcendental Perspective of Westminster's Apologetic.' *Westminster Theological Journal* 48, no. 2 (Fall 1986): 223-39.

Koons, Robert C. *Realism Regained: An Exact Theory of Causation, Teleology, and the Mind*. Oxford: Oxford University Press, 2000.

Krabbendam, Henry. 'Cornelius Van Til: The Methodological Objective of Biblical Apologetics.' *Westminster Theological Journal* 57, no. 1 (Spring 1995): 125-44.

Kretzmann, Norman. *The Metaphysics of Theism: Aquinas's Natural Theology in Summa Contra Gentiles I*. Oxford: Clarendon Press, 1997.

————. *The Metaphysics of Creation: Aquinas's Natural Theology in Summa Contra Gentiles II*. Oxford: Clarendon Press, 1999.

Kretzmann, Norman, and Eleonore Stump, eds. *The Cambridge Companion to Aquinas*. Cambridge: Cambridge University Press, 1993.

Kretzmann, Norman, Anthony Kenny, and Jan Pinborg, eds. *The Cambridge History of Later Medieval Philosophy: From the Rediscovery of Aristotle to the Disintegration of Scholasticism 1100–1600*. Cambridge: Cambridge University Press, 1982.

Kurtz, Ronni. *No Shadow of Turning: Divine Immutability and the Economy of Redemption*. Reformed Exegetical and Doctrinal Studies, edited by Matthew Barrett and J. V. Fesko. Fearn: Mentor, 2022.

Kuyper, Abraham. *Common Grace: God's Gifts for a Fallen World*. 3 vols. Bellingham, WA: Lexham Press, 2015–2020.

————. *Encyclopedia of Sacred Theology*. Translated by J. Hendrik de Vries. New York: Charles Scribner's Sons, 1898.

————. *Lectures on Calvinism*. Grand Rapids: Wm. B. Eerdmans Publishing Company, 1931.

————. *Pantheism's Destruction of Boundaries*. Translated by J. Hendrik de Vries. Bronxville, NY: np., 1893.

Lagerlund, Henrik, and Benjamin Hill, eds. *The Routledge Companion to Sixteenth Century Philosophy*. New York: Routledge, 2017.

Lang, Andrew. 'The Reformation and Natural Law.' Translated by J. Gresham Machen. *Princeton Theological* Review. 7, no. 2 (April 1909): 177-218.

LaRocca, Robert. 'Cornelius Van Til's Rejection and Appropriation of Thomistic Metaphysics.' ThM thesis, Westminster Theological Seminary, 2012.

Lear, Jonathan. *Aristotle: The Desire to Understand*. Cambridge: Cambridge University Press, 1988.

Lehner, Ulrich L., Richard A. Muller, and A. G. Roeber, eds. *The Oxford Handbook of Early Modern Theology, 1600–1800*. Oxford: Oxford University Press, 2016.

Letham, Robert. *The Holy Trinity*. Revised edition. Phillipsburg: P&R Publishing Company, 2019.

Levering, Matthew, and Marcus Plested, eds. *The Oxford Handbook of the Reception of Aquinas*. Oxford: Oxford University Press, 2021.

Lillback, Peter A. 'Interview with Dr William Edgar.' *Unio cum Christo* 3, no. 1 (Apr 2017): 249-64.

Littlejohn, Bradford, ed. *God of Our Fathers: Classical Theism for the Contemporary Church*. Lincoln: The Davenant Press, 2018.

Locke, John. *An Essay Concerning Human Understanding*. London: Penguin Books, 1997.

Logan, Samuel T., Jr. 'Theological Decline in Christian Institutions and the Value of Van Til's Epistemology.' *Westminster Theological Journal* 57, no. 1 (Spring 1995): 145-63.

Lonergan, Bernard, *Collected Works*. Vol. 2, *Verbum: Word and Idea in Aquinas*. Edited by Frederick E. Crowe and Robert M. Doran. Toronto: University of Toronto Press, 1997.

Long, D. Stephen. *The Perfectly Simple Triune God: Aquinas and His Legacy*. Minneapolis: Fortress Press, 2016.

Long, Steven A. *Analogia Entis: On the Analogy of Being, Metaphysics, and the Act of Faith*. Notre Dame, IL: University of Notre Dame Press, 2011.

Lotze, Hermann. *Logic in Three Books of Thought, of Investigation, and of Knowledge*. Translated by R. L. Nettleship, et al. Edited by Bernard Bosanquet. Oxford: The Clarendon Press, 1884.

Lovejoy, Arthur O. *The Great Chain of Being: A Study of the History of an Idea*. Cambridge: Harvard University Press, 1936.

Lowe, E. Jonathan. 'Essentialism, Metaphysical Realism, and the Errors of Conceptualism.' *Philosophia Scientiae* 12, no. 1 (April 2008): 9-33.

Machen, J. Gresham. *Christianity & Liberalism*. Grand Rapids: Wm. B. Eerdmans Publishing Company, 1923.

————. 'The Relation of Religion to Science and Philosophy.' *The Princeton Theological Review* 24, no. 1 (Jan 1926): 38-66.

————. *What is Christianity?* Edited by Ned B. Stonehouse. Birmingham: Solid Ground Christian Books, 2013.

————. *What is Faith?* London: Hodder and Stoughton, 1925

Macleod, Donald. 'Bavinck's *Prolegomena*: Fresh Light on Amsterdam, Old Princeton, and Cornelius Van Til.' *Westminster Theological Journal* 68, no. 2 (Fall 2006): 261-82.

Mangum, R. Todd. *The Dispensational-Covenantal Rift: The Fissuring of American Evangelical Theology from 1936 to 1944*. Studies in Evangelical History and Thought, edited by David Bebbington, et al. Milton Keyes: Paternoster, 2007.

Mander, W. J. *British Idealism: A History*. Oxford: Oxford University Press, 2011.

Mansfield, Aaron. 'Knowledge of the Natural Law in the Theology of John Calvin and Thomas Aquinas.' DPhil diss., University of Oxford, 2021.

Marcel, Pierre. *The Christian Philosophy of Herman Dooyeweerd*. Vol. 1, *The Transcendental Critique of Theoretical Thought*. Translated and edited by Colin Wright. Aalten: WordBridge Publishing, 2013.

————. *The Christian Philosophy of Herman Dooyeweerd*. Vol. 2, *The General Theory of the Law-Spheres*. Translated and edited by Colin Wright. Aalten: WordBridge Publishing, 2013.

Marenbon, John. *Medieval Philosophy: An Historical and Philosophical Introduction*. London: Routledge, 2007.

Marsden, George M. *Fundamentalism and American Culture*. Second edition. Oxford: Oxford University Press, 2006.

Marston, George W. *The Voice of Authority*. Nutley, NJ: The Presbyterian and Reformed Publishing Company, 1960.

Maspero, Giulio and Robert J. Woźniak, eds. *Rethinking Trinitarian Theology: Disputed Questions and Contemporary Issues in Trinitarian Theology*. London: T&T Clark, 2012.

Masselink, William. *General Revelation and Common Grace*. Grand Rapids: Wm. B. Eerdmans Publishing Company, 1953.

————. *J. Gresham Machen: His Life and Defence of the Bible*. Grand Rapids: Zondervan Publishing House, 1939.

Mastricht, Petrus van. *Theoretical-Practical Theology*. Vol. 1, *Prolegomena*. Translated by Todd M. Rester. Edited by Joel R. Beeke. Grand Rapids: Reformation Heritage Books, 2018.

————. *Theoretical-Practical Theology*. Vol. 2, *Faith in the Triune God*. Translated by Todd M. Rester. Edited by Joel R. Beeke. Grand Rapids: Reformation Heritage Books, 2019.

Mattson, Brian G. 'Van Til on Bavinck: An Assessment.' *Westminster Theological Journal* 70, no. 1 (Spring 2008): 111-27.

Maxwell, Paul C. 'The Covenant Theology of Cornelius Van Til in Light of His Interaction with Karl Barth and Hans Urs von Balthasar.' *Criswell Theological Review* 12, no. 1 (Fall 2014): 81-107.

McCall, Thomas, and Michael Rea, eds. *Philosophical and Theological Essays on the Trinity*. Oxford: Oxford University Press, 2009.

McConnel, Timothy I. 'Common Grace or Antithesis? Towards a Consistent Understanding of Kuyper's "Sphere Sovereignty."' *Pro Rege* 31, no. 1 (Sept 2002): 1-13.

———. 'The Historical Origins of the Presuppositional Apologetics of Cornelius Van Til.' PhD diss, Marquette University, 1999.

———. 'The Influence of Idealism on the Apologetics of Cornelius Van Til.' *Journal of the Evangelical Theological Society* 48, no. 3 (Sept 2005): 557-88.

———. 'The Old Princeton Apologetics: Common Sense or Reformed?' *Journal of the Evangelical Theological Society* 46, no. 4 (Dec 2003): 647-72.

McGrade, A. S., ed. *The Cambridge Companion to Medieval Philosophy.* Cambridge: Cambridge University Press, 2003.

McInerny, Ralph. *Aquinas on Analogy.* Washington, D.C.: Catholic University of America Press, 1996.

———. *Praeambula Fidei: Thomism and the God of the Philosophers.* Washington, D.C.: Catholic University of America Press, 2006.

McNeill, John T. 'Natural Law in the Teaching of the Reformers.' *The Journal of Religion* 26, no. 3 (July 1946): 168-82.

McTaggart, John M. E. *The Nature of Existence.* Vol. 1. Cambridge: The University Press, 1921.

———. *The Nature of Existence.* Vol. 2. Edited by C. D. Broad. Cambridge: The University Press, 1927.

McVicar, Michael J. *Christian Reconstruction: R. J. Rushdoony and American Religious Conservatism.* Chapel Hill: The University of North Carolina Press, 2015.

Mijuskovic, Ben Lazare. *The Achilles of Rationalist Arguments: The Simplicity, Unity, and Identity of Thought and Soul from the Cambridge Platonists to Kant: A Study in the History of an Argument.* The Hague: Martinus Nijhoff, 1974.

Mondin, Battista. *The Principle of Analogy in Protestant and Catholic Theology.* The Hague: Martinus Nijhoff, 1963.

Montagnes, Bernard. *The Doctrine of the Analogy of Being According to Thomas Aquinas.* Translated by E. M. Macierowski and Pol Vandevelde. Edited by Andrew Tallon. Milwaukee: Marquette University Press, 2004.

Morello, Sebastian. *The World as God's Icon: Creator & Creation in the Platonic Thought of Thomas Aquinas*. Brooklyn: Angelico Press, 2020.

Morley, Brian K. *Mapping Apologetics: Comparing Contemporary Approaches*. Downers Grove: IVP Academic, 2015.

Mortensen, John R. 'Understanding St. Thomas on Analogy.' PhD diss., Pontificia Universitas Sanctae Crucis, 2006. The Aquinas Institute for the Study of Sacred Doctrine.

Mosteller, Timothy M. *The Heresy of Heresies: A Defense of Christian Common-Sense Realism*. Eugene, OR: Cascade Books, 2021.

Muether, John R. *Cornelius Van Til: Reformed Apologist and Churchman*. Phillipsburg: P&R Publishing, 2008.

Muller, Richard A. *After Calvin: Studies in the Development of a Theological Tradition*. Oxford Studies in Historical Theology, edited by David C. Steinmetz. Oxford: Oxford University Press, 2003.

————. 'Calvin and the "Calvinists": Assessing Continuities and Discontinuities Between the Reformation and Orthodoxy: Part One.' *Calvin Theological Journal* 30, no. 2 (Nov 1995): 345-75.

————. 'Calvin and the "Calvinists": Assessing Continuities and Discontinuities Between the Reformation and Orthodoxy: Part Two.' *Calvin Theological Journal* 31, no. 1 (Apr 1996): 125-60.

————. *Calvin and the Reformed Tradition: On the Work of Christ and the Order of Salvation*. Grand Rapids: Baker Academic, 2012.

————. 'Calvinist Thomism Revisited: William Ames (1576–1633) and the Divine Ideas.' In *From Rome to Zurich, Between Ignatius and Vermigli*, edited by Kathleen M. Comerford, Gary W. Jenkins, and W. J. Torrance Kirby, 103-118. Studies in the History of Christian Tradition. Leiden: Brill, 2017.

————. 'The Dogmatic Function of St. Thomas' "Proofs": A Protestant Appreciation.' *Fides et Historia* 24, no. 2 (Summer 1992): 15-29.

————. 'Historiography in the Service of Theology and Worship: Toward Dialogue with John Frame.' *Westminster Theological Journal* 59, no. 2 (Fall 1997): 301-310.

————. 'Incarnation, Immutability, and the Case for Classical Theism.' *Westminster Theological Journal* 45, no. 1 (Spring 1983): 22-40.

———. 'John Preston on the Purpose and Place of the Natural Knowledge of God.' *Calvin Theological Journal* 57, no. 2 (Nov 2022): 247-70.

———. 'Not Scotist: Understandings of Being, Univocity, and Analogy in Early-Modern Reformed Thought.' *Reformation & Renaissance Review* 14, no. 2 (Aug 2012): 127-150.

———. 'Not Without Scripture: William Perkins, the Light of Nature, and Proofs of the Existence of God.' In *Reading Certainty: Exegesis and Epistemology on the Threshold of Modernity*, edited by Ralph Keen, Elizabeth Palmer, and Daniel Owings, 203-222. Studies in Medieval and Reformation Traditions. Leiden: Brill, 2022.

———. *Post-Reformation Reformed Dogmatics*. Vol. 1, *Prolegomena to Theology*. Second edition. Grand Rapids: Baker Academic, 2003.

———. 'Reading Aquinas from a Reformed Perspective: A Review Essay.' *Calvin Theological Journal* 53, no. 2 (Nov 2018): 255-88.

———. 'Reformation, Orthodoxy, "Christian Aristotelianism," and the Eclecticism of Early Modern Philosophy.' *Dutch Review of Church History* 81, no. 3 (Jan 2001): 306-25.

———. 'Scholasticism Protestant and Catholic: Francis Turretin on the Object and Principles of Theology.' *Church History* 55, no. 2 (June 1986): 193-205.

———. 'Scholasticism, Reformation, Orthodoxy, and the Persistence of Christian Aristotelianism.' *Trinity Journal* 19, no. 1 (Spring 1998): 81-96.

———. *The Unaccommodated Calvin: Studies in the Foundation of a Theological Tradition*. Oxford Studies in Historical Theology, edited by David C. Steinmetz. Oxford: Oxford University Press, 2000.

———. 'Was it Really Viral? Natural Theology in the Early Modern Reformed Tradition.' In *Crossing Traditions: Essays on the Reformation and Intellectual History*, edited by Maria-Cristine Pitassi and Daniela Solfaroli Camillocci, 507-531. Studies in Medieval and Reformation Traditions. Leiden: Brill, 2018.

Murray, John. 'Systematic Theology.' *Westminster Theological Journal* 25, no. 2 (May 1963): 133-142.

———. 'Systematic Theology Second Article.' *Westminster Theological Journal* 26, no. 1 (Nov 1963): 33-46.

Musculus, Wolfgang. *Common Places of Christian Religion.* Translated John Man. London: R. Woulfe, 1563.

Nadler, Steven, ed. *A Companion to Early Modern Philosophy.* Malden, MA: Blackwell Publishers Ltd., 2002.

Nash, Ronald H. *The Word of God and the Mind of Man: The Crisis of Revealed Truth in Contemporary Theology.* Phillipsburg: P&R Publishing, 1982.

Naugle, David K. *Worldview: The History of a Concept.* Grand Rapids: William B. Eerdmans Publishing Company, 2002.

Nelson, Alvin F. 'Internal Relations.' *The Southwestern Journal of Philosophy* 3, no. 1 (Spring 1972): 23-31.

Nixon, Leroy. *John Calvin's Teachings on Human Reason.* New York: Exposition Press, 1960.

North, Gary. *Dominion and Common Grace: The Biblical Basis of Progress.* Tyler, TX: Institute for Christian Economics, 1987.

———. ed. *Foundations of Christian Scholarship: Essays in the Van Til Perspective.* Vallecito, CA: Ross House Books, 1979.

———. ed. *Theonomy: An Informed Response.* Tyler, TX: Institute for Christian Economics, 1991.

———. *Westminster's Confession: The Abandonment of Van Til's Legacy.* Tyler, TX: Institute for Christian Economics, 1991.

Notaro, Thom. *Van Til & the Use of Evidence.* Phillipsburg: Presbyterian and Reformed Publishing Company, 1980.

Oakeshott, Michael. *Experience and Its Modes.* Cambridge: The University Press, 1933.

Oberman, Heiko A. *The Dawn of the Reformation: Essays in Late Medieval and Early Reformation Thought.* Grand Rapids: William B. Eerdmans Publishing Company, 1992.

———. *The Reformation: Roots and Ramifications.* Translated by Andrew Colin Gow. London: T&T Clark, 1994.

———. 'Some Notes on the Theology of Nominalism: With Attention to Its Relation to the Renaissance.' *The Harvard Theological Review* 53, no. 1 (Jan 1960): 47-76.

O'Donnell, Laurence R., III. '*Kees Van Til als Nederlandse-Amerikaanse, Neo-Calvinistisch-Presbyteriaan apologeticus*: An Analysis of Cornelius Van Til's Presupposition of Reformed Dogmatics with special reference to Herman Bavinck's *Gereformeerde Dogmatiek*.' ThM thesis, Calvin Theological Seminary, 2011.

————. 'Neither "Copernican" nor "Van Tilian": Re-Reading Cornelius Van Til's Reformed Apologetics in Light of Herman Bavinck's *Reformed Dogmatics*.' *The Bavinck Review* 2 (2011): 71-95.

Oliphint, K. Scott. 'The Consistency of Van Til's Methodology.' *Westminster Theological Journal* 52, no. 1 (Spr 1990): 27-49.

————. *Covenantal Apologetics: Principles & Practice in Defense of Our Faith*. Wheaton: Crossway, 2013.

————. *God With Us: Divine Condescension and the Attributes of God*. Wheaton: Crossway, 2012.

————. 'Is There a Reformed Objection to Natural Theology?.' *Westminster Theological Journal* 74, no. 1 (Spring 2012): 169-203.

————. 'Jerusalem and Athens Revisited.' *Westminster Theological Journal* 49, no. 1 (Spr 1987): 65-90.

————. 'Jonathan Edwards: Reformed Apologist.' *Westminster Theological Journal* 57, no. 1 (Spring 1995): 165-86.

————. *The Majesty of Mystery: Celebrating the Glory of an Incomprehensible God*. Bellingham, WA: Lexham Press, 2016.

————. *Reasons for Faith: Philosophy in the Service of Theology*. Phillipsburg: P&R Publishing, 2006.

————. '"Something Much Too Plain to Say": A Systematic Theological Apologetic.' In *Resurrection and Eschatology: Theology in Service of the Church*, edited by Lane G. Tipton and Jeffrey C. Waddington, 361-82. Phillipsburg: P&R Publishing Company, 2008.

————. *Thomas Aquinas*. Great Thinkers, edited by Nathan Shannon. Phillipsburg: P&R Publishing, 2017.

————. 'Using Reason by Faith.' *Westminster Theological Journal* 73, no. 1 (Spring 2011): 97-112.

————. 'Van Til and the Reformation of Apologetics.' URL: https://defenseofaith.wordpress.com/2015/11/07/van-til-and-the-reformation-of-apologetics/

Oliphint, K. Scott and Lane G. Tipton, eds. *Revelation and Reason: New Essays in Reformed Apologetics*. Phillipsburg: P&R Publishing, 2007.

Orlebeke, Clifton J. 'On Brute Facts.' *The Calvin Forum* 19, no. 1-2 (Aug–Sept 1953): 13-17.

Orr, James. *The Christian View of God and the World*. New York: Anson D. F. Randolph and Co., 1893.

Ortlund, Gavin. 'Wholly Other or Wholly Given Over? What Van Til Missed in His Criticism of Barth.' *Presbyterion* 35, no. 1 (Spring 2009): 35-52.

Otto, Randall. 'Renewing Our Mind: Reformed Epistemology and the Task of Apologetics.' *The Evangelical Quarterly* 88, no 2 (Apr 2016-2017): 111-25.

Partee, Charles. *The Theology of John Calvin*. Louisville: Westminster John Knox Press, 2008.

Pavlischek, Keith J. 'An Analysis and Evaluation of Cornelius Van Til's Doctrine of Common Grace.' MPhil thesis, Institute for Christian Studies, 1984.

Paley, William. *Natural Theology: Or Evidence of the Existence and Attributes of the Deity, Collected from the Appearances of Nature*. Edited by Matthew D. Eddy and David Knight. Oxford: Oxford University Press, 2006.

———. *A View of the Evidences of Christianity*. 2 vols. London: Vernor, Hood, and Sharpe, 1811.

Payne, Michael W. 'Epistemological Crises, Dramatic Narratives, and Apologetics: The *Ad Hominem* Once More.' *Westminster Theological Journal* 64, no. 1 (Spring 2002): 95-117.

Pelikan, Jaroslav, and Valerie Hotchkiss, eds. *Creeds & Confessions of Faith in the Christian Tradition*. 3 vols. New Haven: Yale University Press, 2003.

Phan, Peter C. *The Cambridge Companion to the Trinity*. Cambridge: Cambridge University Press, 2011.

Pinkard, Terry. *German Philosophy 1760–1860: The Legacy of Idealism*. Cambridge: Cambridge University Press, 2002.

Platt, John. *Reformed Thought and Scholasticism: The Arguments for the Existence of God in Dutch Theology, 1575–1650*. Studies in the History of Christian Thought, edited by Heiko A. Oberman. Leiden: Brill, 1982.

Polanus, Amandus. *The Substance of Christian Religion*. Translated by Elijahu Wilcocks. London: John Oxenbridge, 1595.

Polyander, Johannes, Antonius Walaeus, Antonius Thysius, and Andreas Rivetus. *Synopsis Purioris Theologiae = Synopsis of a Purer Theology*. Vol. 1, *Disputations 1-23*. Edited by Dolf te Velde. Translated by Riemer A. Faber. Studies in Medieval and Reformation Traditions, edited by Andrew Colin Gow. Leiden: Brill, 2015.

———. *Synopsis Purioris Theologiae = Synopsis of a Purer Theology*. Vol. 2, *Disputations 24-42*. Edited by Henk van den Belt. Translated by Riemer A. Faber. Studies in Medieval and Reformation Traditions, edited by Andrew Colin Gow. Leiden: Brill, 2016.

———. *Synopsis Purioris Theologiae = Synopsis of a Purer Theology*. Vol. 3, *Disputations 43-52*. Edited by Harm Goris. Translated by Riemer A. Faber. Studies in Medieval and Reformation Traditions, edited by Andrew Colin Gow. Leiden: Brill, 2020.

Popkin, Richard. *The History of Scepticism: From Savonarola to Bayle*. Revised edition. Oxford: Oxford University Press, 2003.

Poythress, Vern S. *The Mystery of the Trinity: A Trinitarian Approach to the Attributes of God*. Phillipsburg: P&R Publishing Company, 2020.

———. 'Reforming Ontology and Logic in the Light of the Trinity: An Application of Van Til's Idea of Analogy.' *Westminster Theological Journal* 57, no. 1 (Spring 1995): 187-219.

———. *Symphonic Theology: The Validity of Multiple Perspectives in Theology*. Phillipsburg: P&R Publishing Company, 1987.

Pratt, Richard L., Jr. *Every Thought Captive: A Study Manual for the Defense of the Faith*. Phillipsburg: P&R Publishing Company, 1979.

Przywara, Erich. *Analogia Entis: Metaphysics: Original Structure and Universal Rhythm*. Translated by John R. Betz and David Bentley Hart. Grand Rapids: William B. Eerdmans Publishing Company, 2014.

Rasmussen, Joshua. *Defending the Correspondence Theory of Truth.* Cambridge: Cambridge University Press, 2014.

Reid, Thomas. *An Inquiry Into the Human Mind on the Principles of Common Sense.* Edited by Derek R. Brookes. University Park, PA: The Pennsylvania State University Press, 1997.

―――. *Essays on the Intellectual Powers of Man.* Edited by Derek R. Brookes. University Park, PA: The Pennsylvania State University Press, 2002.

Reiter, David. 'The Modal Transcendental Argument for God's Existence.' *The Confessional Presbyterian* 7 (2011): 147-52, 250-51.

Re Manning, Russell, ed. *The Oxford Handbook of Natural Theology.* Oxford: Oxford University Press, 2013.

Reymond, Robert L. *The Justification of Knowledge.* Phillipsburg: Presbyterian and Reformed Publishing Co., 1979.

Rian, Edwin H. *The Presbyterian Conflict.* Grand Rapids: W. B. Eerdmans Publishing Company, 1940.

Riley, Michael P. 'Can One be Both a Dispensational and "Covenantal" Apologist?' *Detroit Baptist Seminary Journal* 21 (2016): 151-66.

Robbins, John W. *Cornelius Van Til: The Man and the Myth.* Jefferson, MD: The Trinity Foundation, 1986.

Roberts, Wesley A. 'Cornelius Van Til' In *Reformed Theology in America: A History of its Modern Development*, edited by David F. Wells, 119-132. Grand Rapids: William B. Eerdmans Publishing Company, 1985.

Rohatyn, Dennis A. 'Internal Relations.' *Philosophical Papers* 4, no. 2 (1975): 116-120.

Rushdoony, Rousas John. *By What Standard? An Analysis of the Philosophy of Cornelius Van Til.* Vallecito, CA: Ross House Books, 1958.

―――. *Van Til.* International Library of Philosophy and Theology, edited by David H. Freeman. Phillipsburg: Presbyterian and Reformed Publishing Company, 1979.

Russell, Bertrand. *Philosophical Essays.* London: Longmans, Green, and Co., 1910.

Sanders, Fred. *The Triune God.* New Studies in Dogmatics, edited by Michael Allen and Scott Swain. Grand Rapids: Zondervan, 2016.

Schmitt, Charles B., ed. *The Cambridge History of Renaissance Philosophy.* Cambridge: Cambridge University Press, 1988.

Selderhuis, Herman J., ed. *A Companion to Reformed Orthodoxy.* Brill's Companions to the Christian Tradition, edited by Christopher M. Bellitto. Leiden: Brill, 2013.

———. *John Calvin: A Pilgrim's Life.* Downers Grove: IVP Academic, 2009.

Seth, Andrew. *Hegelianism and Personality.* Edinburgh and London: William Blackwood and Sons, 1887.

Seth, Andrew and R. B. Haldane, eds. *Essays in Philosophical Criticism.* London: Longmans, Green, and Co., 1883.

Shannon, Nathan D. *Absolute Person and Moral Experience: A Study in Neo-Calvinism.* T&T Clark Enquiries in Theological Ethics, edited by Brian Brock and Susan F. Parsons. London: T&T Clark, 2022.

———. 'A Brief Rejoinder to Kevin DeYoung.' *Westminster Theological Journal* 83, no. 2 (Fall 2021): 267-73.

———. 'Christianity and Evidentialism: Van Til and Locke on Facts and Evidence.' *Westminster Theological Journal* 74, no. 2 (Fall 2012): 323-53.

———. 'Covenant Relation as Prolegomena to Knowledge of God: An Exegetical Study of John 5.' *Neue Zeitschrift für Systematische Theologie und Religionsphilosophie* 61, no. 3 (2019): 333-53.

———. 'Junius and Van Til on Natural Knowledge of God.' *Westminster Theological Journal* 82, no. 2 (Fall 2020): 279-300.

Shepherd, Victor. *The Nature and Function of Faith in the Theology of John Calvin.* Vancouver: Regent College Publishing, 1983.

Sims, Bryan Billard. 'Evangelical Worldview Analysis: A Critical Assessment and Proposal.' PhD diss, Southern Baptist Theological Seminary, 2006.

Sinnema, Donald. 'Aristotle and Early Reformed Orthodoxy: Moments of Accommodation and Antithesis.' In *Christianity and the Classics: The Acceptance of a Heritage*, edited by Wendy E. Helleman, 119-148. Lanham/New York/London: University Press of America, 1990.

Smith, David P. *B. B. Warfield's Scientifically Constructive Theological Scholarship*. The Evangelical Theological Society Monograph Series, edited by David W. Baker. Eugene, OR: Pickwick, 2011.

Smith, Ralph. *Paradox and Truth: Rethinking Van Til on the Trinity*. Moscow, ID: Canon Press, 2002.

Spencer, Stephen R., 'Fideism and Presuppositionalism.' *Grace Theological Journal* 8, no. 1 (Spring 1987): 89-99.

Spier, J. M. *An Introduction to Christian Philosophy*. Translated by David Hugh Freeman. Philadelphia: The Presbyterian and Reformed Publishing Company, 1954.

Sproul, R. C., John Gerstner, and Arthur Lindsley. *Classical Apologetics: A Rational Defense of the Christian Faith and a Critique of Presuppositional Apologetics*. Grand Rapids: Zondervan, 1984.

Steinmetz, David C. *Calvin in Context*. Second edition. Oxford: Oxford University Press, 2010.

Stump, Eleonore. *Aquinas*. London: Routledge, 2003.

Sullivan, Daniel J. *An Introduction to Philosophy: Perennial Principles of the Classical Realist Tradition*. Charlotte: TAN Books, 2009.

Sutanto, Nathaniel Gray. 'From Antithesis to Synthesis: A Neo-Calvinistic Theological Strategy in Herman Bavinck and Cornelius Van Til.' *Journal of Reformed Theology* 9, no. 4 (2015): 348-74.

———. *God and Knowledge: Herman Bavinck's Theological Epistemology*. T&T Clark Studies in Systematic Theology, edited by John Webster, et al. London: T&T Clark, 2020.

Svensson, Manfred, and David VanDrunen, eds. *Aquinas Among the Protestants*. Chichester: Wiley Blackwell, 2018.

Swain, Scott. *The Trinity: An Introduction*. Short Studies in Systematic Theology, edited by Graham A. Cole and Oren R. Martin. Wheaton: Crossway, 2020.

Sytsma, David S. 'John Calvin on the Intersection of Natural, Roman, and Mosaic Law.' *Perichoresis* 20, no. 2 (2022): 19-41.

Taylor, A. E. *Plato: The Man and His Work*. Sixth edition. London: Methuen & Co., Ltd., 1949.

Thompson, Mark D., ed. *Engaging with Calvin: Aspects of the Reformer's Legacy for Today*. Nottingham: Apollos, 2009.

Tipton, Lane G. 'The Function of Perichoresis and the Divine Incomprehensibility.' *Westminster Theological Journal* 64, no. 2 (Fall 2002): 289-306.

———. 'Locating the Mystery: Bavinck and Van Til on Immutability and Anthropomorphism.' *The Confessional Presbyterian* 17 (2021): 17-22, 241-42.

———. *The Trinitarian Theology of Cornelius Van Til*. Libertyville, IL: Reformed Forum, 2022.

———. 'The Triune Personal God: Trinitarian Theology in the Thought of Cornelius Van Til.' PhD diss, Westminster Theological Seminary, 2004.

Trelcatius, Lucas. *A Briefe Institution of the Common Places of Sacred Divinitie*. Translated by John Gawen. London: Francis Burton, 1610.

Troost, Andree. *What is Reformational Philosophy? An Introduction to the Cosmonomic Philosophy of Herman Dooyeweerd*. Translated by Anthony Runia. Grand Rapids: Paideia Press, 2012.

Trueman, Carl R. 'Calvin and Calvinism.' In *The Cambridge Companion to John Calvin*, edited by Donald McKim, 225-244. Cambridge: Cambridge University Press, 2004.

Trueman, Carl. R., and R. Scott Clark, eds. *Protestant Scholasticism: Essays in Reassessment*. Studies in Christian History and Thought, edited by Alan P. F. Sell, et al. Eugene, OR: Wipf & Stock, 2005.

Turner, David L. 'Cornelius Van Til and Romans 1:18-21: A Study in the Epistemology of Presuppositional Apologetics.' *Grace Theological Journal* 2, no. 1 (Spring 1981): 45-58.

Turretin, Francis. *Institutes of Elenctic Theology*. 3 vols. Translated by George Musgrave Giger. Edited by James T. Dennison, Jr. Phillipsburg: P&R Publishing Company, 1992–1997.

Ursinus, Zacharius. *The Summe of Christian Religion*. Translated by D. Henry Parry. London: James Young, 1645.

Van Dixhoorn, Chad, ed. *Creeds, Confessions, & Catechisms*. Wheaton: Crossway, 2022.

Van Doodewaard, William. 'Van Til and Singer: A Theological Interpretation of History.' *Puritan Reformed Journal* 3, no. 1 (Jan 2011): 339-62.

Van Drunen, David. *Natural Law and the Two Kingdoms: A Study in the Development of Reformed Social Thought*. Grand Rapids; Wm. B. Eerdmans Publishing Co., 2010.

Van Nieuwenhove, Rik, and Joseph Wawrykow, eds. *The Theology of Thomas Aquinas*. Notre Dame, IN: University of Notre Dame Press, 2005.

Van Til, Cornelius. 'Calvin the Controversialist.' In *Soli Deo Gloria: Essays in Reformed Theology*, edited by R. C. Sproul, 1-10. Nutley, NJ: Presbyterian and Reformed Publishing Company, 1976.

———. *The Case for Calvinism*. Philadelphia: The Presbyterian and Reformed Publishing Company, 1963.

———. *Christian Apologetics*. Second edition. Edited by William Edgar. Phillipsburg: P&R Publishing, 2003.

———. *Christian Theistic Evidences*. Second edition. Edited by K. Scott Oliphint. Phillipsburg: P&R Publishing, 2016.

———. *A Christian Theory of Knowledge*. Edited by K. Scott Oliphint. Glenside: Westminster Seminary Press, 2023.

———. *Christianity and Barthianism*. Philadelphia: The Presbyterian and Reformed Publishing Company, 1962.

———. *Christianity and Idealism*. Philadelphia: The Presbyterian and Reformed Publishing Company, 1955.

———. *Common Grace and the Gospel*. Second edition. Edited by K. Scott Oliphint. Phillipsburg: P&R Publishing, 2015.

———. *The Defense of the Faith*. Fourth edition. Edited by K. Scott Oliphint. Phillipsburg: P&R Publishing, 2008.

———. 'God and the Absolute.' PhD diss., Princeton University, 1927.

———. *An Introduction to Systematic Theology*. Second edition. Edited by William Edgar. Phillipsburg: P&R Publishing, 2007.

———. *The New Hermeneutic*. Phillipsburg: The Presbyterian and Reformed Publishing Company, 1974.

————. *The Protestant Doctrine of Scripture.* Philadelphia: The Presbyterian and Reformed Publishing Company, 1967.

————. 'Reformed Epistemology.' ThM thesis, Princeton Theological Seminary, 1925.

————. *The Reformed Pastor and the Defense of Christianity & My Credo.* Phillipsburg: The Presbyterian and Reformed Publishing Company, 1980.

————. *The Sovereignty of Grace.* Philadelphia: The Presbyterian and Reformed Publishing Company, 1969.

————. *A Survey of Christian Epistemology.* Phillipsburg: The Presbyterian and Reformed Publishing Company, 1977.

————. *Who Do You Say That I Am?* Nutley, NJ: The Presbyterian and Reformed Publishing Company, 1975.

————. *The Works of Cornelius Van Til.* Edited by Eric Sigward. Electronic ed. New York: Labels Army Company, 1997.

Van Vliet, Jan. 'From Condition to State: Critical Reflections on Cornelius Van Til's Doctrine of Common Grace.' *Westminster Theological Journal* 61, no. 1 (Spring 1999): 73-100.

Vander Kam, Henry. 'Some Comments on Kuyper and Common Grace.' *Mid-America Journal of Theology* 2, no. 1 (Spring 1986): 53-62.

Velde, Dolf te. *The Doctrine of God in Reformed Orthodoxy, Karl Barth, and the Utrecht School.* Studies in Reformed Theology, edited by Eddy Van der Borght. Leiden: Brill, 2013

Venema, Cornelis P. 'Calvin's Doctrine of the Imputation of Christ's Righteousness: Another Example of "Calvin Against the Calvinists"?' *Mid-America Journal of Theology* 20 (2009): 15-47.

————. 'The "Twofold Knowledge of God" and the Structure of Calvin's Theology.' *Mid-America Journal of Theology* 4, no. 2 (Fall 1988): 156-82.

Vidu, Adonis. *The Same God Who Works All Things: Inseparable Operations in Trinitarian Theology.* Grand Rapids: William B. Eerdmans Publishing Company, 2021.

Viret, Pierre. *A Christian Instruction.* Translated by I. S. Seene. London: Abraham Veale, 1573.

Voetius, Gisbertus. 'The Use of Reason in Matters of Faith.' In *Introduction to Reformed Scholasticism*, by Willem J. van Asselt. Translated by Albert Gootjes, 225-47. Reformed Historical-Theological Studies. Grand Rapids: Reformation Heritage Books, 2011.

Vollenhoven, Dirk H. T. *Introduction to Philosophy*. Edited by John H. Kok and Anthony Tol. Sioux Center: Dordt College Press, 2005.

———. *Reformed Epistemology: The Relation of Logos and Ratio in the History of Western Epistemology*. Translated by Anthony Tol. Edited by John H. Kok. Sioux Center: Dordt College Press, 2013.

Vos, Arvin. *Aquinas, Calvin, & Contemporary Protestant Thought: A Critique of Protestant Views on the Thought of Thomas Aquinas*. Grand Rapids: Christian University Press, 1985.

Vos, Geerhardus. *Natural Theology*. Translated by Albert Gootjes. Grand Rapids: Reformation Heritage Books, 2022.

———. *Reformed Dogmatics*. 5 vols. Translated and edited by Richard B. Gaffin, Jr. Bellingham, WA: Lexham Press, 2102–2016.

Waddington, Jeffrey C. 'On the Shoulders of Giants: Van Til's Appropriation of Warfield and Kuyper.' *The Confessional Presbyterian* 7 (2011): 139-146, 250.

Warfield, Benjamin B. *The Inspiration and Authority of the Bible*. Edited by Samuel G. Craig. Phillipsburg: The Presbyterian and Reformed Publishing Company, 1948.

———. *Selected Shorter Writings of Benjamin B. Warfield*. 2 vols. Edited by John E. Meeter. Phillipsburg: P&R Publishing, 1970–1973.

———. *The Works of Benjamin B. Warfield*. Vol. 9, *Studies in Theology*. Grand Rapids: Baker Book House, 1991.

Webster, John. *The Domain of the Word: Scripture and Theological Reason*. London: Bloomsbury, 2012.

———. *Essays in Christian Dogmatics*. Vol. 1, *Word and Church*. London: Bloomsbury, 2001.

———. *Essays in Christian Dogmatics*. Vol. 2, *Confessing God*. London: Bloomsbury, 2005.

———. *God Without Measure: Working Papers in Christian Theology*. Vol. 1, *God and the Works of God*. London: T&T Clark, 2016.

————. *God Without Measure: Working Papers in Christian Theology.* Vol. 2, *Virtue and Intellect.* London: T&T Clark, 2016.

Wells, David F. 'On Being Framed.' *Westminster Theological Journal* 59, no. 2 (Fall 1997): 293-300.

————. *No Place for Truth: Or Whatever Happened to Evangelical Theology?* Grand Rapids: Wm. B. Eerdmans Publishing Co., 1993.

————. ed. *Reformed Theology in America: A History of its Modern Development.* Grand Rapids: William B. Eerdmans Publishing Company, 1985.

Wendel, François. *Calvin: Origins and Development of His Religious Thought.* Translated by Philip Mairet. Durham, NC: The Labyrinth Press, 1963.

White, Thomas Joseph, ed. *The Analogy of Being: Invention of the Antichrist or the Wisdom of God?* Grand Rapids: W. B. Eerdmans Publishing Co., 2011.

————. *The Trinity: On the Nature and Mystery of the One God.* Thomistic Ressourcement Series, edited by Matthew Levering and Thomas Joseph White. Washington, D.C.: The Catholic University of America Press, 2022.

————. *Wisdom in the Face of Modernity: A Study in Thomistic Natural Theology.* Ave Maria, FL: Sapientia Press of Ave Maria University, 2009.

White, William, Jr. *Van Til: Defender of the Faith.* Nashville: Thomas Nelson Publishers, 1979.

Wiley, Daniel. 'Retaking Mars Hill: Evaluating the Presuppositional Interpretation of Acts 17:16-34.' *Evangelical Quarterly* 92, no. 4 (Dec. 2021): 328-50.

Wilhelmsen, Frederick D. *Man's Knowledge of Reality: An Introduction to Thomistic Epistemology.* Englewood Cliffs: Prentice-Hall, Inc., 1956.

Wippel, John F. *The Metaphysical Thought of Thomas Aquinas: From Finite Being to Uncreated Being.* Washington, D.C.: Catholic University of America Press, 2000.

Wollebius, Johannes. *Compendium Theologiae Christianae.* In *Reformed Dogmatics*, edited and translated by John W. Beardslee III, 26-262. Library of Protestant Thought. New York: Oxford University Press, 1965.

Wolterstorff, Nicholas. *Thomas Reid and the Story of Epistemology*. Modern European Philosophy, edited by Robert B. Pippen. Cambridge: Cambridge University Press, 2001.

Zanchi, Girolamo. *Confession of Christian Religion*. Cambridge: John Legat, 1599.

Zemek, George J., Jr. 'Exegetical and Theological Bases for a Consistently Presuppositional Approach to Apologetics.' ThD diss, Grace Theological Seminary, 1982.

# Subject Index

## A

Adam ........ 23, 56-60, 70-71, 71n2, 84, 90-91

Adams, Jay ............................... 220

*ad hominem* argument .............. 110

*Always Ready* (Bahnsen) ............ 121

Ames, William ............ 37, 172, 229

*analogia entis (analogy of being)* ......... 101-2, 199, 199n26

*Analogy of Religion, The* (Butler) .......................... 103, 205

analytic philosophy ...................... 24

Anderson, James N. ............. 24, 28

Anselm ...................................... 164

anthropomorphic language ..................... 41, 41n24

antithesis ......... 73, 89-97, 106, 112, 114-15, 124-30, 178-82, 219-20

apologetics
of Aquinas ........................... 176, 210-11, 211n67
common ground in .......... 105-6, 110-12, 114, 126-27, 140, 140n24
evidence in ............. 91, 111, 113, 135-37
history of ............................. 197
practice of ................ 27n53, 224
presuppositional (*See* presuppositionalism)
Reformed ...................... 230-32

Scriptural ....... 124, 130, 134-41, 140n24, 142, 224, 232
traditional ......... 101-7, 141, 160, 170, 181n37, 190, 197
Van Til's summary of ..................... 106-7, 112-13
*See also* interpretation, principle of; proofs, theistic

apostles ....................... 130, 134-36

Aquinas, Thomas
overview .......................... 208-11
apologetics of .......... 176, 210-11, 211n67
Reformed theologians and .......................... 202, 228
on revelation ..... 209-10, 209n61
theology of ...... 199-201, 202n35
Van Til on ................. 101-2, 199, 199n26, 201-2, 201n32, 207

Arians .................................... 53n2

Aristotelianism, Christian ...................... 144, 214

Aristotle ........... 101-2, 104, 110n45, 164, 197, 211n67

Arminian theology ........... 106, 230

aseity of God ..... 24, 24n42, 39-40, 42, 50, 60-61, 215

Asselt, Willem van .................... 198

Athenian philosophers .......... 138, 140n24

277

# Scripture Index

Also available from Mentor Books ...

*Righteous by Design*
*Covenantal Merit and Adam's Original Integrity*

Harrison Perkins

978-1-5271-1157-8

Righteous by Design is, on one hand, a thorough historical investigation of medieval and counter–Reformation theology, exploring sources that have seldomly if at all been treated in Reformed literature. At the same time, it is also a theological case that original righteousness was natural to Adam before the Fall and that Adam could have merited everlasting life according to the covenant of works. The payoff of this effort in theological retrieval is to underscore the majesty of grace in that sinners are right with God only on the basis of Christ's merits. Thus, this book mounts a case for the Protestant law–gospel distinction through the lens of the imago Dei to highlight the sufficiency of Christ and his work.

*Irresistible Beauty:*
*Beholding Triune Glory in the Face of*
*Jesus Christ*
by Samuel G. Parkison

What hath beauty to do with systematic theology? In this new monograph, Samuel G. Parkison explores this question by examining the relationship between Christ's divine beauty and regeneration and faith. Building on recent scholarship in (a) theological retrieval of the Christian tradition, and (b) Protestant developments in theological aesthetics, this project is concerned with soteriology's aesthetic dimension.

*Death in Adam, Life in Christ:*
*The Doctrine of Imputation*
by J. V. Fesko

The doctrine of imputation is the ground in which salvation is rooted. It is often seen as superfluous or splitting hairs, and yet, without it, redemption automatically becomes reliant on our own works and assurance of salvation is suddenly not so sure. J. V. Fesko works through this doctrine looking at its long history in the church, its exegetical foundation, and its dogmatic formulation.

*No Shadow of Turning:*
*Divine Immutability and the Economy*
*of the Redemption*
by Ronni Kurtz

While divine immutability enjoyed a broad affirmation through much of Christian theological antiquity, it has fallen on harder times in modernity. This book aims to swim upstream from this claim and demonstrate that divine immutability does not handicap soteriology but is a necessary and vital component of God's economy of redemption as triune changelessness protects and promotes the redemption of God's creatures.

*For the Mouth of the Lord has Spoken:*
*The Doctrine of Scripture*
by Guy P. Waters

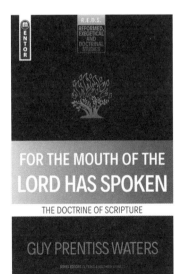

There is no book better than the Bible. It is God's own word. He breathed it into existence. He does wonderful things in and by it. But there is hardly a book more assailed, mocked, and assaulted than the Bible. New Testament Professor Guy Prentiss Waters delves into the doctrine of Scripture. Addressing the revelation, inspiration, inerrancy, sufficiency and perspicuity of the Bible, he also engages with what some other prominent theologians had to say on the subject.

*Chosen in Christ:*
*Revisiting the Contours of*
*Predestination*
by Cornelis Venema

Cornel Venema revisits the important doctrine of predestination to re–familiarize the church with truths about God's sovereignty in salvation. But he does not merely re–visit old ground but also engages a host of historic and contemporary challenges to the doctrine. He addresses the subject from exegetical, historical, contemporary, and pastoral vantage points.

*Cracking the Foundation of the New*
*Perspective on Paul:*
*Covenantal Nomism versus Reformed*
*Covenantal Theology*
by Robert J. Cara

The New Perspective on Paul claims that the Reformed understanding of justification is wrong – that it misunderstands Paul and the Judaism with which he engages. This important book seeks to show that this foundation is fundamentally faulty and cannot bear the weight it needs to carry, thus undermining the entirety of the New Perspective on Paul itself.

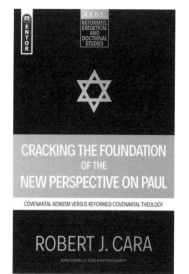

*The Primary Mission of the Church: Engaging or Transforming the World*
by Bryan D. Estelle

This book argues for the separation of the church and the state. Additionally, Estelle claims that the historically reformed position is that Christ is ruler of all; however, he manifests his rule in different ways. These basic categories, i.e., that God rules the church as a redeemer (a spiritual kingdom) and rules the state and all other social institutions (the civil kingdom) as creator and sustainer, has been widely held by Reformed thinkers for centuries until the modern period.

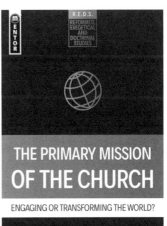

*Reforming Free Will: A Conversation on the History of Reformed Views*
by Paul Helm

In the light of what powers and faculties are human beings responsible individuals in the everyday? In his theological, historical and philosophical examination of reformed orthodox views of free will and divine sovereignty Paul Helm considers determinism and compatibilism and their historical development between 1500 and 1800.

# Christian Focus Publications

Our mission statement –

STAYING FAITHFUL
In dependence upon God we seek to impact the world through literature faithful to His infallible Word, the Bible. Our aim is to ensure that the Lord Jesus Christ is presented as the only hope to obtain forgiveness of sin, live a useful life and look forward to heaven with Him.

Our Books are published in four imprints:

### CHRISTIAN FOCUS

popular works including biographies, commentaries, basic doctrine and Christian living.

### CHRISTIAN HERITAGE

books representing some of the best material from the rich heritage of the church.

### MENTOR

books written at a level suitable for Bible College and seminary students, pastors, and other serious readers. The imprint includes commentaries, doctrinal studies, examination of current issues and church history.

### CF4·K

children's books for quality Bible teaching and for all age groups: Sunday school curriculum, puzzle and activity books; personal and family devotional titles, biographies and inspirational stories – because you are never too young to know Jesus!

Christian Focus Publications Ltd,
Geanies House, Fearn, Ross-shire,
IV20 1TW, Scotland, United Kingdom.
www.christianfocus.com